LET THERE BE
Light

LIBERATING THE HEART OF HUMANITY TO CREATE
HEAVEN ON EARTH

AMANDA ERIN KELLY, MSc

Let There Be Light

Copyright © 2024 by Amanda Erin Kelly

All rights reserved. No portion of this book may be reproduced in any form without written permission from the publisher or author, except as permitted by U.S. copyright law.

Title: Let There Be Light: Liberating the Heart of Humanity to Create Heaven on Earth
Published by Illumina Wisdom
Written by Amanda Erin Kelly, MSc
Cover Design by Amanda Erin Kelly

Print ISBN: 979-8-9918822-0-0
E-Book ISBN: 979-8-9918822-1-7
Audiobook ISBN: 979-8-9918822-2-4

First Edition, November 2024
11.11

Printed in the United States of America

www.amandaerinkelly.com
www.illuminawisdom.com

Let There Be Light

Liberating the Heart of Humanity to Create Heaven on Earth

Amanda Erin Kelly, MSc

Illumina Wisdom

CONTENTS

Author's Note	3
Let There Be Light	7
Introduction: Awakening the World	9
1. Let There Be Light Healing Back to Wholeness	35
2. Light and Love The Eternal Essence of Your Being	44
3. Reclaim Your Power Why Outsourcing Keeps you Stuck	54
4. Light Is Truth Anchoring into Heart Wisdom	62
5. Living in the Light The Biology of High-Vibrational States	71
6. Choosing the Light: The Inside Job How to Take Responsibility for your Life	80
7. The Enlightened Heart The Life-Changing Power of Gratitude	87
8. Out of the Head, Into the Heart How to Connect with the Light and Live a Heart-Centered Life	95
9. Light in the Darkness Preparing for the Descent into the Underworld	105

10.	The Brave Heart Alchemizing the Shadows	114
11.	The Long Shadow of Limiting Beliefs Deconditioning and Unlearning to Reconstruct Your Reality	130
12.	The Golden Great Reset The Deeper You Dive, The Higher You Rise	138
13.	Confronting the Collective Shadow Challenging the Status Quo	152
14.	The Truth Shall Set You Free From Surviving to Thriving	179
15.	Patriarchy and the Paradigm of Separation It Ends With Us	190
16.	The Big Shift: Rise of the Divine Feminine The Resurrection of a Radiant Future	201
17.	Soular Power The Source of Light and Life	213
18.	Creating Heaven on Earth The Rainbow Pillar of Light	225
19.	We Are Not Alone The Diamond Web of Connection	235
20.	Living the Prophecies: Co-Creating Heaven on Earth Astrology, Prophecy, and the Birth of Christ Consciousness	243
21.	You Are The Miracle Mastering the Way of Love	255

Epilogue: We The People Writing Humanity's New Story	265
Resources	269
About the author	271
Endnotes	273

This book is dedicated to the children of the world.
To the future generations of humanity,
To the spirit babies bearthing into our world with incredible frequencies of light,
To the heart of humanity,
And to the inner child within each of us.
May all souls find peace, love, and liberation,
May we remember our purity and innocence as Children of Love.

AUTHOR'S NOTE

This book was born of a spontaneous inspiration to create a 21 day series called the Light in the Darkness, beginning December 1, 2020 through the Winter Solstice and Jupiter-Saturn Great Conjunction on December 21, 2020.

I woke up that morning with the idea, sat down with my mocha, and outlined the topics for the 21 days, setting the stage for the shift in consciousness and Awakening through current events and creating the framework for the journey into wholeness. I trusted the guidance and simply spoke from my heart and the wisdom and knowledge I had integrated into my conscious awareness and embodied until that point.

Little did I know how much I would have to say, much less that a couple years later I would have the inspiration to transcribe those words into a book.

Much has shifted in these short four years both personally and collectively, however I have only anchored more deeply into the wisdom that wished to be shared. I have endeavored to set the stage even more comprehensively through the introduction, and to fill in gaps, add nuance, and share relevant resources, which I include at the back.

My Gene Keys are Truth and Illumination, and the contents of this book outlines what resonates as Truth within my heart and soul. All I share is for the purpose of collective liberation, healing, and empowerment.

This journey is continually unfolding as we collectively evolve, reclaim our remembrance, and blossom into our wholeness. If you come across something in these pages that does not have a proper resource or could use updating, please do not hesitate to reach out. My intention is to keep a living library of resources, accessible on my website and in my community.

To access these resources and additional free tools and support for the practices outlined in this book, please head to my website thisartcalledlife.com, where you will also find access to my online community and school, Illumina Wisdom School.

Medical Disclaimer

The author has made every attempt to provide information that is accurate and complete, but this book is not intended as a substitute for professional medical advice. The content of this book is for informational purposes only and is not intended to diagnose, treat, cure, or prevent any condition or disease. The content does not take into account your individual health, medical, physical fitness or emotional condition or needs.

You understand that this book is not intended as a substitute for consultation with a licensed practitioner. Please consult with your own physician or healthcare specialist regarding the suggestions and recommendations made in this book. The use of this book implies your acceptance of this disclaimer.

How to Navigate This Book

Naturally, I do recommend you read this book from start to finish, cover to cover, however long that may take, in order to have the full picture. Some of my favorite lines land at the end of chapters, at the end of sections within the chapter, and some in the heart of paragraphs in the heart of a chapter.

It is also worth noting that I shared the chapters in a specific order for a specific reason.

All that said, to actually work with it, you may find that taking it one chapter at a time will help you to integrate the wisdom, implement the practical steps, and work through the reflection, self-inquiry, and journaling prompts.

Take a few deep breaths to settle into your body, and breathe golden light into your heart space. Drop into your heart, and with a curious mind stay open to receiving the messages shared within.

You may wish to have a journal and pen handy, or a dedicated note on your favorite notes app at the ready. Get cozy with a cuppa, put on soothing music or healing frequencies, or settle into your favorite spot in nature.

What may be ideal for some is to read it cover to cover then start over and return to each chapter, step by step, to spiral deeper. This process may help you to anchor into the full picture as you then go deeper into the inquiry.

Using the additional tools, resources, and content available through my website this artcalledlife.com/let-there-be-light and my school will facilitate the process of inquiry.

Finally, this work is best done in support of like-minded community. Please find links to the community on my website.

Acknowledgements

It would be impossible to thank every person who has played a role in the inspiration, mentorship, guidance, and creation of this book. Thank you to my reflections and my mirrors who illuminated both my light and my shadows and helped to show me both where I needed to grow and remind me of the light and power within.

Thank you to my parents who brought me in to this beautiful world, to my sister who has been there through thick and thin, and to my precious nieces who remind me of the innocent joy of our pure nature, with a delicious blend of sweetness and spice, sass and laughter.

Thank you to my healers and mentors, to those who gave me feedback and encouragement along the way, and to the many beautiful sparks of light who I've had the honor of crossing paths with in this lifetime of many lives.

LET THERE BE LIGHT

The Cover Image

The background cover image is a real photograph. I took it from an airplane window on a flight down to a retreat I went on a couple short weeks after my cancer treatment ended, September 2016.

This image popped into mind when the idea for this book came through, and it served as the working cover image. Naturally, it felt right to keep it when it came time to think seriously about the cover. Our Earth, illuminated by Heaven. See color image on my website: https://thisartcalledlife.com/let-there-be-light

INTRODUCTION: AWAKENING THE WORLD

"To be hopeful in bad times is not just foolishly romantic. It is based on the fact that human history is a history not only of cruelty, but also of compassion, sacrifice, courage, kindness. What we choose to emphasize in this complex history will determine our lives. If we see only the worst, it destroys our capacity to do something. If we remember those times and places—and there are so many—where people have behaved magnificently, this gives us the energy to act, and at least the possibility of sending this spinning top of a world in a different direction. And if we do act, in however small a way, we don't have to wait for some grand utopian future. The future is an infinite succession of presents, and to live now as we think human beings should live, in defiance of all that is bad around us, is a marvelous victory."
~ Howard Zinn

'It's Over.' It was dark and stormy, and I looked out over the New York City skyline and saw a cluster of dark, ominous clouds hovering over Lower Manhattan. As I stood there, I felt this deep knowing wash over me: It's Over.

A few hours later, the clouds began to lift, and the skyline lit up in gold as the setting sun reflected off the buildings. Then the sky turned pink, and I stepped out to see it more clearly and gasped: a double rainbow arched over the valley, framing the skyline.

Hope. Renewal. The Rise of a New Earth. The Resurrection of Eden. The time had finally come.

I knew a monumental shift was underway, the way I had known back in 2012 when a 'random' thought suddenly popped into my head out of nowhere, entirely out of context, as I sat in the library in London writing my papers for grad school: The System, The Shift, The Awakening.

I didn't know what it meant, but I knew it meant something big, and that it was coming.

***

Life in its ever-increasing ephemeral complexity is shape-shifting before our eyes. Everything is changing and nothing is as it seems. Covid. Lockdowns. Confusion. Pandemic. Economic collapse. Mass job loss. Social Division. Mental Health Crisis. Inflation. Migrant and border crises. Chaos. War. Governments being toppled. The looming threat of World World Three. Two assassination attempts on a former president during the United States election season followed by the sudden swapping of one presidential nominee for another unelected candidate in the opposing party. Politicians that lie to our faces and make a mockery of democracy (while glossing over the fact that the United States is a federal constitutional republic). Gaslighting, propaganda, and censorship controlling the global masses' perception of reality. Unnatural Monster Storms eviscerating entire regions the size of countries. Election results that blindsided many. Many of us are left to wonder: is *any* of it real?

One would think this is the description of a dystopian novel, a fictional Orwellian future. Yet, this is the 'reality' we have found ourselves in, the nearly 8 billion humans alive on Planet Earth in 2024, simultaneously living out every dystopian narrative ever written.

Life is a stage, and the Truth is indeed stranger than fiction.

Indeed, the world around us is crumbling and the world as we knew it is rapidly disappearing, life changing in unprecedented ways at an unprecedented pace to the point that even the word unprecedented itself is beginning to sound like a hackneyed cliche.

Pervasive collective anxiety, fear, division, and separation are polluting our perception and communication. Misinformation, propaganda, and the deliberate distortion of science are fomenting confusion so people can't discern what is true or who to believe because we've become so disconnected from our bodies and inner guidance systems.

For so many—Life. Feels. Heavy. Our future—entirely uncertain.

People are recognizing that everything feels weird. Nothing feels right. Life feels *off*. Many are seeing through the deception and are perceiving the establishment and distorted system for what it is.

It seems as if all the darkness in our world is surfacing all at once and no one quite knows what to do about it. Indeed, the world is undeniably changing. All can see it, feel it, and sense it on some level, but so many feel lost and confused as to what is actually happening and why. And most don't know how to grapple with it. Grief, rage, denial, and helplessness consume so many to the point of confusion and apathy. So many long for things to go 'back to normal' but by now recognize they won't.

Yet this is precisely what we must recognize: we *cannot* go back, and what was considered to be 'normal' was in fact not at all a normal state for our bodies, our minds, our hearts, or our souls. The world we *thought* we knew was an illusion, a facade. A failed experiment.

If we allow ourselves to pause and tune in, we will begin to hear the whispers of our hearts and souls that know we can't go back to the way things were before. The sword of Truth is piercing through illusion and illuminating the distortion, yet many are left without a sense of direction, much less a map or tools to move forward or rebuild.

Yet in the face of the chaos, the light of everlasting hope burns eternal and calls us to have steadfast faith in the strength and ultimate goodness of humanity.

In fact, this sequence of historic events is perfectly aligned with Pluto—the generational planet ruled by the god of the underworld signaling transformation, death, and rebirth—entering Aquarius as well as the United States' own Pluto Return, which means it entered the same position it was in 1776, coinciding with the Declaration of Independence. A nation's Pluto return coincides with revolution and the rise and fall of empires as it reveals the darker underbelly of a society for transmutation end evolution into a higher state of being.

The Apocalypse is upon us. Revelation is underway. Disclosure is here.

Apocalypse is a work of Greek origin meaning to reveal; an 'uncovering' of divine knowledge. It is to be sure the end of times, but not in the manner most might believe.

We are living in the age of prophecy, responsible for ushering in the future of humanity, a new Golden Age of Light.

Hope is here. As the saying goes, it's always darkest before the dawn.

***

I learned this lesson the hard way. In 2016, I was diagnosed with cancer at the age of 30. As a fit hot power yogi who could simultaneously do a handstand and touch her toes to her head, it was a slap-in-the-face wake-up call where I felt the rug be swept out beneath my feet and my world was flipped upside down. But when I got really honest with myself, I also knew that my life pre-diagnosis didn't feel right. I wasn't living the life I knew deep down I was meant to live. I realized this was my opportunity to change.

Many who experience a personal cataclysm in the form of a health crisis, an accident, sudden job loss, a relationship ending, or the death of a loved one face such a reckoning. Some might call it an ego death; others might call it an awakening.

Crisis can evolve into opportunity for change if we look at it through the correct lens. In fact, the Chinese character for crisis, when flipped upside down, means Opportunity.

This is precisely what is happening to humanity as a whole: our inverted matrix is being flipped upside down so that it becomes right side up once more. We have reached the Crisis point—now is our opportunity to rise up, put the world right, and return to our organic state.

To quote Leonard Cohen's Anthem, "There is a crack in everything, and that's how the light gets in." Our minds and hearts are being cracked open so that the light of Truth can flood in to restore us to the Truth of our wholeness, our holiness.

Awakening catalyzes a dark night of the soul. As higher frequencies of light from the Sun amplify and stream into the planet, they illuminate the shadows and force a purge of darkness and deception within the collective. Humanity is in the midst of collective ego death, the proverbial dark night of the soul—which is truly a dark night of the ego as we face the shadows of our false identity—and we are being called to surrender into deep trust and faith that the light at the end of the tunnel awaits, to heal the pain and separation in our world, to release all that is not True and Good, to be the light ourselves.

Collectively we are walking the Hero's journey together, returning to the remembrance that we are all one.

Religious dogma is a relic of the old paradigm, however many of the untainted core teachings in religious texts contain deep wisdom. In the Book of Genesis from the Bible, God said, 'Let there be light.' This simple statement contains profound Truth: it is time for humanity to Let the Light guide the way, to allow the light of our hearts to shine forth and to remember the Light of higher consciousness resides within us all, uniting us through the Heart of Source to usher in the dawn of a new Golden Age of humanity.

It is time for a resurrection and regenesis of our sacred hearts and blessed home: to create Heaven on Earth.

'It's Over' meant the timeline of darkness is over. The timeline the ruling elite tried to instigate with the tragedy of 911 is over. The timeline of death, destruction, and global domination perpetuated by a tiny group of corrupt and power-hungry entities is over. It's Over.

It's over for the dark forces that have attempted to control and enslave humanity, to entrap us in the inverted illusions of the inorganic matrix for millennia. Right is wrong. Unhealthy is healthy. Disease is normal. Control is freedom. God is fear.

It's always about numbers (many of which they co-opt and invert so we stay in separation from the Truth, like 13 and 666). Nine is a number of completion, while 11 is a master number, alignment, new beginnings, enlightenment, intuition. When united, 911 means emergence, profound spiritual awakening, and enlightenment, and there is compelling evidence based on astronomical alignments to suggest that Jesus (Yeshua) Christ's actual birth date was September 11th. It is only fitting in our inverted reality that they would choose a deeply encoded date to enact destruction and tragedy.

Emergence became Emergency. Birth became Death. Hope became Fear. And now, It's Over. We are restoring order to the world and returning to the organic blueprint of love and harmony.

Technological innovation and intellectualism bereft of a guiding higher consciousness rooted in morality threatens the very fabric of our future humanity. However, the power of our illuminated hearts will reveal the true Edenic reality that awaits.

The Light has Won. It's time to reclaim the Truth, which is Love and Unity.

Welcome to the Great Awakening. Where the Light Always Wins.

The System, The Shift, The Awakening: Bridging Science and Spirituality

If you're thinking: How on Earth could this collective chaos be an Awakening? Well, as anyone who has ever done a detox knows, it gets worse before it gets better.

Metamorphosis and transformation require the release, even death, of the old so that the highest version of what is possible can take its place.

Like the phoenix rising from the ashes, fully formed from the energy of total transformation, a New Golden Age is blossoming.

Death must always precede rebirth.

Humanity is evolving and the planet we live on is shifting in dramatic fashion. What is coming is the rebirthing of humanity as we evolve into higher consciousness and the rebirthing of Earth herself. We can't take the distortions of the old paradigm with us.

While things may look grim on the outside, in Truth, this is a collective initiation on a global level.

What is happening right now is a blessing because the Truth is, the 'reality' created by the inverted matrix was enslaving our consciousness. We are now being liberated from the shackles of tyranny into love and sovereignty.

What we see over and over in the face of trouble is how community steps up to help one another—humans helping humans, souls supporting souls.

United We Stand points to a greater spiritual truth driving the collective evolution of we the people—that of Unity Consciousness. The familiar phrase 'United We Stand, Divided We Fall' originated in the fourth verse of a patriotic ballad, The Liberty Song, 1768. It is time to reclaim our founding principles and recognize that our individual liberties are upheld through the unification of We The People, harmonizing in commUnity.

A country and culture that has exalted individualism and independence is now ready to evolve into its next iteration: remembering that we are stronger together. Divisiveness has been weaponized against the population, and it is time to rise above the noise and unite for our future. It is time to build a more beautiful future of love, harmony, and abundance for all. We have shown time and again how incredibly resilient and capable we are when left to our own devices, and now it is time to integrate the wisdom of hyper-self-reliance to radiate the brilliance of the diamond when our unique fractals merge into a whole that is far stronger than its facets.

How do I know this?

First, please don't take any of what I share as the absolute ultimate Truth. Do your own research, and above all, use your intuition and discernment. I'm sharing my perspective and what I believe to be true, rooted in a more profound sense of knowing deep within my heart that higher truth is guiding us to pervasive universal truths we are remembering now: We are all one, we are all love.

All I suggest and humbly request is that you stay open to these ideas and read with a mind of curiosity. If it doesn't resonate, leave it. Always only take what resonates and leave the rest. You don't have to agree with me or everything I say, and I'm not asking you to; I'm simply sharing my perspective and what I feel to be true for me and what has helped me in the hopes that it may be of benefit to you. With that said, I will share what I know to be true for me and what I believe to be the path that we are on, knowing that so much more will come to light as we continue to evolve and expand our consciousness.

***

In 2012, I was sitting in the library of my graduate school in London writing papers on Consumer Psychology, the Evolution of Competition and Cooperation, Decision Making, perspective-taking, and financial decision-making through the lens of social and cultural psychology and inter-temporal discounting. I read books like *The Darwin Economy*[1] and *The Structure of Scientific Revolutions*[2], and the nerd in me relished it. Post-dissertation, I interned at an organization that investigated corruption in both public and private sectors through the lens of transparency.

By that point, I'd already lived in three countries, including a half year studying abroad in Paris at the Sorbonne, 14 months teaching English in Tokyo, followed by eight months of travel through Asia, nearly six of which were spent in India doing a full-immersion yoga teacher training course at an ashram, meditation courses, and volunteer work. Between Paris and Tokyo, I spent a couple of summers working in high-end fashion in Midtown Manhattan. I tutored SAT, ACT, and Math and Science to a number of the 0.01% families in Manhattan, the Hamptons, and London and volunteered in the slums and impoverished rural areas of India.

Having entered college in Biology Pre-Med and switched to Psychology after freshman year, this eclectic and nomadic path at first glance seemed not just unconventional but straight out of left field. Yet, as we know, Hindsight is 2020, and looking back, I can now see how seeds were being planted and threads were being woven into a tapestry I could never have envisioned then. I was perfectly positioned to become a professional dot-connector.

So there I was, looking out the library window, writing my papers and loving every moment of it. I always arrived early to get my preferred window seat in the far room on the fourth level of the library, the centerpiece of which is the most ironically inefficient spiral staircase in existence, and I often stayed until after dinner.

One day, sitting in said spot in the library, a random 'thought' came through quite out of the blue: The System, The Shift, The Awakening. I had no clue what it meant, nor did I have any prior context for these terms—especially not 'Awakening'—but it felt so profound I *knew* it meant something. Something Big. And that it was coming. Eventually. I tucked it away in the back of my mind, yet the clarity of the moment had been emblazoned upon my memory.

Fast forward to 2020—I realized something wasn't quite right about the pandemic narrative and the imprinted memory flashed into my mind. I knew the time had come. The Shift was here, the Awakening was happening. Which also meant the System was crumbling.

I would now call that 'thought' a download, or a channeled message from my Higher Self or the realms of Higher Consciousness. I now embrace my intuition as my superpower and Claircognizance as the most prevalent and powerful Gift that has been awakening within. I also have an entirely new appreciation for the phrase Hindsight is 2020.

Much shifted for me in the interim. Halfway between 2012 and 2020, I was diagnosed with cancer. As it goes with many people, this crisis point served as an awakening for me. My intuition—which, again, in hindsight, had always guided me on my major life decisions—came to the fore as I unwittingly and entirely not by choice embarked on my first deep initiation into my spiritual essence, rebirthed so literally to the point I was bald and had to rebuild my body.

Beginning with my very first CT scan, my intuition guided me on the path of healing. I knew from that day that I was being guided and protected, as my uncle had passed the night before from his own battle with cancer. They'd given him six months, and he went within days. I believe he was my angel who saved my life as that very night after he passed, I woke up with sharp shooting pains in my left shoulder. First thing that morning, I looked up my symptoms and called my doctor to request a CT scan. While 'it doesn't work that way' as I was told by the receptionist, sure enough, I got the scan that day, and it showed a grapefruit-sized growth inside my chest, compressing my chest and my lungs.

At some point during the diagnostic process I also received a message from the ether that 'It was not my time to die. It was my job to heal the family pattern of dying from cancer.' Logically, it's impossible to know such things, as some rational PhD in Philosophy tried to argue with me a year or so after the ordeal. Yet in that moment I knew it was true with every fiber of my being. It gave me hope and kept me going because I knew this was much bigger than young little me.

After treatment ended, the true healing journey began, and it spiraled me ever deeper into the realms of trauma, energy, and the search for that deeper essence of Truth within.

Then 2020 hit, the dots began to fully click, and I knew beyond a shadow of a doubt that many of my deeper feelings and suspicions about our inverted matrix reality were in fact correct, that—as I'd experienced in the belly of the beast that is our medical system—our system was upside down and backward. By that point I was already fully on board with spirituality and seeing 11:11—a sign of alignment—on the daily.

There we were, living the Great Awakening, and I knew that the download I'd received in 2012 had been a prophecy in its own right, now bearing out.

Dreams, Prophecies, and Quantum Science

What is happening now has never happened before in the history of the Universe. Yes, you are living amidst the most extraordinary transformation in galactic history. YOU are playing a starring role in the greatest show in the Universe simply by being here on Earth right now.

The transformation has just begun, and its significance is a magnitude of galactic levels as we are living in the times of prophecy.

Many are remembering prophecies[3] of the Natives, such as the White Buffalo woman prophecy, and rare White Buffalo Calves are being born, three within Spring of 2024. The Eagle and Condor prophecy represents the uniting of the tribes, and in March of 2024, tribe elders from North and South America convened to signify the prophecy's unfolding. The Prophecy of the Rainbow Warriors also speaks of this time of unification, while Biblical prophecies such as the Second Coming of Christ are coming to bear within all those who follow the path of Christ Consciousness. The second coming is truly the birthing of Christ Consciousness within each of us. According to Hindu belief, this time signifies the end of the Kali Yuga, and of course, many are familiar with the End of Times prophecy as predicted by the Mayans. The End of times does not mean the end of the world, rather, the end of the Dark Ages, an era, and the end of Time itself. Apocalypse means to reveal, and what is being revealed is the Truth of our Spiritual Nature and the quantum reality we reside in.

Over the past few years, I have had numerous dreams with a prophetic or revelatory quality, several involving water. Waters rising only to suddenly give way to a bright new reality; what could only be described as the 'firmament' breaking, allowing a deluge of water to flood down, instantaneously flipping the world only to reveal a peaceful and pristine realm; a goddess holding a lightning bolt; darker aspects about our matrix reality being revealed; a sense of waiting in the underworld, pearls of wisdom embodied, unafraid of the power within, prepared to emerge; enveloped in the golden energy of divine union, held in the serene bliss of oneness.[4]

Weaving together these dreams and prophecies with quantum science and the evident crumbling of our current reality, it has become increasingly easy to see the bigger picture as a unified whole, especially as so many of us are uncovering these same truths held within the treasure chests of our hearts.

The old systems and structures are breaking down because the ego-based patriarchal paradigm of deception, distortion, lies, illusion, separation, limitation, and enslavement is over. We are shifting into a new paradigm based on Truth, love, harmony, and abundance, and all that does not align with these frequencies is falling away so that we can rebuild anew.

The Sword of Truth is coming down, and the House of Cards is Falling as the Scales of Justice restore balance so we can build a world on a firm foundation of Truth, Justice, and Liberty for All.

Spoiler alert: It's Science. This Shift is ALL about frequency. Our planet—the entire solar system, in fact—is being bombarded by high-frequency scalar waves from the center of our Universe that are catalyzing a full-scale shift of gargantuan proportion into a higher state of vibration, consciousness and being.

The rise of Quantum Physics has begun to shift our collective consciousness, and science is only beginning to catch up with eternal Spiritual Truths—that we are one, part of a greater consciousness, experiencing this miracle called life through our unique fractal of expression.

Quantum Biology[5] is now showing that genes are not our destiny. Rather, the expression of our genetic material can, in fact, be impacted by our environment, flipping the Darwinian paradigm on its head.

The HeartMath[6] Institute is also disproving the Cartesian dichotomy that the Mind and Body are separate entities—and that the mind is the superior intelligence. It is now recognized—whether or not entirely accepted—that 80% more information travels from the heart and body to the brain, which leaves just 20% of the communication top-down from brain to body. Furthermore, the heart contains its own neurological network, indicating a true Heart Intelligence.

While the Mind may be the Placebo, the Heart is the Source and the Womb the center of our Life Force.

Plasma Physics[7] expands on our quantum understanding, offering clues to the nature of consciousness and universal intelligence. Plasma is considered the fourth state of matter beyond the traditional solid, liquid, gas model. A superheated gas, plasma strips electrons away from atoms to form an ionized gas. Why does it matter to us? Because plasma comprises over 99% of the visible Universe.[8] It is the Northern Lights of the Aurora Borealis, lightning bolts, stars, nebulas, and most importantly, our very own star—the Sun.

Plasma is the essence that makes life possible. It is the Source of Life itself. Plasma flows through our veins.

Everything is energy, including us.[9] In times past in Eastern Europe, when a storm threatened, they would ring all the church bells nonstop to dissipate the looming threat. Interestingly—and unfortunately—they removed the bells from church towers throughout Europe in World War II. However, this points to a view that frequency had the power to impact weather itself.

Perhaps there is more to this than mere superstition. Water is a conductor of electrical energy, so perhaps frequency has the potential to impact precipitation. Our own bodies are made up of 70% water, up to 99% at a molecular level.[10] Emotion is energy in motion while our hearts pump blood through our bodies via electrical impulse—what if frequency is the key to unlocking the mysteries within? Our water bodies hold both the pain and the wisdom of the past, containing the eternal consciousness of the cosmos that is ready to be purified and radiated. Our own bodies are the fountain of youth, the eternal spring of life carrying the living waters holding codes of remembrance primed to be unleashed as the spark of life ignites within the chamber of secrets, transforming the heart of darkness into the diamond heart of eternal victory.

We must upgrade and evolve our understanding of physical reality to include the quantum before building new systems and structures designed to support the whole human being and a thriving global community.

As we move through space, Earth is traversing the Photon Belt,[11] a powerful ring of light in our galaxy of the Universe that exists at a higher frequency. Every 26,000 years Earth passes through this luminous river, ushering in a profound change as humanity shifts in consciousness and collectively undergoes an evolutionary leap. Acting as a cosmic catalyst, this phenomenon triggers spiritual awakening and profound transformation as the light unlocks latent gifts buried in our dormant DNA.

A photon is the smallest possible particle of light, or a 'quantum of light' that carries electromagnetic force, or radiation that carries energy proportional to the radiation frequency but has zero rest mass. Photons are the individual 'packets' of light that make up the X-Ray radiation. Microwaves are made of photons, and biophotons are present in brain waves emitted by neurons.

Just like microwaves, radio signals, and wifi, we are being bombarded by light frequencies beyond the visible spectrum that impact our cells in a very tangible way. We are impacted by energy, whether or not we can consciously or palpably feel it.

Go ahead and rub your palms together quickly right now—you can feel the friction, heat, and energy vibrating around your hands and pulsating between them if you slowly, gently separate your palms and pulse the air between them for a few seconds.

We can feel the Sun's heat on our skin and immediately feel calmer and more connected when walking barefoot in the grass or sand. Our skin absorbs ions from the Earth and light energy from the Sun, impacting our mood and physical well-being.[12] This is all proven by science,[13] yet facts like these rooted in ancient Earth wisdom have been relegated to the shadows because there is no profit to be made from natural remedies.

Real Science confirms ancient wisdom: we are energetic beings composed of waves and frequencies, connected to the cosmos above, made of the elements of the Earth below, and one with all of her wonderfully varied inhabitants.

The task now is to remember this Truth and recognize our birthright as powerful creator beings, as powerful healers, to remember that we are magical manifestors, that we are Kings, Queens, priests, and goddesses in earthly human form here to be stewards of Earth and all of her brilliant creatures as vessels enacting Divine Will. The potent light codes streaming in from the cosmos trigger this cellular awakening, unlocking buried memories of our magic and power.

Everything is Energy—Including You

Humanity as a collective has been experiencing wide-ranging, often inexplicable symptoms. Extreme fatigue, sleeplessness, restlessness, anxiety, feeling pressure, stress, a sense of disorientation, heightened sensitivity, colds, coughs, sore throats, a sense of apathy, loss of desire for food, emotional ups and downs, night sweats—the list goes on.

If you've been feeling it, it's not just you, and it's clearly not just Covid. Nor is it just EMFs. Or the chemicals in our food, soil, water, and air from chemtrails, pesticides, pollution, and corruption of our food management, all of which have a detrimental impact on our well-being, to be sure.

All pose a threat to our thriving, but in reality, the poisoning of our Earth is an attempt to mask the Truth and block and prevent the ascension of frequency and consciousness occurring on the planet now.

Many such symptoms may also be related to the frequencies blasting off the Sun in the form of Coronal mass ejections, solar flares, and solar storms. The Schumann Resonance[14]—Earth's electromagnetic frequency, or 'heartbeat,' that typically resonates at 7.83 Hz, equivalent to an Alpha or theta brain wave—has been spiking relentlessly. We feel it down to our DNA. The symptoms we are experiencing often result from a forced cellular detox. We are purging the toxicity within, deep down to a cellular level as old viruses, bacteria, and parasites come up to the surface to be cleared, as well as old emotions and past traumas. Many call them Ascension symptoms.

Duality at its finest and the journey of transformation in a nutshell—we feel worse before we feel better.

Quantum physics has demonstrated beyond doubt that everything is energy, including us, the Earth, the moon, and the stars. Not only are we all made up of energy, we are all connected. By extension, it stands to reason within this quantum paradigm that massive fluctuations in the Earth's energy and that of the cosmos would directly and dramatically impact us mere humans.

Hospitals have long since recognized that emergency rooms are swamped on the night of the full moon. Sharing publicly the notion that you felt impacted by the full moon, however, still typically gets us labeled as witchy or woo-woo, though it seems by the day, more and more are recognizing that there is more to our reality than meets the eye. Many are returning to natural remedies and a way of life rooted in communion with the land, reclaiming their healing and magical powers such as clairvoyance, embracing their 'witchiness,' and remembering their lineage as Priests and Priestesses. However, such terms are undeniably predominately used in a derogatory or dismissive manner, relegated to the realm of woo.

But we are beginning to remember what has been lost: the essence of the sacred. The moon serves as a reminder of our mystical essence and the untapped mysteries of the cosmos above and the Universe within.

Women's cycles have, of course, long been known to sync with those of the moon. We are all birthed—brought to Earth—from the waters of the womb, waters so intimately influenced by the moon. Given the moon's impact on the ocean's tides, it stands to reason that if a cosmic body like the moon can have such a dramatic impact on the world's giant bodies of water, and humans are comprised of 70-80% water, up to 99% at a molecular level, it's no great leap to conclude that the moon would have some impact on our comparatively minuscule water bodies. While few studies have been conducted on the moon's impact on humans, data does corroborate the uptick in odd behavior and occurrences on the night of the full moon. A full 40% of medical professionals believe in the moon's influence on human behavior.[15]

Astrologers, of course, accept as fact that the moon and planets have a profound and intimate impact on each of us to the point of influencing our personality and evolution in this lifetime based on the specific alignments at our time of birth. But let's advocate for the devil in the mind prone to doubt.

Now, if the moon, which is about a quarter the size of the Earth, can have such a noticeable and measurable impact on Earth and her residents, imagine the possible influence a planet like Jupiter might have, which is 11 times wider yet large enough to hold over 1,000 Earths inside.[16] The Sun, for perspective, is roughly 11 times wider than Jupiter and can fit 1,000 Jupiters if it were hollowed out. To round out this comparison, the Sun is approximately 109 times larger than Earth, and an estimated 1.3 million Earths could fit inside.

To be sure, Jupiter is quite a bit farther from Earth than the moon and rotates around the Sun in a much larger orbit than Earth, so naturally the relationship is different. However, it seems only logical that such massive cosmic bodies could also have some energetic influence on Earth depending on their locations and alignments. Everything is energy, and everything is connected after all.

From a quantum perspective, it only stands to reason that other planets in our solar system could influence Earth—and therefore us—on an energetic level. Astrology rings true for many and is an ancient discipline in its own right, while the ancients looked to the stars for guidance and direction on literal and figurative levels. Stonehenge, the pyramids, and most ancient megalithic sites[17] were constructed according to particular astronomical alignments, especially the solstices and equinoxes.

The reverse here is also true: we 'mere' humans can profoundly impact the planet's frequency, both for better and worse. As Mother Earth's frequency shifts, it ripples into the cosmos. Known as the Maharishi effect,[18] mass group meditations on peace have been correlated with a measured reduction in violence. This effect has been studied and recorded numerous times.

When united for peace, we can collectively shift the incidence of violence, and world peace then becomes a viable reality rather than an impossible dream. If smiles, yawns, and random acts of kindness are contagious, perhaps it's not such a stretch to believe that peace and joy can be, too. Humanity collectively raising our vibration will ripple out into the cosmos, influencing the quantum web of creation in which we reside.

In sum, our behavior is influenced by everything around us; why would it be any different for the massive planets orbiting our own Sun? Nor can we underestimate the impact we each have as a node of connection in the greater web of life. We are part of a greater whole, that of not just the Earth but the solar system, which is, in turn, part of the greater mysteries of the galaxies and the whole Universe—unique notes in the One Song of Creation.

As we remember that we are integral threads in a vast tapestry of life with a responsibility to uplift the greater whole, we begin to weave golden threads of possibility into the fabric of existence that can alter the course of our collective destiny. We are returning to unity consciousness—the understanding that all is connected, which is precisely what quantum physics has proven.

Wherever your viewpoints currently reside, the fact remains we are fully entering the quantum paradigm, and quantum science has long established the Truth of our energetic nature and that of the cosmos. The disconnect is that quantum Truth has not yet trickled down into our human systems and structures, and this separation between science and practice is finally being unified. It is incumbent upon each of us to accept this quantum leap of a paradigm shift and embrace the process of inner evolution as the outdated structures around us crumble.

At long last, we are bridging science and spirituality, unifying our understanding of the Universe, the cosmos, ourselves, and our place in the greater whole. Even if it is all just a hologram, to win the game of life, we must embrace the role the greater cosmos plays if we wish to continue leveling up, to remember that we are both nothing and everything all at once, humbly wielding the power of the Universe within as vessels of the divine. At this point, we become true magicians who can out-create any obstacles or cosmic hiccups on our path.

The Quantum Leap

Humanity is in the midst of a shift far beyond anything we have experienced. According to many, we are completing not just a 2,200-year shift of the ages from Pisces to Aquarius, not just a 13,000-year cycle, or even a 26,000-year cycle. These numbers are mind-boggling enough from our limited human perspective. We are shifting out of the Age of Pisces into the Age of Aquarius, closing an entire astrological cycle. With the generational Planet Pluto moving into Aquarius[19] for good as of November 19, 2024 (based on the Tropical zodiac),[20] we will continue to see the old systems and structures based on hierarchy, power-over, and control crumble as we move into an era marked by an ethos of humanitarian and egalitarian ideals. Many see this new cycle as not just the start of a 20-year cycle but the mark of the beginning of the Age of Aquarius.

These shifts in ages and cycles are massive transitions in and of themselves. However, consider that many recognize that humanity's ascension is also triggering the ascension of the entire galaxy, which is now moving into the center of the Universe. What is happening right now is of gargantuan galactic proportions.

As we enter the Age of Light, our consciousness will expand and elevate to embrace the notion that we are not just physical bodies but beings of light having a very dense physical experience where our subtle energy bodies move at a slow rate. Our bodies are vehicles, or vessels as I often refer to them, for our greater soul consciousness—our higher self that is light.

Esoteric wisdom has recognized since ancient times these subtle bodies that exist beyond sight but are quite real. Quantum physics has proven that we and everything in the Universe are made up of energy oscillating at different speeds and vibrations. Every body has its own energy field, from every human and creature on the planet to Planet Earth herself.

These esoteric traditions have always known about and understood Earth's energetic grid, what many people refer to as ley lines, and every ancient temple, pyramid, and site of worship was constructed along these gridlines or at potent intersections to amplify our personal alchemical initiatory processes and help integrate the subtle energy bodies into a more powerful whole.[21]

Alchemy is simply the process of transforming and integrating our shadows—or our 'sins'—into embodied wisdom as we return to a state of unified wholeness—or (w)ho-liness—as a being of love. This integration amplifies and elevates the frequency of our energy as we release the denser emotion-based frequencies, which can then be perceived as light. This is what 'enlightenment' is—bringing light into our being as we return to a purified state of consciousness that is vibrationally aligned with frequencies of love and above, lightening our load so that our life experience is light and free. This alchemical purification and embodiment of light is the true Gold the alchemists sought—the Spiritual Gold of our ascended essence, pure, rich, and royal. Nature's true abundance is the essence of our divinity.[22]

Earth School

Earth is a very dense existence. Incarnating in these physical bodies requires our souls to drop in frequency, which is difficult. Yes, life on Earth is hard. Many consider Earth one of the most challenging schools in the universe. And yet it is both a playground and a potent crucible for our souls to alchemize the density and polarity of the 3D—the fear, the trauma, the anger, the shame, the blame, the separation. The result of this intense pressure is the most brilliant diamond imaginable.

When it comes to integrating the self, the whole is greater than the sum of its parts. Integration aligns us with and helps us access what is known as the light body to ascend our consciousness and form into higher levels of awareness.

After millennia of darkness, during which we were cut off from spiritual wisdom, modern science is finally rediscovering these ancient truths. We are at long last at the brink of emerging from the Dark Age through a beautiful merging of science and spirituality. This understanding will catapult us into a new paradigm of wholeness and a Golden Age of Light, Love, and Harmony.

This journey entails both personal and collective evolution as we transcend the limitations of our minds and our current understanding of physical existence. We've forgotten our true nature and have been kept in the dark, wandering lost souls muddling their way through a twisted tunnel of human suffering. Searching for the light, forgetting that all we seek lies within.

The End of Times that is upon us is no doomsday armageddon. It is something to be celebrated and welcomed with open arms as elitist structures crack and crumble. It is a Shift, a transition into a new state of being that aligns with our highest Truth—that of love and abundance for all.

The Apocalypse is indeed upon us. The true meaning of Apocalypse is a Great Prophetic Revelation; it is a disclosure, a revelation, an uncovering of knowledge. The Truth of who we are and the reality of our world is being revealed. It is 222 as I type this—a calming message of balance, harmony, and stability that calls on us to have hope, faith, and trust. Through faith and trust in the path being laid before us, we can restore balance and harmony to the world.

We are entering a New Earth of higher vibration where we will feel lighter and freer, embodied in our Truth of unity and oneness, free from the shackles of fear and limitation. Yet, we are the ones who must build it as vessels for the new consciousness pouring down into the planet through us.

'Vessels' is precisely what we are, and we are being called to empty our vessels of the old and expand our vessels to hold more light, to upgrade our vessels to be a match for the most powerful force in existence, the frequency behind all existence: Love.

We are being asked to hold these new frequencies to enter into this new era, this Golden Age of Heaven on Earth, so that the New systems and structures we build endure, erected on unshakeable foundations of harmony to create a world of peace and abundance for all.

More and more people are attuning to these increased frequencies, returning to the universal Truth of Love. Christ Consciousness is Universal Consciousness, far beyond the man named Yeshua that the world knows today as Jesus Christ. Yes, he taught us the Way of Love; he is an exemplar, a way shower, who did indeed seed the blueprint for the Christ impulse on Earth. Krystic Consciousness is Eternal Source Light, the energy of pure God-Source-Creator Consciousness. Christ—sometimes spelled Kryst, Krystic, Christic—consciousness itself goes far beyond the man we know from the Bible, whose pure teachings taught direct communion with God-Source universal consciousness. Crystalline consciousness is embodied in our crystalline essence—who we are at our core, in our purest form.

Healing back to Wholeness, coming back into mind-body-soul-spirit alignment, integrating soul fragments—whatever path one takes, whichever terms resonate, it's all leading us back to the same Truth: Love and inner union. This is the ultimate goal of Yoga: inner union. The root term of Yoga, yuj, means 'to yoke,' 'to join,' or 'to unite.'

Many believe that during Jesus' lost years,[23] he traveled to mystery schools around the ancient world, including Egypt and India, to train in advanced initiatory practices to accomplish what he incarnated to do: anchor the blueprint for Christ Consciousness by showing us how to resurrect the light body ourselves. Achieving inner union and wholeness is the key to unlocking the miraculous within.

By integrating all aspects of yourself through the crucible of the journey that compresses the coal so intensely that all impurities dissipate, the reward of facing and embracing our shadow is activating the crystalline diamond within, radiating a rainbow light that fractals through the infinite facets of our multidimensional being.

Inner peace is the foundation. This journey is about rediscovering, or cultivating, a sense of inner peace where we can remember our connection to divinity, find stillness in surrender, and come into alignment and union with these higher frequencies of source light. Surrender to peace, and all will be revealed.

Life As We Know It

As we undergo the profoundly transformative swells of a massive paradigm shift like no other in recorded human history, more of us are awakening to the notion that perhaps there is more to this thing we call life than we have been led to believe. More than ever, we are compelled to contemplate life, its purpose, and the very meaning of our existence.

The uncertainty of what the future holds can shake us to our core. But, as we go deeper into an 'inner-standing' of universal truths, we begin to shift our frequency out of fear, stress, and anxiety and into a space of curiosity, excitement, and possibility. Our view of the world and ourselves expands, and with it, our sense of the potential of what the future holds.

My spiritual journey—my process of 'awakening' if you will—has been a slow and gradual one. I did not experience a mind-blowing, world-altering, earth-shattering moment where everything changed in a flash. Some experience it like that; most don't—quite the contrary. Over time, seeds are planted, and finally, a piece of information or a momentary experience bursts the bubble, and the dots begin to connect. As my journey has unfolded, I've been piecing the puzzle together and constructing an understanding of the big picture. My intuition has guided me along the way, but as I muddled through my first three decades, still mostly unconscious of the true workings of the Universe, I turned down the dial of my intuition many times.

Every time I trusted that deep knowing, magic and life upgrades happened. But far too many times, I allowed societal expectations to trump the calls of my heart and whispers of my soul.

I went through life uncomfortably numb, suppressing my feelings and ignoring the nudges of my soul, scared to live life according to my deepest, most authentic desires. I was guided to India at the age of 23 after having left the structures and expectations of New York City behind over a year prior when I made the unconventional choice to move to Tokyo to teach English. In India, I dove head first to an immersive yoga teacher training at an ashram. It was as authentic a yoga immersion as you could imagine. Four am wake-up calls, spartan living quarters, hours of yoga practice, chanting, karma yoga duties, yoga philosophy classes, and even neti pots and panchakarmas.

After a six-month stint in India spent meditating, learning about Buddhist and Hindu philosophy, and volunteering in a rural village, I was sucked back into the epicenter of the matrix, New York City. Stress, overwhelm, and the pressure to achieve and perform dominated my life yet again, no matter how hard I tried to carve an aligned path within that system.

Then, in 2012, the phrase 'The System, The Shift, The Awakening' popped into my head. A cancer diagnosis, a healing journey, and a personal soul awakening later, here we are in the midst of the shift, on the brink of a global awakening spurred by the crumbling of an outdated system based on the old paradigm.

Welcome to the quantum realm where Heaven on Earth becomes our reality and heart and soul lead the way.

In October 2020, just over six months into the Covid pandemic, I recorded a YouTube video entitled 'A Spiritual Perspective on 2020' on the 'portal day' 10/10. From a spiritual perspective, ten is a number of wholeness, possibility, and new beginnings, and October 10th also happens to be World Mental Health Day [24]—divine timing and alignment.

Four years later, I am editing this on the eve of October 10th, as chaos reigns through the threat and devastation of monster storms with a highly contentious US election looming. Everything is just as relevant, if not more so, as it was when I first shared that video and the series that followed that December, which would, unbeknownst to me at the time, become this book.

For so many, this has been a time of chaos and turmoil, uncertainty and fear, not to mention grief, despair, and worry—all the feels that are not very comfortable or fun to be feeling. And, of course, our mental health at a collective level has been severely impacted.

And yet everlasting hope and faith are guiding us through the storms of chaos to emerge cleansed, purified, unified, and whole.

The upheaval of the past several years is evidently much more extensive than the fallout caused by an 'escaped' pathogen—we're in the midst of a paradigm shift. In the realm of science, everyone operates within an accepted understanding of how the Universe works, and then occasionally, there's a momentous breakthrough and our fundamental understanding of science and the world shifts because of that new theory or perspective.

Copernicus and the Sun is the clearest example: when he said that the Earth revolved around the Sun and not the other way around, it catalyzed a massive paradigm shift because it fundamentally changed how people perceived the world and their place in it. Now, people are experiencing a great deal of fear over our world, and personal realities are becoming unrecognizable with the greater economic and socio-political repercussions of the global lockdowns and subsequent global chaos and political unrest, and for some, the loss of everything due to unnatural weather disasters. This shift is frightening for so many because it shatters their version of reality, and they are not anchored in themselves or a higher truth.

This paradigm shift is more worldview-shattering than the one brought about by Copernicus because it's more than a paradigm shift—it's a shift into a whole new Age of Humanity.

It is not easy to grapple with the proverbial rug being pulled out from under you as everything you thought was true starts to crumble, which is what is happening in society now. Our systems, structures, understanding of ourselves and the world, and our very belief systems are breaking down. And that, of course, is disturbing to confront because what is at stake is nothing less than our lives and our livelihoods.

Our health is at stake. Our government is at stake, even the structures and rules of society that no one is clear on anymore. Regarding information these days, who can we trust? People are quick to remove those who hold different beliefs from their lives entirely. That was never a thing before. People could hold different viewpoints and still get along. What happened to honest and open discussion? It isn't easy to discern what's true and what's not in this age of anxiety and disinformation. Collectively, we are grappling with deep, profound existential questions and issues.

Facing the darkness is daunting, and we can feel lost, wandering aimlessly through it. Yet, from a spiritual perspective, this is a beautiful time to turn inward because we can create the light for ourselves from within. This is precisely what we are being called to do—to go inward. To shine the light takes soul searching; it takes shadow work, it takes digging deep and confronting uncomfortable things, which is precisely what this book endeavors to shed light upon.

Amidst all this darkness, there is hope. The light at the end of the tunnel shines brighter and brighter for those willing to lift their perspective out of the shadows and above the fog and turn in the direction of Truth, our True North.

My intention in sharing this perspective is to spread hope and start to plant the seeds of inquiry so that others can understand what is going on from a bigger perspective.

The Truth is that humanity is entering a new era, a whole new age of human evolution, as we rise to a new level of collective consciousness. The way I and much of the spiritual community understand this process is that we are ascending in consciousness to become Human 2.0, Homo Luminous, beings of Light.

In the spiritual war for the soul of humanity, the light has already won, but we do have to choose it.

Coming out of the Spiritual Closet

Spirituality is still widely regarded as wacky and woo-woo and just for the witches and weirdos. Some relegate anything with a paranormal or a potentially spiritual tinge as straight-up psychosis. While spiritual psychosis is a real danger when people open up and access realms they're not ready for without having the proper tools or protection in place, a spiritual awakening is more Real than our inverted false matrix 'reality.' It reveals the truth of our reality, which many have not yet been ready to face.

It took me a while to fully embrace my spirituality and claim it publicly. Encouraging conversations with both those on the spiritual path and those who were not but were open enough to resonate with much of what I shared about my journey and understanding gave me that initial boost to start sharing back in 2020. Here we are, and my understanding of this emerging reality has only deepened, and my conviction of these truths has only strengthened.

As any history buff knows from the time of England's coffee houses and their role in the emergence of the Industrial Revolution,[25] the sharing of ideas is what moves humanity forward. The World Wide Web and social media have granted us instantaneous access to information, global communication, and connection, spurring the rate of technological innovation over the past few decades to exponential levels. However, we have also witnessed a marked move by technocratic global governance to suppress and control access to certain information, to suppress voices that dissent against chosen narratives that perpetuate the paradigm of patriarchal control. Many can now clearly see that Truth has been suppressed through cancel culture and outright censorship.

While Truth is a lofty concept, and perspective plays a significant role in how we perceive it, I believe in higher, Universal Truths with a capital T. Many within the spiritual and conscious communities are tapping into the same wisdom. It can't be all coincidence, and at this point, the sheer breadth and quantity of believers belie the notion of brainwashing.

To be sure, there is distortion in many of our teachings because we have lost the mystery schools of old and our direct connection to the divine. Discernment is our greatest lesson of this time, yet so many of us are connecting to the greater Truth that has been eluding us: There is something greater than us that we are all connected to and a part of. We are spiritual beings having a human experience, and we are here to Awaken the beings of Love that we are. Most who follow the path authentically arrive at this Truth through personal experience.

Again, please do your own research. Critical thinking is key. More than that—do your own soul searching.

It's really about hearing these ideas and then sitting with them yourself, contemplating and tuning in to your intuition. Do these notions ring true for me? What feels authentic, what feels right? We all have our own Truths and realities in the current separation-based paradigm, but I believe we are all coming to a broader understanding. We're arriving at different rates and following different paths, but that doesn't make one person's path better or worse than the next because they all eventually lead us back home to the Truth of love that radiates from the light within.

We're all on this journey together. And that's what this is all about: Unity, harmony, forgiveness, compassion, love, and recognizing that we are all sparks of divine human consciousness in the most challenging school in the Universe, which is simultaneously the most magical playground available to us: Planet Earth Academy.

Most of us have to repeat lessons, classes, and even whole grades over and over. But the more aware we become of our thoughts and energies, and the more responsibility we take for how we show up and respond to our circumstances, the faster we move through these lessons and the quicker we ascend to the next grade or level of the game.

We must come together and support each other on this journey because it's not an easy one. Still, I can tell you that if you commit to your growth, you will come out on the other side like the most resilient butterfly with glimmering golden wings, and energies are amplifying to facilitate your transformation. So what's taken me four years to learn and embody might have taken someone else 20 years, while it might take the next person only four months. We each have our journeys, yet the current energies enable rapid growth and upgrades for those who choose to ride the waves. Each of us has our own journey, so we must remember not to compare. When we reach the final level of the game, we remember that we are not meant to do it alone, in every sense of the expression.

My journey has been a process of diving deep into myself and uncovering what lurks in the shadows, the ignored parts of self. As I often say, the deeper you dive, the higher you rise.

Time is accelerating, and this incredible shift is allowing us to do this work more quickly, to awaken, ascend, and raise our vibrational frequency more rapidly because the Earth herself is shifting. From these perspectives, we are all shifting collectively together, along with the planet.

As we live in a world of free will, we do have an individual choice in the matter. We live in a 3D world and are ascending into what many call 5D consciousness. Many say we are already in 4D, where time begins to dissolve, and that many of us are going beyond 5D up to 12D. Each of these realities coexists on different vibrational frequencies. To me, what matters more than these distinctions is how we show up in the world and to those around us. All of it is a choice our soul must make, and what matters most is simply focusing on keeping our vibration aligned with love and expansion.

These higher dimensional frequencies are being anchored into our planet as we move through a very high-frequency part of the galaxy, and within these frequencies, there is no room for density. The new era, or the new reality that we're shifting into, is essentially a frequency shift into a higher dimensional experience of our world. It's just a frequency shift. But it's a big deal. Everything that does not align with these higher frequencies must be released. Fear, hatred, anger, lack, scarcity, and pain do not align with Heaven, so we cannot create that reality if we still hold on and exist as a vibrational match for the denser, separation-based reality.

Healing back to wholeness, embodying our Truth, and living in alignment with our soul is the path I endeavor to walk and embody so that I can authentically serve my mission of lighting the way on the journey of alchemizing our shadows into a life of beauty, love, and abundance.

I know this journey isn't easy, and I am sending so much love and compassion to you wherever you are on your journey. I share what follows with you because this wisdom has been profoundly helpful for me as I navigate the unknown. It's a matter of simply taking that first step and being bold enough to get curious.

Fundamentally, all there is to do is BE the light. That's it. Keep your energy, vibration, and frequency light. The shift is about BEing in these high vibrational states of gratitude, love, joy, and harmony.

However, simple does not necessarily mean easy, and many of us are here to unravel complex webs of illusion.

For those who might not yet fully understand what this means or how to achieve it, want a primer on what is actually going on in the world right now, or would like to connect the dots of their own journey with the words woven within, read on.

This book is for you.

When I say love and light, I mean the kind of light that was born from the darkness.
The kind of light Birthed from the crucible of the womb of alchemy
Diamond Light formed under pressure and radiating the full spectrum of brilliance through its multifaceted nature
The light you had to walk through the tunnel in utter darkness with only the guiding inner light of faith to find on the other side
The light of the Heavens you could only return to after going through the depths of hell
This light isn't empty. It is full, radiant, Whole.
Pure and Holy, only because you walked through the flames of alchemy to rise like the sun, illuminating the world with sheer power and grace

Chapter One

Let There Be Light

Healing Back to Wholeness

"And God said, Let there be light: and there was light. And God saw the light, that it was good: and God divided the light from the darkness."
~ Genesis 1:3

As I opened my eyes the morning of December 1, 2020, I received a crystal clear message: record a video series entitled 'The Light in the Dark,' leading up to December 21, 2020, the Winter Solstice. This date was considered by many to be the dawning of a new era marked by the Saturn-Jupiter Great Conjunction.[26] A New Golden Age. An Age of Miracles.

Amidst hope inspired by the season of light, we were, of course, simultaneously facing what many mid-'pandemic' were referring to as a 'Dark Winter.'

The days approaching the Winter Solstice were getting shorter, and even in Miami, the temperature had plummeted overnight. I woke up that first day of December with the urge to put on a sweater and hunker down with some hot cocoa. Reminders of long, dark winters spent in New York City, New Jersey, London, Tokyo, and Paris came rushing in—the long, cold, dark winters I'd come to Miami to escape. Flashbacks of the perpetually cold fingers and unacknowledged seasonal depression I experienced every Winter of my life pre-2018 flooded my brain.

Memories of a heavy sense of darkness in the Winter leading up to my cancer diagnosis in March 2016 penetrated my hopeful outlook. As grounded as I have become in hope and faith, as fully I now embrace the light, I remember all too well the depths of darkness I've experienced and fully understand the depths of despair, grief, anger, fear, and frustration so many experienced in 2020.

Not immune to any of it, I'd faced deep grief in the early months of 2020 with the sudden passing of my Nana right before lockdown began, on the same day our beloved family dog was put down. She and I had a special bond, and over the months waves of grief washed over me.

Weeks prior, I'd experienced the fear, confusion, and emotional and hormonal roller coaster of what I soon learned was a chemical pregnancy. Not in a space of wanting in that situation, an internal battle raged as I was relieved and grateful to my body for taking care of it while in quiet despair at the loss, knowing full well it would have gone against every fiber of my being to terminate actively, all while being confronted with the deeper fears of possible early menopause and infertility that loomed as a worry post-chemo until I could see the doctor for testing. I'd been lucky in many regards, and it seemed there was still hope, but it was an emotionally traumatic experience, followed weeks later by the grief of further loss. Still stuck in a soul-sucking job with a narcissistic boss, I was grappling with many new layers of my own dark night of the soul in those first months of 2020 when everything in our world changed. Grief, however, can become one of the most powerful catalysts for transformation and expansion. That was the year my life completely changed—for the better.

That morning, I awoke with that strong urge to speak about the surge of light streaming into the Earth precisely because the amplification occurred in the midst of Winter, as we plunged into the season of darkness. The contrast and polarity of light and dark have never been more pronounced, and it is crucial to ground down and embody these light frequencies. More light is streaming into the planet than ever, forcing us to purge the shadows that strive to block it. Our world has been plunged into crisis, chaos, and fear, and light is needed all the more to balance, transmute, and transcend the dark. We need to fully understand the dark and the light to heal, rise in our power, and build a more beautiful future.

With the holidays, December ushers in a symbolic season of hope. The promise of light amidst the season of darkness. Hanukkah is known as the festival of lights, an eight-day celebration honored by lighting candles on the Menorah. Kwanzaa is primarily symbolized by seven candles, representing the seven principles: unity, self-determination, collective work and responsibility, cooperative economics, purpose, creativity, and faith.

Christians light advent candles for Christmas and decorate with sparkling strings of fairy lights while celebrating the Christmas Star, or the Star of Bethlehem, and the birth of the Son, the bringer of hope. Ancient goddess and Earth-based traditions celebrated Winter Solstice and the Rebirth of the Sun on December 25, after three days of darkness as the sun seemingly stands still after Solstice for three full days. From the darkest of nights comes the hope and promise of Rebirth as the light finally overcomes.

I have since learned that some religious scholars hypothesize that the Star of Bethlehem was a 'great conjunction' of planets, much like the Jupiter-Saturn conjunction that occurred on December 21, 2020.[27]

While these Holy Days are associated with light, hope, joy, and the promise of renewal, for many, the holidays can evoke stress, sadness, and grief, serving as reminders of who or what has been lost, perhaps amplifying feelings of loneliness and loss. During this season, many confront the duality of light and dark from this deeply internal perspective.

The contrast has become increasingly pronounced, and it's time for us all to fully confront, embrace, and integrate both the light and the dark and anchor them by virtue of the potent alchemy contained within these concepts through tangible methods of embodied understanding.

Because the light illuminates the dark, the light illuminates the shadows we tend to sweep under the rug. We can no longer ignore the uncomfortable aspects of life we attempt to suppress, repress, or ignore. Given the chaos and turmoil the world has faced, it is more important than ever to focus on the light, to integrate, ground, and anchor it within.

Embracing the light isn't about spiritual bypassing. It's not about toxic positivity. It doesn't mean pretending everything's fine when it's not. That does not serve you. Ignoring the shadows, both within and without, is a form of repression and suppression, which is what got the world into this crazy state of existence in the first place. These coping mechanisms will not serve anybody in the long run, particularly not yourself.

Awakening allows us to see the illusion, inner alchemy and embodiment is what ends the karmic looping and generates the of fulfillment and ascension.

Integrating the light is incumbent upon fully facing and embracing the shadows. This is the key to embodiment: facing the darkness head-on and alchemizing it into the spiritual gold of wisdom. We are going through a collective purge whether we like it or not, bringing stuff up and out of the darkness and into the light. So we might as well get on board; otherwise, we may drown in fear and confusion.

Awareness is critical because we need awareness to fully acknowledge that it exists. We cannot heal what we cannot see. We cannot heal what we cannot face. This is true at the individual level as well as at the collective level. If we are unaware of what's in the dark, of what's been hidden, suppressed, and swept under the rug, there's no way to heal it.

The Golden Reset

We are in the midst of a massive upheaval at the collective level of society, but the global crisis is unveiling our inner demons as well. Lockdowns, isolation, and pervasive disillusionment have forced many to turn inward and face their shadows. A Great Reset is indeed upon us, but one that serves and supports our highest possible timeline of Truth, love, and sovereignty, free from agendas of control and manipulation.

For the light to win personally and for the collective majority, we need to anchor light by getting grounded in our bodies and embodying trust and faith that the light at the end of the tunnel is growing brighter, because we are allowing it to shine through us by blossoming our hearts open.

We must go through the heart of darkness to find the treasure we seek, buried deep within. To reach the other side of the dark tunnel, we must transmute the shadows that lurk in our blind spots and fully integrate darkness and light. This is the journey we are all being called into. It is imperative that every one of us show up and do the work to anchor in the higher vibrational frequencies of the light. This is the work of the light workers, the healers, the visionaries, the soulpreneurs, the creatives, the lovers, the truth warriors, and every awakening soul that is beginning to remember what has been forgotten and forsaken. These are the battles the light warriors have come to win.

This is your work—yes, *you* reading this right now because this book came into your field and you picked it up for a reason. Whether or not you *feel* ready, it is time to release fear and step into your power. To step into and fully reclaim our power, we must acknowledge and integrate the shadows because it's when we integrate the dark the light becomes complete.

When darkness is integrated into the light, it becomes a prism of the infinite spectrum of light in which light becomes whole and we remember our holiness. Healing Back to Wholeness is the recognition that we are already whole, but we have been living in a paradigm of separation, polarity, and duality based in fear that perpetuates the illusion of lack. We need to heal the fear and unworthiness; we need to see it and feel it so that we can face it, embrace it, integrate it, transmute it, and release it. We do this to remember our true nature and the divine Truth that we are already whole. Holy.

From that frequency of wholeness, the light beautifully reflects our multifaceted and multidimensional nature. When we heal the separation within created by trauma and unhealed emotional pain, we integrate the light and the dark, the fear and the love. Fear is simply the separation from love. It underlies hatred, anger, and all the dense, heavy, negative emotions. To heal ourselves and the ills of humanity, we are being called to bring the fragments back together to reintegrate into wholeness and inner union, which we will discuss further as we deepen on this journey.

Inner union is the integration of masculine and feminine energies within to return to harmony. Yin and Yang merge to create that perfect balance. Without the dark, the light cannot be fully expressed. To fully step into the light, genuinely be light, reclaim our power, and shine as a beacon of hope, we must face the shadows head-on and not live in fear of them.

We must enter the heart of darkness, walk through the fire, and let all separation burn away so that we can rise from the ashes more whole, complete, and healed than ever before. Every time we go through this crucible of transformation and transmute the density and transform it, we become even more powerful. We need to feel it to heal it.

Collectively, the shadows have been bubbling and erupting to the surface. And this is why we're facing global chaos and crises. Chaos, fear, confusion, and uncertainty run rampant because we're not clear on how to grapple with the dark and haven't been taught how to do so. And most of us just don't want to because it feels so darn uncomfortable and scary. So, many have stuck their heads in the sand rather than grapple with the demons. There is no blame or shame for anyone who has done this—because we *all* have..

We've been taught to ignore the shadows, suppress and repress those 'darker' emotions individually, and collectively ignore the dark shadows in our society. We have been told that everything is hunky-dory when it's not. We've been gaslit and manipulated by political puppets and corporate media propaganda and told that conspiracies are false theories and fed further lies to distract us from digging deeper. Now is the time we must go within and find the spark to reignite our inner light and stand powerfully in our Truth.

First and foremost, we must tune in to our intuition to get clear on what is true. Our intuition always knows what is right and what is in genuine alignment with our soul's highest good, which is always aligned with the highest good of all. At a deep soul level, we always know what is good, authentic, and correct for us.

What is right? What is good? What is true? We have been conditioned to ignore inner whispers that counter societal programming, to turn down the dial on our intuition. We are not comfortable trusting our gut or following those niggles. We are not comfortable trusting ourselves.

One of the most significant issues we face is a lack of self-trust because the more of us that do tune in and tap into that inner guidance system, the power that resides in our inner knowing, the less we can become manipulated and the more we come fully alive and shine our light bright.

Digging deep and doing the inner work is the most demanding work we can ever do, but we need to do it because this is the task of this lifetime, and the future of humanity and the Earth depends upon our healing. All the shadows are being exposed and 'coming to light' so we can collectively alchemize them into a Golden Age of Light.

As the shadows are being illuminated, the current paradigm based on fear, separation, lack, and scarcity is falling away. The patriarchy is falling, but on the other side of this crumbling of the old structures and systems, of the old ways of being that aren't working for us and haven't been for quite a while, the opportunity to enter a whole new era and birth a New Earth is here. We are already doing it, those of us who have chosen to answer the call of the higher Truth of the Universe.

Earth is ascending and we are ready to release the old. The old paradigm is hanging on with the grip of death. But we are ready for Rebirth. We are ready to Birth a New Earth.

On December 21, 2020, Jupiter and Saturn aligned for 'The Great Conjunction,' a rare occurrence. According to many, this date marked the end of a 26,000-year cycle. The ancients predicted this End of Time and modern astronomy and astrology corroborate the magnitude of this moment through the planetary alignments. Since 2012, we've had numerous powerful astronomical alignments that many have correlated with the start of the New Era.

I don't believe one singular date ushers in this reality; rather, we are in a multi-year transition period. In the grand scheme, 12 years is negligible in a cycle of 26,000. I believe over the next several years, we will only see an increase in collective upheaval; however, simultaneously, many more will experience a profound awakening or catalyzation of their ascension. So I believe we are here, entering an entirely new paradigm and a wholly new era of humanity, and it is our task to anchor the blueprint for an entire New Age of Humanity. This is our legacy.

Because the shift is so massive energetically speaking, we individually and collectively have to choose it because our dense physical bodies encumbered by heavy trauma and low-frequency emotions are not a vibrational match for the new era. We cannot just sit here passively and expect the healing to happen. We must actively co-create the world we want: Heaven on Earth is available to us as long as we choose it. It starts within. We must actively choose the light and transmute the dark.

It begins within, and like a ripple in the ocean of consciousness, our frequency triggers those around us to start their journeys. Seeds are planted, more profound intuitions triggered. Bit by bit, step by step, we will rise. As we keep choosing, we ascend into the light one step at a time, one person at a time. Together, we rise.

Take Your First Steps

Awareness is the first step in healing because we cannot heal what we cannot see; we cannot heal what we cannot feel. Numbing our body stops us from feeling. If we are to change our circumstances, life, and world, we need to heal these traumas and emotional wounds.

First, cultivate stillness. Start your day with warm lemon water. Breathe. Meditate. As you get comfortable with these simple practices, allow the thoughts to come up and allow yourself to see what is festering in your subconscious so you can begin to do the deeper emotional healing surrounding the events and circumstances that created these beliefs. Observe. Journal. Cry if you need to. Release. Integrate. Then let go of the old thoughts.

When triggers come up, get curious. Investigate the root and determine what is underlying that trigger. Is it really because that person cut you off in traffic? Or is there something deeper that truly triggered you? There is usually a much deeper root than the immediate situation of someone cutting you off on the road. It could relate to a deeper wound about feeling disrespected, not being seen or heard, or being unable to take up space. It could be a worthiness wound. See how quickly that can spiral! And yes, that's precisely how it works.

These wounds can be buried deep; sometimes, minor situations can trigger them. Whenever a trigger arises, it's an opportunity for us to get curious about where it is coming from.

Grounding down and getting centered in your body is critical to this process. So many of us are in our heads, completely disconnected and disembodied. Ascension is about going inward, deeply embodying these higher frequencies. Where many go wrong is the desire to escape their bodies and this reality, to travel through the astral and have literal out-of-body experiences at the expense of cultivating a deep connection with their physical body and a deep appreciation of this physical experience.

To heal, we need to feel *safe* to feel. We must feel safe in our bodies. Put your feet on the Earth and connect to nature as much as possible; go to the beach, a forest, or a park, hike, exercise outside, or walk to the store instead of driving. Be out in nature, feet on the ground, sun on your face, as much as possible as this helps us cultivate a connection to Earth and our physical bodies.

As much as possible, physically connect to the ground directly through your skin, cotton, or any non-synthetic material. Rubber soles on our feet block the beneficial ions from penetrating the skin.

Even more critical is direct exposure to sunlight. Vitamin D is essential for optimal immune health, so soak up as much direct sunlight as possible, preferably in the morning and evening, without sunblock, which blocks Vitamin D absorption. If you have fair skin, build your way up to twenty minutes in the morning and evening. When you do need sunblock, stick to organic, chemical-free brands.[28] Also, wean yourself off sunglasses as our eyes absorb most of the light codes we receive. I have light blue eyes—if I can do it, so can you. Receiving light directly through our eyes helps to activate the pineal gland.

Keep your immune system strong; keep your body strong. Vitamin C,[29] vitamin D, and zinc,[30] along with a spectrum of nutrient consumption, will boost immunity to any pathogen that may come along. Studies have found all cancer patients to have low Vitamin D levels, with a majority having an actual deficiency.[31] I was deficient, and supplementing both orally and with direct sunlight was one of the first things I did before treatment even began. I literally got a tan. To this day, I can tolerate more sun on my skin and my pale blue eyes, through which we receive many benefits. Remove the protection, and remove the dark shades. Covid patients were also found to be low in Vitamin D across the board. And yet they told us to stay inside. Hm.

Eat the rainbow as much as possible by consuming real natural foods. Consume as many different nutrients as possible, and supplement with high-quality supplements as needed. One issue we face is our soil has been depleted, and the use of pesticides and genetically modified crops has diminished the nutrient content of crops nearly across the board. An apple today is not the same as an apple sixty years ago. Supplementing with high-quality products can dramatically improve overall well-being. Personally, I load up my system if facing illness, especially water-soluble vitamins like vitamin C, as the body naturally excretes what it doesn't utilize. Of course, consult a holistic or integrative practitioner. A complete blood panel can determine deficiencies and imbalances.

Magnesium is an essential nutrient in which we're collectively highly deficient, with an estimated 75% not consuming enough and nearly half entirely deficient.[32] Magnesium will be highly beneficial to most because it is implicated in over 300 bodily reactions, including enzymatic reactions. It helps us sleep and improves digestive regularity, two critical considerations as so much of our overall health and functioning ties back to sleep and gut health. The most bioavailable form is Magnesium glycinate; it is less likely to cause digestive issues and effectively reaches muscles and organs.

Breathwork is a potent healing modality because it helps move the energy and shift some densities.[33] Simply returning to the breath and taking a few long, deep inhales and exhales can calm the system almost instantaneously in times of stress or overwhelm.

Throughout this book, we will build on this information, but those are a few simple, practical steps you can take right now to jump-start or support your journey. You can find more free resources on my website. The Body Temple Blueprint offers a comprehensive program to support all the levels of your being and build a strong foundation of mind-body health and vitality.

Chapter Two

Light and Love

The Eternal Essence of Your Being

"If you want to find the secrets of the universe, think in terms of energy, frequency, and vibration." ~ Nikola Tesla

Emotional States and Energetic Frequencies

Our true essence is that of light. Every one of us, at our core, is a beautiful being of light. We have simply forgotten this.

To Know Thyself is the ultimate goal of the pilgrimage that is Life, and it is the core tenet of the journey of healing back to wholeness and that of this book: to remember who you are.

The shadows of darkness have shrouded the Truth, but we are in the midst of a monumental shift that is lifting the veil. When I initially received the idea to discuss the light in the dark in 2020, I thought it would mean the literal season of darkness—Winter—ushered in with December when the days become darkest. Yet this season of darkness is truly one that is lasting several years as all of the darkest shadows of humanity come to light. If we zoom out even further, however, this period of darkness has lasted millennia.

Humanity is finally exiting the Dark Ages.

Profound hope looms on the horizon as the light of the sun is shining brighter, illuminating the way forward ever more clearly for those who choose to leave the past behind and follow the golden path to an age of miracles. A future of brightness, wonder, and beauty is within reach. A world based on Truth, harmony, love, and joy awaits.

Many of us, however, are still lost in the dark, blinded to the promise of a bright new reality. With all this loose talk of being the light, shining your light, the light versus dark, what do we mean by 'the light?' To most unfamiliar with the global shift in consciousness, it probably still sounds a bit like intangible woo-woo fluff.

Light, love, and shadow energies are related directly to frequency and energy. Energy manifests as emotions in humans. All emotions resonate at a particular frequency—fear, anger, shame, and hopelessness resonate at very low or constricted frequencies. At the same time, love, joy, gratitude, and bliss vibrate at much higher or more expanded frequencies. Gratitude is the threshold into the higher states of love, beauty, and magic, which is why it is so powerful. Our emotional, feeling, or vibrational state truly does create our reality as our external becomes a vibrational match for our internal frequency. As within, so without.

Every emotion has a particular frequency, a particular vibration. According to the scale of emotions, at the bottom are the frequencies of hopelessness, helplessness, and depression, one of the lowest states you can be in. Shame registers as the lowest.*

Note: I am only using the terms 'high' and 'low' to facilitate our understanding of these concepts through a linear model, as most of our minds still categorize information in this manner. This model is still rooted in hierarchy, inherently a manifestation of separation consciousness. It is technically more accurate to refer to these states from the perspective of contraction and constriction versus expansion. To most effectively conceptualize this idea, however, seeing it as a scale from low to high is still easier. Low correlates to the constricted states of being, and high correlates to the most expanded states of consciousness.

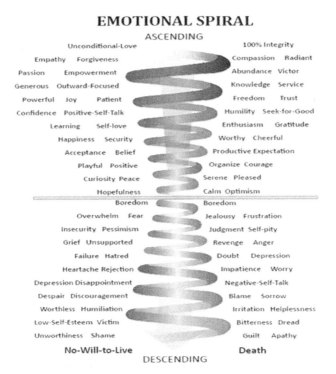

The scale of emotions slowly ascends, increasing in frequency, through the heavier, denser emotions until we reach a particular threshold. At this point, we transcend density and elevate into higher vibrational frequencies that allow us to attract our dreams and visions.

It is crucial to understand this not just for manifestation purposes but also for physical healing of the body. The body cannot heal itself in these lower, denser emotional states. Energy is blocked, and traumas and emotional wounds keep us in the patterns of stress, fear, anxiety, and depression, which hinder the immune system's ability to do its job. Shifting out of these states, healing the wounds, releasing the blocks, and elevating our states are crucial to our vitality, well-being, and ability to attract love, abundance, and success.

Anger is a much higher frequency than sadness, despair, and helplessness. So once you shift into a state of anger, you shift into a greater sense of power, but power with a sense of control or domination is still a low vibration. The desire to control perpetuates the hierarchical paradigm of 'power over,' which has created much of the global discord we are currently facing. This form of power is the power that corrupts. It is false power.

Underlying anger is often grief, so once we truly process the anger, bitterness, and resentment, we frequently uncover the pain of hurt, abandonment, loneliness, and betrayal. So even though rage is a powerful emotion, allowing ourselves to fully embrace and release the sacred rage will often move the energy only to enable us to go even deeper and experience a profound cathartic release of deeply buried pain. A sense of peace settles in as soon as this sensation is released.

What I love and find very fascinating is the science behind the state of gratitude. Gratitude is the gateway between the lower, denser, heavier emotions and the higher, more expansive emotions. Cultivating gratitude is profoundly important because it can shift us into those higher states of expansion.

This is why cultivating a gratitude practice is so vital. Numerous studies have found that it improves many areas of life, from relationships to physical health to business success. Creating a new habit doesn't generally happen overnight. Just like one session at the gym to exercise our muscles and build strength will not miraculously change our body overnight, cultivating any new practice or energy so that it becomes our habitual state of being takes concerted focus and repetition. Changing our lives, changing our emotional state, changing our frequency—that also takes consistent practice.

We must show up for ourselves daily and practice being in that different state. We have to practice existing in the lighter, higher, more expansive emotions like love, joy, freedom, bliss, and abundance until it becomes our natural state. All these emotional states expand our energetic field, and cultivating these elevated emotional frequencies so they become our state enables us to experience expansion and elevation in our lives. This is what embodiment is: rewiring the brain and the body. Embodiment of these expanded states is how we become the creators of our reality.

Running Through Golden Fields of Joy

Think about when you played as a kid; you likely felt the world was wide open and full of possibilities. You were free, living fully in the moment. Play helps us to be present in the moment, in the Now. Incorporating play and joyful experiences into our lives as much as possible allows us to not only cultivate these emotional states that are a frequency match for the healing, love, and abundance that most of us desire, but also to stay present in the moment rather than ruminating over the past or worrying about the future, neither of which exist except in our minds.

Imagine running with childlike abandon through a golden field of sunflowers, laughing and free. Deep blue spread across the infinite expanse of the sky above, and warm, radiant sunshine beams down on your face. Smile. Breathe it in. Return to this field of sunflowers anytime you feel heaviness seep in. This field of sunflowers came through in the activation for the Key of Joy in my series, The Golden Keys to Abundance, which brought us on the most beautiful, playful journey through a golden field of smiling flowers, and imagining myself in this scenery helps me to remember that joyful feeling and inevitably brings a smile to my face.

Play is something we need to consciously create more of as adults because as we grow older, we become burdened with a sense of responsibility for what we 'should' be doing, achieving, or succeeding at based on some formula of external validation. We get stuck in the spin cycle of doing and discount our state of being. This is a major facet of where we've gone wrong in society, and from a big-picture perspective, it helps us to understand why we are in this global state of disconnection. We have suppressed our natural state of childlike innocence and joy.

While we must face the shadows and go through the dark tunnel, incorporating joy on the journey gives our soul the nourishment it needs to keep going. I also believe that healing can come through joy itself, especially once we reach a certain state of our evolution.

To counteract the heaviness of the dark, we must consciously create and cultivate moments of joy and play in our lives.

What is Darkness?

We've discussed what the light means from a practical perspective and, in doing so, touched on the natural polarity of the darkness. However, there is an important distinction I would like to make before delving in: the difference between the shadows and the darkness itself.

Darkness in and of itself is not sinister. Nor is it evil. Darkness is Source itself—the void, the womb, the origin of creation, the Mother energy. The feminine polarity is the void space from which all potentiality and possibility are generated. The womb is the fertile ground from which all life is birthed. Darkness often gets conflated with the shadows that lurk within the darkness, hidden from our perception; the darkness itself isn't what needs healing; it's the shadows contained within that require facing and integration.

When we refer to the dark, we typically mean the shadows that lurk in the dark, fester in our subconscious beliefs, conditioning, and programming, take root in our bodies and energetic fields, and even wind around our DNA. We must confront the shadows swept under the rug and the proverbial skeletons in our closets.

Shadows include heavier, denser emotions, outdated beliefs, false programming, and emotional trauma. The shadow consists of the physical trauma that gets stuck in the body as well, but it's primarily the suppressed or repressed emotions from our past that we don't want to unbury. Our body remembers. If we go even deeper, it's not even from our current lives alone. We inherit not just our physical and genetic traits from our family lineage, but down the line through epigenetics, we also inherit trauma and sexual trauma going way back to ancient civilizations.

Our souls can even carry trauma and karmic imprints from other lifetimes, timelines, and dimensions. Since the fall of humanity, we have been living in a world of polarity and separation. The fall in consciousness created an opportunity for absolute individuation, and now we have the opportunity to bridge the realms of physicality and spirituality together, bring them back into wholeness, and integrate the separation and the duality.

This is why this work of healing can feel so challenging—it forces us to go places we never wanted to go. Yet the light is always there to guide us back to Truth and love. It comforts us and shines hope into the darkest of nights. Remember, what you resist persists. Allow yourself to surrender to the process, and Let it be Easy.

The darkness of Source itself, the void of the womb, the mother herself, is there to hold us until we are ready to be reborn into the light, shadows integrated, more whole and brilliant than ever.

This is what we're here to do as humans—to learn our soul lessons to heal the separation and return to wholeness and love. To remember who we are. This has been our job over lifetimes, generations, and the entire span of humanity: to remember the force of source creation that flows through us.

We are here at this critical time in humanity's evolution because we have experienced enough to handle the intensity of these times. We are here to transmute it all.

From a galactic spiritual perspective that recognizes that the soul is eternal, we all chose to be here in this lifetime. And we all specifically chose to be alive here for this show we are witnessing—the Greatest Show on Earth, ever. We chose it and were chosen—all of us. I heard a fascinating tidbit from an intuitive: for each of us here right now, there were over a million other souls who wanted our spot on the Earth—right now—to be part of this show. There are roughly 8 billion of us on the planet presently. And all of us are the lucky chosen ones who get to attend the most challenging school and play a role in the greatest show in the galaxy.

Looking at it from this perspective might be deeply triggering for some or conjure skepticism: *What, why would I ever have chosen to experience the excruciating pain of my trauma? Why would people choose to experience the horrific suffering that is occurring at this very moment?* I get it. I most certainly do. The dark forces took the experiment too far.

But all the muck that we are going through, all of the grief, uncertainty, and upheaval is so that we can do this work to liberate the consciousness and souls of humanity because we are at the brink of a massive transition point. Only powerful souls can face the depths of darkness humanity is confronted with, and many choose to incarnate into lifetimes of hardship and even abject horror to balance karma from a previous lifetime. The oppressor becomes the oppressed. When we learn the lessons and integrate the wisdom, we transcend, ending the trance and the looping cycles of karma.

Advanced souls, strong souls, and those who chose to go through the most challenging school because they had radically important lessons to learn are the ones incarnated here now. As hard as the Earth school is, it's also a magical playground full of pleasure and possibility where we get the opportunity to experience the magic of physical creation in all of its duality. And yes, this is how important what is going on right now is from a galactic, universal perspective.

Here on Earth, most of us are stuck in our tiny little egos like, Oh my gosh, the sky is falling. Things are crumbling from the 3D earth perspective, but that's precisely why we are here—to create not just a new paradigm but a whole new era. All built on a false foundation must go.

We are shifting into a new golden age of light. We are awakening to our true infinite potential. As complex, challenging, and painful as it might be for so many of us, we need these outdated systems and structures to be dismantled because they're not working for us. It's time to create something better, enter the golden age of light, love, harmony, and peace, and collectively come together to rebuild.

This Shift ushers in a new paradigm of cooperation rather than competition. We are here to bridge the polarity, to transmute fear into love, dark into light. That transmutation process thrusts what's been hidden in the darkness into the light, looking into the shadows and integrating them and healing them, creating a fuller expression of the light—for us to be even more whole and complete.

Through this healing process, the light becomes brighter and more vibrant. It radiates from a whole new depth of brilliance, encompassing an even vaster spectrum of color and luminosity than we could imagine because we've been stuck under the fog of shadows. Like light beaming through a clear glass prism, what seemed like simple, clear glass radiates a beautiful rainbow, almost like magic.

Rainbow frequencies are associated with higher realms of consciousness and the primary chakras, or energy centers, within our energy body, so as we raise our frequencies, seeing rainbows often becomes much more frequent. But it goes beyond the rainbow—there's so much more vibrancy to life that we can't even fathom. When we're in a state of fear or the lower denser emotions, we get stuck in a constricted state akin to tunnel vision, we cannot see possibility. This is precisely why it's so hard to heal, transform, and change our lives when we live in fear or survival mode.

This is exactly what the collective is experiencing right now, so it's of the utmost importance that we step up and shine brighter than ever because humanity needs us. Our neighbors and loved ones need us. Every person in your life needs you to step into your power and shine your light. Together, our lights merge to create a brilliant rainbow of infinite possibilities.

The Battle of the Light vs the Dark

Growth isn't always easy, but it's always worth it. To reiterate, light represents elevated consciousness, higher frequency, and more expansive emotions and states of being. What most of us refer to as 'the dark' is lower consciousness and denser, more constricted emotions and states of being. No matter where we are on our journey, even those of us who predominantly embody the light, we confront experiences that elicit these heavier shadow frequencies, which is why I distinguish between passing emotions and states of being.

As we continue to elevate, these frequencies impact us less and the bounce back becomes faster and faster. We can catch ourselves much more readily and consciously choose to shift out of that. To choose to return to the frequencies of love, gratitude, trust, and compassion. Ultimately, the deeper we dive, the higher we rise.

The spiritual battle is waged against our consciousness and within our hearts and minds above all. True mastery and wholeness blossoms from integrating and embracing the shadow, not rejecting or denying it. We remember it is all worthy of love. Once we return to a state of wholeness and remember our divinity, our energy field becomes impenetrable as we are surrounded by a forcefield of protection generated by pure divine love.

In the battle for our souls, our purity becomes our power, not our weakness. Our remembrance of our innocence and worthiness becomes our greatest shield of protection, and our radiance of Truth the greatest weapon against the illusion of darkness.

Shine Your Light

Gratitude shifts us into these expansive states of love, joy, bliss, harmony, and abundance and helps us to transmute bitterness, fear, or lack. Embodying the higher states allows us to reclaim our power as the creator of our lives.

To return to the esoteric or spiritual perspective, light is Truth, the source of life force energy itself. We are all light beings having a physical experience here on Planet Earth. Healing and raising our vibration is the journey of returning to our natural state of divine light. It is a state of grace. This is the Truth we are returning to.

A spark of the divine lives within all of us. It's often just hidden, buried under the shadows of our fears, traumas, and repressed emotions, under the pain and suffering we experience in life. Much of the heavy shadows we carry are not even from our lifetime, but we carry them deep in our tissues, our cells, and our DNA, wound tightly around the molecules that contain our unique sacred blueprint. The fear, anger, hurt, pain, and suffering extend back to our ancestors, carried down the generations through our DNA. Epigenetic research has proven this.

Our job is to heal the ancestral trauma, unravel the past, and release it from our DNA to shift our timeline and birth a new version of humanity—beings grounded in the light rather than the fear and the heavy, dense emotions.

Embodying the light so that we can be free and live fully and beautifully is, in fact, the most practical thing we can do. This is how we heal humanity and build a more beautiful future.

The Light is Love

Light is love, the eternal essence that resides within. It all comes back to love. The basis of life is love—it is the Source of creation. Love is a force of attraction that holds atoms and molecules together, an energetic force of gravitational pull. The light is like the spark within us, our life force essence born of eternal love, and our fundamental creative force.

Our light is our inner fire. We have been shutting down our life force by turning down the dial on our light and, in essence, turning away from life. Every time we choose to turn down that dial of our fullest expression and our deepest joys and passions, every time we turn down the dial of what lights us up, we are turning down the dial on life itself because the light is life. It is the spark of passion that urges us to create and expand. It's love.

Love is what compels us to grow. It compels us to expand and repair this disconnection, the sense of separation. This is our job right now. That is what it means to go through the dark, to release what's holding us back from being our most whole, most authentic expressions of ourselves, to liberate our souls, and to step into the light. The light is our Truth. Deep down, it's what we know to be true, the intuitive knowing guiding us our whole lives.

Emerging from our cocoon of darkness requires us to tune in to our intuition, to that inner core of our being that knows what's honest, authentic, and pure, and allow that to lead. Allow love to lead. Choosing the light will enable you to embody this state of expansion and freedom that lights you up, fuels your fire, and ignites your passions.

You being lit up is you being the light. Living your life fully, completely, and beautifully aligned with your Truth is you being the light. Light is Truth. It's simply the Truth of who we are. Shining your light means living your Truth and being your fullest, brightest, most beautiful expression.

So to recap: what is the light? The light is you living your life fully, being your fullest expression of you. It is you reclaiming and stepping into your power. It is remembering who you are—a spark of the divine that is pure eternal love.

Chapter Three

RECLAIM YOUR POWER

Why Outsourcing Keeps you Stuck

"Intuition is seeing with the soul." ~ Dean Koontz

"The only real valuable thing is intuition." ~ Albert Einstein

The Time to reclaim your power is Now. I won't bury the lead here: no one else can heal you, but you. You are your own healer. The sooner you recognize this, the faster things begin to shift.

Of course you can receive profound support and guidance from highly skilled healers and well-trained professionals. But what a good healer truly does is show the way and hold the space for you to uncover the power and possibility you contain within.

The matrix has conditioned us to outsource our expertise and look for a savior outside of ourselves. Both science and religion have disconnected us from the true source of power, grace, and light: ourselves. Seeking a savior will only serve to keep us stuck and small and is simply not going to work for our highest good because it places the power outside of us. Seeking a savior or looking 'up to the experts' keeps us down and disempowered—below, lesser than, subordinate. The Truth is, we are all far more powerful than we have led to believe; than we have been allowed to perceive.

There are many layers to this discussion, but the whole purpose of going through the dark night of the soul and doing the shadow work and digging in, diving deep, and showing up for yourself in these seemingly complicated and challenging ways is so that you can reclaim your power.

It is all in service of your highest good. It is all in service of your greater potential: confronting obstacles and challenges, facing dark nights of the soul, and getting clear on what's blocking and limiting you; when we choose to face those demons, we ignite the fire of transformation. Walking through the fire will ultimately empower you. Fire cleanses us by burning away the impurities, toxic thoughts, energies, and emotions that prevent us from fully embodying our brightest light and fullest power.

Placing our power outside of ourselves happens unconsciously. It is not something we consciously choose or decide to do; it happens primarily because of our programming, conditioning, and how our caregivers and society raise us. We have been trained to give away our power through our culture, our family, our societal programming, our education, and our collective trauma-based states of victimhood.

When we consider our limiting beliefs and general belief systems, where do they come from? They come from society, culture, the programming and conditioning from our first several years of life, and childhood environment. The often reality-shattering Truth is that we don't even realize how deeply mired we are in these programs. Even the most intelligent, highly educated amongst us are susceptible to the programming; in fact, those who are highly educated often have a more challenging time releasing their grip on their current understanding of reality, in large part due to educational indoctrination and ego attachment to their lauded ivory tower education conferring the highest knowledge and Truth available.

But that 'knowing' is based on the logical brain rather than the intuitive heart wisdom this consciousness shift calls us to connect with. Out of the head, into the heart—this is the lesson of the time. The mind can easily be swayed; true strength resides within the conviction of the heart's wisdom.

My cancer journey hit this home. When most of us see a white lab coat, AKA a doctor or a scientist, we assume they are the experts. We believe that they will provide the best solution available, but let's take a step back here—they may be brilliant, skilled, and knowledgeable about their profession (I am certainly not denigrating the intense technical training that doctors have undergone in their specialty), but how much time do they spend with YOU? An oncologist spends possibly 20 or even 30 minutes with you if you're lucky, but how much time do they really spend with you in the grand scheme of life? How well do they know you?

Are they inside your body? Are they inside your mind? Do they know your heart's innermost secrets? Consider that for a moment. Yes, they can run tests. They can order the appropriate tests and lab work and interpret it in ways that most of us cannot—a crucially important resource for us to have when we hit crisis mode. I'm personally very grateful for these medical advances. I applaud our advances in diagnostics, lifesaving procedures, and interventions, especially those in the Emergency Rooms. I'm not trying to detract from all the good that many doctors do. Nor do I deny that the majority are well-intentioned.

That said, sometimes their guess is as good as yours, especially regarding chronic conditions. When it comes to treatment, they might recommend a protocol they have seen work for other people, but that doesn't necessarily mean it is the best option for you. Especially in the world of cancer where the options have serious strings attached (cut, poison, or burn) and the odds are often still not very high, there are times when we have to dig in and ask ourselves, is this right for *me* right *now*?

If we allow ourselves to tune in and listen to our heart and intuition, the answer may be No. That's a scary prospect for most people to consider, much less confront, acknowledge, and accept. We often don't realize that other options exist and fear the option of making such monumental decisions for ourselves. Taking responsibility for becoming our own expert isn't necessarily easy, but it is highly empowering. When we stop blaming our circumstances, doctors, treatment, bad luck, or bad genes, our perspective and energy shift, and suddenly, we can perceive possibility.

Cancer is an extreme example as we are discussing matters of life and death. But let's face it: cancer rates are rising dramatically, and many genuinely are facing such matters. But even in the case of a cold or something that requires an antibiotic, we are being called to tune in and consider the consequences, side effects, and repercussions of these choices. Sometimes, antibiotics are valuable. That said, antibiotics are also extremely overprescribed, usually because they don't know what else to do, and some classes of antibiotics can come with severe side effects. While rare, they do happen.

Antibiotics are not a cure-all, and they wreak havoc on the gut,[34] which is implicated in many different forms of disease. Antibiotics destroy bacteria, including the good ones that aid digestion. The gut is the largest source of serotonin[35] in the body. A gut out of balance can lead to a brain out of balance.[36]

Crises, obstacles, and challenges present opportunities to tune in and listen to yourself. *The doctor is telling me that I should take this medication, but how does it feel for me if I consider the side effects of it, what it might do to my body, and how it might impact my gut health?* We can step back and say, all right, is this for my ultimate good? Is this going to benefit me in the big picture? Is there a natural alternative? Zooming out, asking questions, and tuning in with your guidance system is what it means to take responsibility for yourself.

Do your research. This is critical on the path of reclaiming your power. We have so much information and resources at our fingertips in this day and age. However, when we take the initiative to do the research, we often find conflicting information, especially in the age of social media. There are agendas at play aiming to filter information about politics, healthcare, and every other issue that has become politicized over the years. Pay attention to the source—who is funding the research or the website? Especially the 'independent fact-checkers'—who is funding them? Sit with it and consider what rings true; who do you trust more? *Why* do you trust them? Collect as much evidence as you can, take a deep breath, then go from there. Common sense can carry us a decent amount of the way, but pay attention specifically to whether what is shared carries an energy of fear or love, or whether it feels constrictive or expansive to you.

Reclaiming your power often requires you to question the status quo; to be the annoying patient; to be the person who asks about the fine print before signing on the dotted line. Many would prefer to breeze through the minutiae, blast right through the decision process, and disregard potential consequences or side effects. Your ignorance and complacency are precisely what they bank on: the ones who profit from the status quo don't want you to see the fine print, check ingredients, or read up on side effects.

Taking responsibility and doing the research is not an easy task, not in this crooked world. Most of us want somebody to tell us what to do in scary situations, especially when dealing with medical issues, because they seem so complicated and come with high stakes life or death consequences. Most of us don't want to stand in the aisle checking the ingredient list of every product. But this is what it takes to change. And once we change ourselves by becoming healthy and empowered, we can come together and change the system.

Ultimately, however, nobody knows you the way *you* know you. You know whether that niggling thing is serious. A doctor may brush off your symptoms for months, but you know deep down something is wrong. Sometimes, it is up to you to put your foot down and demand that test and not walk away until they give it to you.

When I was diagnosed with cancer, I didn't realize quite how dire my situation was, but I knew something was wrong. One morning, after an extra bad night of pain-induced sleeplessness, I got up and Googled my symptoms—yes, the thing you're not supposed to do—which, being a fit, healthy Yogi who could do a handstand and touch her toes to her head at the same time, didn't add up. I self-diagnosed with a pulmonary embolism, unwilling to entertain the alternative: cancer. Both cases called for a CT scan.

I called my doctor's office and said, "I need to see the doctor this afternoon. I need a CT scan." The receptionist replied, "It doesn't work that way. You can't just 'get' a CT scan; you need a reason. At any rate, you won't get one today; you need insurance approval." I insisted on getting the earliest appointment available that afternoon. I went in, I told the doctor my symptoms, and he sent me down for an X-ray. He said to come back up after the X-ray to review the results together. I at least felt heard and validated. So when I returned, we sat down and he pulled up the screen. He paused. Then he scrunched up his face and went, *Hmm*.

He turned the screen, pointed, and said, "See this white film over your left lung? I don't know what that is." He pivoted to look me in the eye and said: "Looks like you've earned that CT scan after all."

I was not medically trained. I didn't even know what a CT scan was, but when I read about it, I knew that that was what I needed, and I needed it that day. Sure enough, I had a grapefruit-sized growth inside of my chest, which ultimately turned out to be cancer. And although it was large, we caught it before it spread.

The upshot is: My intuition may have saved my life.

I obviously didn't *want* to be right about it. I hadn't even allowed myself to entertain cancer as a possible diagnosis. But I ultimately knew something was very wrong inside my body. This is not about my ego feeling vindicated; it's about my intuition being validated in a powerful, lifesaving way.

Inner knowing is the most profound wisdom, but most of us have been completely disconnected from that. What if I had waited? The mass was compressing my heart and my lungs. I had two millimeters of breathing space in my left breathing apparatus. My left lung was pretty close to collapsing. If I didn't trust the intuitive inclination that led to the confirmation that something was very off—that there was a giant grapefruit-sized growth inside my chest —I wouldn't have taken the next proactive steps necessary to begin healing even before I had a formal diagnosis in hand.

Trusting your intuition and yourself is crucial to reclaiming your power because you won't take a no for an answer when you know what is right for you. You cannot be gaslit, manipulated, controlled, or compromised when you know your Truth.

If we allow ourselves to connect and tune in, we know our bodies best. We know ourselves best. We are the experts on us when we lean in and begin to trust our inner knowing.

When you know something is right or necessary, you stand up for yourself and your beliefs and keep going. You continue to pursue what you desire. You stay focused on the vision when you're clear on what you want to manifest and have absolute conviction in how you are meant to serve the world.

Humanity must tune in and connect with what is truly for our highest good rather than listen to the so-called experts because these times are mired in confusion. Conflicting information abounds. The unfortunate reality is experts can get so lost in the data that they lose sight of reality.

The majority of the top-down narrative does not align with our highest good. We are bombarded by uncertainty, fear, chaos, finger-pointing, canceling, and deception. Fear dominates, rather than love and compassion. Division and separation are the agenda, rather than unity.

United we stand, Divided we fall. This is not just a guiding principle; it is one of the highest Truths of all rooted in Christ and Unity Consciousness.

Our current stark reality presents a beautiful opportunity for us to exercise our self-guided trust and intuition, to practice standing in our power more and more by questioning what is being said, what we're being told, and asking: *what is right for me, right now?* What makes me feel good, in an 'aligned with my soul' kind of way, not in a hedonistic, self-indulgent manner?

What makes me feel healthy? What makes me feel alive? Because, what are we here for? We're here to Live our lives. Life is for living—fully, completely, and beautifully.

Reclaiming our power and reclaiming our sovereignty is key right now. I believe in a higher power and that we are one with this higher power. Seeking a savior outside of ourselves keeps us in separation. It keeps us in a state of disempowerment because it implies that we can't help ourselves.

When we feel helpless, we don't have the ability to heal ourselves or our lives. Religion places the power outside of us, and so many well-intentioned individuals are waiting helplessly to be saved. Sadly, recent scientific dogma is edging ever closer to religious-like doctrine.

We are far more powerful than helpless sheep dependent on their masters to guide them to food and safety. I believe that ascended masters like Jesus—who I connect with as Yeshua—are way showers who incarnate to show us the path to Truth and remembrance. They come into human form to guide us and reveal the potential we hold within. They realize this potential within themselves so that we can recognize it resides within us, too. Free from distortion, these teachings show us how to walk in their footsteps in a very literal way. *'You will do greater things than me.'*

We are our own saviors. We are the ones we have been waiting for. We are the only ones who can save ourselves. Just like the adage 'You can lead a horse to water, but you can't make it drink,' the same is true for us. We have to choose the path, choose to show up, and do the work ourselves. We can follow the way of Jesus, walk the path of love, and immerse ourselves in his teachings. But we are the ones who have to show up and do it—to live it and embody it. We can't wait for somebody to swoop in and fix everything for us.

If we're not willing to show up and take the aligned action that will support our growth in the direction of our vision, things will not shift. Walking this path takes a concerted effort, but it is worth it.

The saying is not 'What would Jesus think, believe, or feel.' It's 'What would Jesus *Do*.' To walk the way of Christ you must get up and take that first step and keep going.

Reclaiming power requires taking responsibility for your life and cultivating an internal locus of control. In psychology, your locus of control is your sense of autonomy. It's akin to the idea that you are the creator of your life, the director of your destiny. You are the author of your dreams and the artist of your masterpiece. Responsibility is an empowered state of being and way of living.

For many, it requires deep healing from trauma and narcissistic abuse (which can literally rewire the brain and hijack the nervous system into freeze mode) to move forward. So as you navigate this path and get honest about the pain of your past, be gentle with yourself. Have patience. Remember though, miracles are possible because you are a miracle.

Reclaiming your power is simply embracing the notion that you have control over the direction of your life. Taking responsibility means holding yourself accountable for your thoughts, feelings, and emotions, for what you consume in a physical, mental, emotional, and energetic capacity. That includes food; that also includes media and social media. It includes books, podcasts, YouTube, Netflix, TV, movies, and the news. What are you allowing into your consciousness? Where your attention goes, your energy flows.

Awareness is the first step. Become aware of your thoughts. What is your overall mindset—optimistic or pessimistic? Growth-oriented or fixated on failure? On the scale of emotions, where do your thoughts, feelings, and emotions predominantly reside—in higher vibrational states of love, gratitude, and joy, or lower vibrational states like fear, anger, sadness, grief, and despair? We must feel and process emotions when they arise so that we can integrate them and release the density and grip they hold on us.

We cannot dwell—or wallow—in those low frequency emotional states and expect to be able to manifest extraordinary lives. It's simply not how the law of attraction, manifestation, or divine co-creation works. Like matches like: we want to raise our vibrational states to match what we want, like love, joy, and abundance. And we have the power to do that ourselves.

Put yourself in the energy of joy and love by doing things you enjoy and feeling the experience of having all you desire, and BE in a state of gratitude. Gratitude is the threshold; it is the key. Gratitude is a powerful tool to help you shift.

We already have all the tools to help us reclaim our power. It's about bringing all the pieces together: mindset, thoughts, beliefs, emotions, feelings—all of these layers create our reality and determine the experience of our lives.

The Truth is, these are the only things we truly have any control over: our inner state, perceptions of, and responses to our external reality. We cannot control everything in our lives, but we can control our reactions and responses to our circumstances, which ultimately dictate our experience of our lives.

Think about where you are in life, what you're doing, and who you surround yourself with. Is it filling you up? What are you putting your energy into? Who are you giving it to? Is that thing or person uplifting you or draining you?

Begin to consider these inquiries for yourself. This is the first step in reclaiming your power: becoming acutely aware of your circumstances and what you allow into your energy field.

By taking responsibility for what you can control in your life, including your thoughts, feelings, emotions, beliefs, mindset, and what you consume and give your energy to, you take one step closer to becoming the powerful creator you are meant to be.

Chapter Four
Light is Truth
Anchoring into Heart Wisdom

"The truth is not always beautiful, nor beautiful words the truth." ~ *Laozi*

Out of the head, into the heart. My personal lesson, and that of the collective.

This is how we create Heaven on Earth: by liberating our hearts and operating and creating from a frequency of love.

It's time to open Pandora's box and uncover the hidden treasures buried deep within.

Trust, patience, and surrender are key components to opening the heart of Truth. We are being called to surrender to our heart space and allow ourselves to open to the love and support of our guides and God Source Consciousness (or whatever term you prefer for this energy).

Truth is your natural state. Truth is all there is. We all originate from Truth but have become disconnected from birth. Light is life, and if the light is Truth, then Truth is the essence of life. This chapter aspires to elaborate on the grandiose concept of Truth and offer practical ways to help you reconnect with the higher Truth weaving the cosmos.

Let's Start with the Heart

The heart holds the highest form of wisdom. Attuning to our heart center will always lead us to our true North—the heart keeps us anchored in our Truth. When we 'trust our gut,' we descend into the wisdom held in lower energy centers, known in spiritual traditions as the chakras. The gut is the center and source of our more animalistic instincts. This is where the real work begins: to access our higher intuition, we must unblock and balance each energy center, starting with the lower centers. Truth blossoms from alignment, mind, body, and soul; brain, womb, and heart.

Our gut contains nerve clusters, including a giant cluster referred to by some as our second brain. Each of our digestive organs is enervated by an extensive neuronal network, known as the Enteric Nervous System.[37] Because of all that we intake through our food and our environment, our digestive system is responsible for digesting an astonishing amount of information that our brains, in their current state, couldn't even come close to fathoming, much less processing. When we consider that the neural networks in our abdomens process far greater quantities of information, much detected by our senses, we can begin to see the wisdom behind the adage 'trust your gut.'

Our conscious brains are limited in the amount and speed of information they can process, and at our current phase in evolution, we are only using an estimated ten percent of them. To fully tune in to the wisdom of Truth, we must tune in to our instincts and tap into our intuition to reconnect with our gut and heart wisdom. I call it Body Wisdom. Attunement requires what many call 'shadow work' to clear the blockages and densities that get in the way of energy flow and heal this connection with inner trust and Truth. Because doing the shadow work and facing our demons is not an easy process for anyone, it's essential to anchor in the light of possibility so that we stay focused on the goal and stay focused on the light and not get mired in the shadows.

We can begin by taking a leap of faith to reconnect with our intuition and learn to trust ourselves to embody this heart-centered wisdom. But when we are still holding on to the shadows that encompass the trauma, pain, and emotional wounds from the past, it is impossible for us to fully trust ourselves, to fully trust life, or to tune in to our intuition. Remember, this is a journey, one that spirals us deeper into ourselves and deeper into trust.

Narcissistic abuse can shatter our sense of trust in others, in the world, but most insidiously our trust in self. Disentangling from the web of deception, lies, and gaslighting can be a harrowing and disheartening process, especially if we have begun to question ourselves and distrust our capacity to discern truth from fiction. Unraveling the doubt and shame requires patience, however the liberation of our light reveals the pot of gold within, and the journey brings us closer to our remembrance of the divinity within.

Ultimately, it serves to empower us, strengthen our boundaries, and liberate our hearts into the expansive beauty and wonder of immaculate divine love.

Healing is about reconnecting with the Truth of who we are. It is about remembering the light within and the spark of divinity that we are. Many ancient wisdom traditions describe our life force energy rising through the energy centers in our body; every tradition discusses these same energy centers, or chakras. So the journey begins with recognizing this universal energy that resides and flows within us all, that we are energetic beings having a human experience.

Our energy is supposed to rise up and flow fluidly; however, if we have trauma or emotional wounds, there are gaps, blockages, or distortions in our energy field that prevent the smooth flow of energy. We must commit to deeper healing to clear out blocks, learn to trust our intuition, embody our heart's wisdom, and allow our life force energy to flow and rise up to fuel the power, passion, and purpose contained within our blueprint.

What follows is the strength to speak our Truth from a space of love and embodied harmony. It begins with trust at the root, the foundation: trusting life, trusting your intuition, and trusting yourself, which then blossoms into a deeper knowing, a more profound wisdom of what is right, what is good, and what is true.

Finally, we arrive at the point of owning, speaking, and expressing our embodied Truth, a manifestation of unblocking the throat chakra.

What is Truth?

In our current matrix reality paradigm, people often speak of His Truth and Her Truth, My Truth versus Your Truth. We frequently see this in divorce or breakups—there's his truth, there's her truth, and then somewhere in the middle lies the actual Truth.

Many are so ingrained in their perspective, their personal version of reality, that they cannot accept that somebody perceives the Truth differently. This opens the realm of beliefs and perspectives on life based on societal, cultural, religious, and familial constructs.

We must go further and transcend these ideas of personal truths and build the capacity to hold multiple truths at once. We can respect that other person has a different belief from us, and honor how their life experiences and circumstances would form their perspectives.

However, the trap I see with even this 'evolved' perspective on Truth is that it's still rooted in the paradigm of separation. When we elevate our perspective to yet another level of consciousness, I believe a higher Truth exists above all our individual beliefs and perspectives, a common Truth we are guided to on our unique paths. Each path is unique, yet there is a common destination we are all being guided toward: Love.

Our unique 'truths' guide us through the personal lessons and experiences we came here to evolve through until we open up to see the grander Truth. His Truth, her Truth, your Truth, my Truth; that's the 3D version of Truth. Truth with a capital T is Unity Consciousness—Oneness.

Society has become extremely polarized, especially in the United States through the realm of politics and social justice issues. There's the Truth that exists for those who vote Blue. And then there's the Truth for those who vote Red. But the bigger Truth with a capital T lies not just in the middle that it's all one bird, it lies way above all of the chaos and noise. Many, through their distorted lens of Truth, are not just supporting but blindly asking for tyranny, censorship, and segregation because they're operating from a limited 'truth' that is truly a belief based on fear and manipulation. While the fear may feel very real to those individuals operating at that level of consciousness, their beliefs are based in illusion and deceit. Higher Truth transcends personal beliefs. The sad truth is that we are living in a post-truth society.

A greater Truth shines through the cracks of the inverted fear-based matrix of the 3D paradigm, which is why we're experiencing so much chaos and instability. The more light flows in, the more the darkness comes to light. The light is guiding us back to Truth. Whether or not people are ready to see it, the light of truth is illuminating the ugly shadows of the system. To see it clearly, we must shed the layers of illusion, remove the shields that have been blinding us from seeing clearly, and allow the Truth to be seen, reconciled, and healed.

Confirmation bias perpetuates deeply ingrained beliefs as people seek out information that confirms their current worldview. Our social media feeds, social circles, and information sources curate echo chambers to continually affirm our sense of what is true. The lack of respectful debate and discussion with those who hold different beliefs is only sowing division in our world.

Alternatively, many experience cognitive dissonance[38] when confronted with facts or viewpoints that challenge their currently held beliefs. The more someone digs their heels in on an issue—the more their ego is attached to being right—the harder it is to admit they might have been wrong, not just to others but especially to themselves. The Truth hurts, but only to an ego operating in distortion.

Shadow work is the process of removing the blinders. It can be deeply confronting and uncomfortable. But on the other side lies the liberation of our minds into Truth and our hearts into Love. The mind then becomes a tool in service to the heart, the ultimate chalice of wisdom.

The fact is, sometimes the Truth is not what you want it to be. Often, there are layers of shame, guilt, or grief that we aren't ready to deal with or don't believe we can handle. So we shove it down, suppress it, and repress it so as not to confront those uncomfortable feelings. Ultimately, avoidance is counterproductive and at odds with our highest good and optimal wellbeing; the same goes for the collective shadows. Having difficult conversations is hard. Not having them is harder.

It's time to face the skeletons in the closet. We cannot continue to repress and suppress our traumas and emotions. Dark, dirty secrets about our world are coming to light, shadows so dark that we can only grapple with them when we have the tools to grapple with the shadows within while remaining anchored in the light. The Truth must come out for us to rise in our power and reclaim our world.

Beliefs come from our family, our culture, our religion, and our social and societal conditioning, and the fact is most of these deeply rooted beliefs come from the first seven years of our lives when our subconscious is a sponge of the world around us.[39]

At that age, we move through life in a delta state, absorbing everything around us. For the most part, we're not consciously able to discern Truth. At the age of seven, how aware were you of Truth beyond your family life or immediate world? Kids are very aware on many levels, but that's ultimately been part of our collective downfall because we're unaware of how much they're aware of. They absorb everything they hear, everything they see, and every way we respond to their needs—or don't. Children raised with unresponsive or unavailable parents carry that separation with them. Children raised by parents with poverty consciousness carry that lack with them. Children who are told 'you can't' or 'people like us can't do that' carry that limitation through life. Until they break the pattern.

We can trace the roots of our beliefs about love, wealth, worthiness, relationships, and almost every aspect of life back to our childhoods. If our parents fought about money, said money doesn't grow on trees, or said money is the root of all evil, there is a perfect setup for a lack or scarcity mindset. Even the most seemingly innocuous moments of our childhoods can deeply imprint on our psyches. That holds true for how our parents were raised, and it holds true for how we raise our children. Blaming our parents is not the solution—becoming the pattern breaker is.

Because we can trace so much of our belief systems and programming back down the lineage to our ancestors' traumas and the societies in which our parents were raised, it becomes much easier to forgive our parents and choose to be the pattern breaker and lineage healer. We can take up the torch and say, 'This ends with me.' We can choose to heal for our children's sake and the whole lineage, forward and back. We can choose to be the liberators.

However, the programming gets passed on without this conscious choice and committed action. This conditioning literally programs us: how we think, how we speak, how we act. Truth is so much bigger than our conditioned realities. Truth is connection and oneness, love, and harmony. We live in a 3D world of polarity and separation, but the Truth we are returning to is so much more beautiful than that: we are returning to the promised land of milk and honey.

We don't arrive there by holding our hands out, waiting for manna to fall from the sky. Walking in truth is a profound test of the soul. We get to the Promised Land by letting go of our ego's desire to control and surrendering to Divine Will, taking actions in accordance with God's guidance with full faith in Love's decree.

Our Natural State

To reconnect with Truth, connect with nature. Nature is the world's cathedral. Think about a time you looked up at the night sky out in nature: distant from a city's noise and light pollution, yet closer to an ineffable sense of peace and connection; or for those who have been fortunate enough to witness the ethereal dance of the stunning Aurora Borealis, the absolute awe and rapture so many experience. Or a time you felt reverence looking out over the vast expanse of the ocean or the sense of wonder you felt watching the sunrise or sunset. The sense of feeling attuned to the breathing life of a forest or the majestic power of a mountain. The soothing scent of fresh rain, the sweet fragrance and brilliant beauty of flowers, the feeling of blades of grass or fine sand under your bare feet.

Most of us have had a moment when we dropped into a profound sense of serenity and deep connection when communing with nature. I feel so connected when I go to the beach and gaze out over the water, watching the waves roll in and out. Living by the beach was my priority during my healing journey, and as my circumstances allow I answer when the mountains and forests call. Simply lying in the grass or walking outside to feel the breeze on my skin, the sun on my face, and the fresh air filling my lungs, I've learned that I don't have to go to some distant locale to feel connected to nature. Even cities have parks. Daily exposure to nature is my favorite medicine.

Wherever in the world you may be, find a way to connect with the natural world around you. Walk out your door and look up at the sky: gaze at the stars and moon at night, delight in the trees, blue sky, and heavenly clouds by day. This profound sense of connection and oneness penetrates our being when we are out in nature because this oneness is Truth.

The simplest way to reconnect with ourselves, uncover the deeper truth within, and open to the higher truth that is available to us all is to connect with nature.

Nature is so powerful because we are made up of the same elements that make up Earth. The same water flows through our veins and makes up our cells, the same minerals from the soil build our bones, the same air flows through our lungs, and the same ball of fire in the sky above that warms our skin and makes all life possible sparks our life force and ignites the light within.

When Hippocrates said 'Let food be thy medicine,' food came purely from nature.

The Truth is, we are all connected to all the kingdoms, above and below. We are all one, connected to a higher consciousness, journeying back to this Truth as we return to love.

What we can do is begin to heal the existential sense of disconnection that we feel—a disconnection from self, from soul, from source. Healing the illusion of separation, first with self, is key because Truth lies within our hearts. *Heart* rearranged spells *Earth*. Source guidance and wisdom from Father God and Mother Earth and you will find your way Home.

The Light of Truth is always there with us, no matter how much we doubt or have lost faith in life and feel stuck in a state of disconnection. We must let go, trust, have faith, and surrender to the process. It's not easy. But even through our doubt, the inner light of Truth is always there within and guiding us every step of the way.

First, we must heal the untruth of thinking that we are separate, that we are disconnected, that we are isolated or alone. Much of this goes back to childhood emotional wounds. We must heal the untruth of believing that we were unloved. This isn't to minimize poor parenting. The unfortunate reality is that most of our parents never received true love either and didn't know how to love unconditionally. Most parents have passed down their own unhealed wounds, limiting beliefs, and traumas to their children, perpetuating generational cycles of lack and trauma.

So, how do we begin to heal ourselves and break these patterns? Begin by loving yourself. Inner child healing is powerful.

Loving the inner child that lives within and telling that inner child that no matter what happened in the past—whatever caused the pain of feeling hurt, scared, alone, not seen, not heard—that they are not alone, sets us free. You, as a fractal of the divine, are there to hold them and offer the protection they desire while they reflect the purity and innocence that resides within your heart.

You can go within and re-parent your inner child and love that inner child back to life. Sit in meditation and reconnect with that smaller version of you that still lives within. Hug them and love them, apologize, forgive, and speak words of affirmation to the little child within that only ever craved unconditional love and acceptance. Send your inner child beautiful heart beams of love and light. Embrace them with unconditional forgiveness and eternal love. You're effectively beaming love into yourself, loving your inner child self back to life, and integrating all past versions of you into wholeness.

This is where the collective healing begins: it begins with each of us going deep into those wounds and excavating the gunk from our past that we've swept under the rug or relegated to the forgotten realms of the subconscious. We may consciously forget as we move through life uncomfortably numb. Yet we carry the energetic imprint of pain, hurt, fear, sadness, loneliness, rejection, abandonment, and betrayal. We carry it all until we acknowledge, feel, integrate, and release it. If we don't, the dam eventually bursts and the cycles repeat until we learn the lesson and walk through the fires of alchemy.

As we deepen into this process, memories, feelings, and sensations will surface. More will come to light. The light of Truth helps us to remember because they've been stuck deep within all along, and that's what's been holding us back. It's often the deeper wounds and trauma that cause physical illness and disease. Mental and emotional dis-ease manifest as physical disease in the body. Deeper traumas and wounds from the past that may not even be ours; they could go back generations, often festering deep within the body.

Whispers of pain, discomfort, or imbalance become urgent calls, and if they continue to be ignored, they manifest as full-blown alarm sirens in the form of cancer (as what happened to me) or acute chronic or degenerative conditions. The body keeps the score[40] in a very real way, and this fact is rooted in the pain of disconnection, a disconnection that is perpetuated in the very systems and structures of not just our society but in the medical system itself. This is why, as technology advances and billions[41] have gone towards research, they are no closer to 'finding' a cure for cancer, and as a global population, especially the West, we are getting sicker and sicker.

Trauma, toxicity, and disconnection from Truth are the root causes of the perfect storm underlying the majority of diseases. You can't pop a pill to heal that.

We must take responsibility for ourselves and begin the work of inner healing. We all have inner wounds, so start hugging that inner child and sending them so much love. From there, question everything: your beliefs and what the media tells you. Question me. Question religion, question spiritual teachings, especially 'New Age,' which is riddled with false prophets and fake gurus.

But start by questioning any belief that creates a shackle of limitation around what is possible for you. Question it all, go through your process, and trust the journey you are being guided to go on. One baby step at a time.

Through doubt and disbelief, perhaps you will come to a point of surrender where you will have to trust and keep taking steps as you continue on this journey because once you take steps forward, there is no turning your back on the Truth, no matter how difficult the path may feel.

Once you see it, you can't unsee it. This journey calls us to surrender to faith. Our heart is always there to guide us back to the path of Truth, to the way of love.

Remember to continually return to your heart because your heart is where your deepest wisdom lies. That is where the light of Truth resides, the source of your inner power.

Chapter Five

Living in the Light

The Biology of High-Vibrational States

"Just like a single cell, the character of our lives is determined not by our genes but by our responses to the environmental signals that propel life."
~ Bruce H. Lipton, Ph.D.

This next phase of our odyssey bridges the material and spiritual, anchoring the esoteric essence of the light into our living biology. Let's now journey deeper into the biology of high vibrational emotional states and *how* to 'live in the light.'

Emotions are a form of chemical feedback. In a cycle beginning with our thoughts, emotions create chemicals in the body. Our thoughts create our emotions, and our emotions create feeling states via biochemical pathways. These chemicals then send signals to our genes that impact gene expression: "Turn on!" or "Turn off!"[42]

Emotions impact our biology at the level of our DNA, which codes for genes, and these genes code for proteins. Gene expression impacts how proteins are created, and proteins are the building blocks of life. Proteins are involved in chemical reactions, our immune system, and our digestion; they're the elemental components of our bones and muscles. Proteins are quite literally the physical manifestation of the codes that create life.

To recap:

- Emotions impact gene expression.
- Gene expression controls the protein production in our body.
- Proteins are the building blocks of our body and catalysts of life.

So emotions then directly impact protein construction in our body, and it is the expression of protein that is the expression of physical life.

Emotions, then, are the fundamental basis of our very being; vitality in every sense of the word. Emotion is 'energy in motion,' so emotions and feelings dictate our life experience as this energy moves and is expressed within our body. And because that is what life is—our experience of this physical existence—our emotions and energetic states rule our life. Once we learn to master our emotions, we become unstoppable.

Consider this against the fact that so many of us were taught that children should be seen and not heard, to stuff our emotions down, to 'keep it together,' have a stiff upper lip, not wear our feelings on our sleeve, or in the case of young boys to 'be a man,' we can begin to piece together the puzzle of disconnection and disease.

As the adage goes, where our attention goes, our energy flows. Emotions are energy in motion, and emotions want to flow. So when they are repressed and stuffed down, they get lodged into our bodies. The associated chemicals then directly impact our physical biology when they aren't allowed to flow and release. Catharsis is healthy because it moves stuck energy, while tears carry memory of our past pain out of the body.

It's quite fascinating and profound when you begin to boil it down and start to put the pieces together to understand the nuances of how emotions impact our physiology at a biochemical level, which subsequently impacts our health and vitality.

It all connects; it all comes together. And this is how the healing happens. We reconnect all the scattered pieces of ourselves and return to a sense of wholeness.

Most of us prefer happiness to a lower vibrational emotional state like anger, grief, resentment, sadness, despair, hopelessness, or helplessness. Those are not fun states to be in. But if we get into biochemistry, the truth is we actually can become addicted to those emotional states at the level of biochemistry.[43] It may sound wild, but subconsciously, when we are accustomed to being in these lower vibrational states, we create more situations and circumstances to perpetuate them so our bodies can feel those chemical rushes.

If this sounds unbelievable or outlandish to you, consider adrenaline. Adrenaline junkies are widely known for actively seeking out death-defying situations to get that sensation of feeling high and on top of the world. As a downhill skier, I love the rush of the wind on my face as I zoom down the mountain, feeling almost like I'm flying. *Fast cars and Freedom* gained popularity for a reason. At our core, our souls desire freedom. In our world, many will go to extreme lengths to interrupt the monotony of mundanity, addicted to the fleeting rush that overrides the undercurrent of dissatisfaction.

Most of us don't realize that even in our more mundane lives, we get stuck in loops and patterns to get our own biochemical fixes. It may not be as obvious as an adrenaline rush and may feel significantly worse. However, our bodies do get addicted to these states. We feed the beast through dwelling, rumination, looping, and numbing. We break the cycle by choosing to. Or life will swoop in and force us to surrender to that higher power.

Living in the frequency of higher vibrational emotional states sets us up to heal, thrive, and shift our internal biochemical states. Our bodies can code for better proteins and grow, repair, and heal when we exist in expanded states. Stress states do the opposite—our genes receive signals that trigger inflammation, which eventually manifests as disease.[44]

By reducing stress, focusing on love and joy, and living in states of gratitude, bliss, harmony, and wholeness, one of the highest frequency emotional states, we shift our entire state of being on every level. Imagine the incredible, beautiful, vital life we could all live once we shift out of constriction and into expansion. Imagine if we allowed ourselves to let go of the baggage and feel worthy to simply Be. Our bodies would be in homeostasis, constantly repairing, naturally healing.

Natural healing is not the inexplicable miracle it's been made out to be. Think about cuts: our bodies know exactly how to heal the wound. Skin regenerates, and bones mend after they break. The power of belief to generate healing has been proven by placebo. Religion has taught us that only Jesus and God could perform miraculous healings. However, in reality 'miracle' healings occur quite regularly. They are typically recorded as medical anomalies, or in the case of cancer 'inexplicably' disappearing—'radical remission.'[45]

The Truth is that the majority of individuals who experience such healings have shifted their frequency state by implementing specific modalities. Many apply multiple approaches. They nourish the mind, body, and soul, healing the disconnection and allowing the body to return to its natural state of love and expansion. Most shift their diet and lifestyle, and most meditate or pray. Often, the mere choice to take back control and take proactive steps forward shifts our internal biochemistry dramatically enough to catalyze the healing process.

Disempowerment is a very depressed frequency state of being. What if Depression itself is rooted in a state of spiritual disconnection? When our soul feels stifled, we cannot truly thrive. It is my belief that the majority of mental health conditions also stem from a core sense of disconnection from our spiritual truth. This line of inquiry stems purely from my inner musings, yet is anchored in profound clarity derived from the golden threads weaving the tapestry of a greater truth.

Trauma creates a fractured state of self and engenders a state of inner separation. When our soul feels fractured, it can manifest as mental instability. Psychosis may be rooted in a sudden spiritual awakening without any tools to ground, resulting in a fractured experience of reality. Bipolar, depression, and anxiety can all be seen as disconnection from our core sense of self and from our true soul path. Dissociative identity disorder could be a manifestation of one's consciousness accessing direct awareness of past lives or multidimensional aspects of self.

What if Neural divergence is a sign of a spiritually activated mind, one that has the capacity to process information in different manners and access information from different realms? While there is high correlation with other matrix factors such as food chemicals and a diet high in refined sugars contributing to conditions including autism and ADHD, and an alarming correlation between increased autism rates with the increased vaccine schedule, there is a wide spectrum and many adults are now looking at lists of symptoms on social media and saying 'Oh, I'm like that too!' *(Hi...)* While I am not denying that perhaps many went undiagnosed, the more I connect the dots I do also wonder if there is another side to this story, and I believe labels do not always serve. What if neural divergence is a particular form of genius unrecognized by the current system?

None of this is to deny chemical imbalances that exist in the brain, but as we have seen the root cause of many of these chemical imbalances may be energetic in nature.

We also wonder why traits like Narcissism and Psychopathy are on the rise in society. Many who find themselves on the path of awakening and spirituality have dealt with narcissistic energy in their life, myself included. Profound opportunities to reclaim our power and create firm boundaries arise from gaslighting and projection and it is all rising in the collective to serve this collective awakening. This could be the subject of an entire chapter unto itself, but I would like to address the phenomenon of the apparent epidemic of narcissistic tendencies.

Naturally, our culture of consumption inherently perpetuates externalization and separation. This goes much deeper than vanity and competition, however. Young minds in modern society develop inside schools that look like prisons following rules of authority that run counter to their natural instincts to play, all while sitting under artificial lights, which are known to increase risk of depression, obesity, and sleep disorders, to name a few.[46] Narcissism could be rooted in never having one's own needs met, deep unhealed trauma buried under so many layers of shame it's nigh on impossible for them to face. Psychopathy could be rooted in suppression perpetuated by an unnatural system that stifles life force and empathy.

Indigenous cultures around the world often see psychosis as a sign of a natural shaman, the 'birth of a healer'[47]—someone who is open enough to access multidimensional realms of consciousness with ease. Such gifts are nurtured. Could it be possible that what we label as a disorder may, in some cases, actually be a gift, if nurtured with the appropriate tools and guidance?

Such wisdom has been lost to the modern world, however as our DNA awakens, we are beginning to remember and uncover the wells of wisdom buried deep within our subconscious. Many now seek the ancient wisdom of the priestesses and the shamans and are here to resurrect and modernize the teachings. Many are recognizing that societal norms are antithetical to our innate nature.

Even in the West, we hear anecdotes of children having imaginary best friends, speaking with angels, or seeing ghosts; what if, instead of suppressing signs of psychic gifts and dismissing them as imagination, we get curious, nurture them with love, and give them space to develop?

This is what I see happening already—children are being born with clear open channels, displaying high degrees of intelligence and curiosity, and in some cases even speaking as a voice of cosmic angelic wisdom.

It is my personal belief that if we take the responsibility to heal the trauma we carry, within just few generations we could see the disappearance of all disease—both mental and physical—and the dissolution of global conflict. This is how we give birth to Unity Consciousness: by healing inner conflict, rebirthing into inner union, and giving birth to the next generations in the frequency of pure love through sacred divine union of healed partners.

We as a society have become disconnected and separated from this idea that our bodies are inherently quite miraculous and that they know exactly what to do. They guide us toward what is aligned and away from what is not. Our bodies carry the wisdom of our souls and know precisely what is in our highest good, but we've, by and large, been severed from our intuition by trauma and conditioning.

We've become a society that kowtows to authority while blaming and shaming the very source and solution to our ills: our Body Temple.

People pleasers place their needs below that of others. So they stop asking questions and stay silent when their bodies and souls are urging them to speak. Society has conditioned us to respect authority and obey the rules and order of conduct. This, however, has come at the expense of our natural instincts and inclinations. We've been disconnected from our inner knowing, so we don't trust those inner niggles. Instead of 'My body knows what to do. It's sending me these signals for a reason,' we blame and shame our bodies for betraying us, for being weak and slowing us down. What if this blame and shame and limited self-perception is the very thing that creates and perpetuates disease?

Our bodies are miraculous wisdom-keepers that repair themselves if we give them the time, space, and natural support to do so. The more unnatural junk, fake, and dead food—chemicals, additives, pesticides, GMOs, antibiotics, hormones—we put into our body, the more that natural state is blocked. Imagine what happens to a child fed a diet of chemicals as their sensitive minds, bodies, and souls develop, is it any wonder we see such a rise in illness and behavioral dysfunction as they grow?

Emotions can catalyze forward momentum as we make proactive choices to better our lives. Changing our emotional state will impact our life, health, biology, and vitality, as we tend to make choices more aligned with supporting our body temple. It will impact everything in a profound, dramatic, and direct way. This isn't some crazy alternative, woo-woo nonsense. It is literal physical, biological, and chemical science.

The irony is that all the spiritual, 'alternative' and 'woo-woo' stuff is now proving to be real through quantum science. When we're in the lower vibrational states, we are in a state of constriction, of dense matter. You can feel it in your body; you feel heavier. Think about being in a state of fear or anxiety; your energy contracts, as does the body.

When we feel disempowered, our shoulders slouch, our heads drop, and we feel lethargic. These heavier, denser states directly impact our physiology. You can tangibly feel it, and you can see it in somebody else.

These telltale signs enable us to monitor ourselves. How am I feeling right now? Am I hunched over and contracted? Or am I feeling expansive and joyful?

Research has shown that power posing can change our inner state through changing our outer state.[48] To change your state instantly, you could throw your arms up in a high V like a cheerleader or a champion celebrating 'Victory!' Fun fact: I was a cheerleader in college and can tell you from experience that going through the literal motions adds that pep to your step—not necessarily the other way around.

Fake it til you make it isn't the vibe; however, shifting our physiological state until our mind, energy, and emotions can catch up helps us come into complete mind-body-soul alignment.

Studies have shown that simply sitting up straight in your chair, shoulders back and chest out, shifts you into a state of power. When we adjust our posture as such, we feel empowered—power from within, infused with confidence. Will and power are still on the lower half of the vibrational scale, but they rank highest on the scale of the lower vibrations.

Gratitude, remember, is the threshold that elevates us to vibrations of light, appreciation, joy, bliss, freedom, love, and wholeness. In these states of expansion and abundance, we feel like anything is possible, everything is available to us, and we're in a state of trust and faith. Tapping into a sense of trust and faith and knowing that everything will work out for you—even if you're in the midst of the dark tunnel and you're not clear on where that path is leading—is being in your true power. Cultivating trust and faith helps us to stay in these higher vibrational emotional frequency states.

A simple gratitude practice could be listing three things you're grateful for every evening, or starting your day each morning with this list. I like ending my meditation with a little prayer/gratitude practice. The state of gratitude brings you into a state of appreciation, which brings you into a state of joy and love. As you can see, it builds upon itself. Ultimately, we reach a state of wholeness, unity, and oneness within and without, a sense of feeling connected with everything: source, nature, and everyone around us.

Wholeness is feeling complete and connected as a perfect expression of your divine self. Returning to wholeness is the ultimate goal. Wholeness might be a difficult concept to wrap your mind around if it's not something that you've thought about or experienced much of before. It's a sense of feeling connected to everything, complete and perfect, exactly as you are. Grounded, confident, serene, and content. Polarity and separation cease to exist. The masculine and the feminine are unified in this state, and notions of good versus evil, wrong versus right, and love versus hate all cease to exist through the lens of unified compassion. Bridged together and brought back into a unified whole, you become a more complete expression of the light. You become the diamond.

In this state of wholeness and connection, we enter the realm of infinite possibilities. Instant manifestation becomes possible. Life blossoms before our eyes and everything becomes magical and beautiful. It's biology, it's physiology, it's physics—it's the quantum reality we live in.

These phenomena converge to enable us to live in our highest vibration embodied in our highest potential, which is, for most of us, beyond what we even believe is possible. Putting our faith and trust in possibility and being open to the fact that the realm of possibility is available to us allows us to stay open to opportunity and magic beyond our wildest imagination. Ideas we think are logically crazy might actually come true. Miracles become reality.

Living in the light is living in a state of gratitude and appreciation, knowing and expecting that all is working out for us. We are complete and whole as we are. Inherently worthy and innately divine.

Part of the healing journey is returning to the remembrance that we already are All we seek.

Releasing the blocks of limitation allows this deeply buried Truth to return to the light, knowing from our deepest core that we are whole and perfect as we are, perfect expressions of the light.

But to find this buried treasure of Truth bound by chains of fear and suffering, we must unravel all of the trauma, pain, and emotional wounds that go back to before we can remember, before even this lifetime. This body, this incarnation, carries inherited baggage from our ancestral lineage, and it is our task to free our lineages from the bondage of the illusion of separation.

The task is upon us to look at the shadows, release them, and integrate them. Heart wisdom is the ultimate source of wisdom, so the work is to come back home to ourselves and into our deep inner knowing of the Truth of who we are—to trust our intuition.

Again, we must unblock the lower energy centers to unlock our intuition, raise our life force into our heart wisdom, speak our Truth, and ultimately be fully connected to Source, free from distortion. The more expanded the frequency of our emotions, the more energy we have, the more information we receive, the more aware we are. Then it all flows full circle up the spiral as we continue to spiral closer into the pillar of light that we are: the unified field of oneness.

Your feeling state is key. So tune in with yourself: how are you feeling right now? And if you're not feeling amazing—which is very understandable in these chaotic times of revelation riddled with confusion and division—use the tools and reminders in this book to shift your state. Start with a long, slow, deep breath.

Getting myself back into a higher vibrational state takes meditation, breathwork, gratitude, simple deep breaths, and moving my body to move the energy. My top priorities are hydration, clean eating, and morning warm lemon water. I listen to frequencies; I rest, I nurture, I journal, and I give myself self-care. I tune in and listen. I dance and occasionally go to sound healings, and as the need or desire arises, I seek support and mentorship from other healers and guides. We all need support. I've figured out what works for me, but these tried and true tools work for many. Our journeys may be unique, but we are all built of the same stardust and source energy.

Most importantly, follow your joy and get in the flow. What lights you up? What brings you joy? Watch a comedy, laugh, connect with your loved ones, call up your best friend. Do something that brings you joy and work that gratitude practice. For me, writing and sharing the messages that come through and wisdom I've gained on YouTube or my programs gets me in the flow zone, as I am lit up by being in my purpose. Find what that is for you, and do more of that.

Sometimes, we do just need to distract ourselves from the stress of life because there is so much craziness in the world right now. Often what we perceive as a distraction is the medicine we need to bring us joy and innocent comfort.

Allow yourself to experience pleasure; allow yourself to experience joy. We have forgotten that life is meant to be experienced fully, including fun, beauty, and magic. Go back to being a child. Live in that childlike joy as much as possible. Allow yourself to unleash that creative, playful, carefree being that lives within, and let them run free!

And finally, Laugh. Laughter is the most potent and delightful elixir for the soul.

CHAPTER SIX

CHOOSING THE LIGHT: THE INSIDE JOB

How to Take Responsibility for your Life

> *"The best years of your life are the ones in which you decide your problems are your own. You do not blame them on your mother, the ecology, or the president. You realize that you control your own destiny."* ~ Albert Ellis

Choosing the light is not all rainbows, magic, and sunshine (although yes it definitely gets to include plenty of that!)—it demands taking responsibility for your life. It's about owning your choices and how you experience life. We have a choice in every moment, whatever life presents to us, whatever experiences we're going through, we always have a choice as to how we will show up and how we will respond.

Many of us have a negative connotation with the word 'responsibility,' associating it with a sense of burden. But when you break the word down, it becomes response-ability—your ability to respond. That perspective shift instantly lightened my perception.

It's quite empowering to take responsibility for your life because you are now in a position to change the outcome and how you show up and experience life. You truly are in the driver's seat; you, indeed, are the director of your movie.

Choosing the light is a choice you make to take personal responsibility for how you show up, how you choose to perceive your reality, how you choose to shift your circumstances and your choices. There are aspects of your life you can control and factors you cannot. We can't fully control our external reality; as much as we want to put the intentions out and manifest, we can't control others or life's randomness. So first, we must take control of our inner environment so our external begins to reflect the internal and all that is not aligned with our inner state begins to fall away naturally.

It must begin within. To affect the external, we must take personal responsibility for our internal world. That includes our thoughts, our emotions, and our feelings. They all feed into each other. Thoughts inform our emotions, which inform our physical feelings, which create a chemical response in the body; it's these states that determine how we show up in each moment and which impact our external reality.

Taking a step back to gain awareness of our thoughts empowers us to shift the quality of our thoughts. We can challenge our worry and anxiety and remind ourselves that the past is the past and that the now is all we have. We can return to our center, breathe, and feel gratitude for this moment.

Try it right here, right now. Shut your eyes and take a few deep, slow breaths. Did you notice any shifts in your thoughts and physiology?

Take stock of your current state as well as your dominant states. Without judgment, is your baseline operating state a denser frequency or a frequency of trust and expansion? Are you dwelling in lower emotional states of fear, anger, or hopelessness, disempowered to the point of giving up? Or do you move confidently through the world, empowered in your actions?

Without judgment, sit with it. Imagine a time in your life where you felt low, where you wanted to give up, where you felt like things were hopeless, or where you felt scared, anxious, angry, or even where you felt like you wanted to take control of the situation too much. Control is a higher vibration than the rest, but the need to control keeps us in constriction, matter, and the physical material.

Control has its shadow side, yet you can use it on the path to empowerment. I prefer to think of the higher sense of control, such as taking control of our life, as power within: the true state of feeling empowered to handle whatever comes our way. I also associate this form of control with discipline and structure. However, I will also use it in this context because so many understand the empowered sense of feeling in control of a situation.

We elevate into the higher vibrational states by choosing how we respond to crisis, trauma, and tragedy. Do we give up and fall into those darker states and dwell there? Or do we take control of how we respond and all the layers in our capacity to shift? What feels better in a state of crisis: helplessly doing nothing to change your situation, waiting for an illusory savior, or taking small, aligned actions in the direction of finding a solution?

Paradoxically, the highest form of self-control is total surrender. Through surrender, we relinquish control of our ego, and allow divine to take over, enabling us to step into a version of ourselves in total power of our life as we have full faith that we are moving in the direction of our destiny. Let go and let God does not mean sitting back and waiting for a miracle to drop in our lap. It means releasing control of our ego which gets lost trying to figure out the 'how' and allowing God Source Consciousness to get in the driver's seat, take the wheel, and flow through us as a vessel of divinity as we take steps forward and move through the world.

I recently asked, 'God, what is it you want me to do?' The answer was instant: Speak. *Okay.*

As a shy little girl with an abject fear of public speaking whose most consistent feedback on her straight-A report cards was '*Amanda needs to speak up more in class,*' finding my voice and having the courage to put myself out there was a huge journey of healing in itself. Then, once I finally felt healed from cancer and many of my past wounds traumas, I was dealt another harsh blow of betrayal and narcissistic abuse; I was blindsided and left with a rattled nervous system and nearly healed abandonment wounds ripped wide open again, not by a romantic partner. I had to re-learn how to trust everyone: men, women, and most of all myself, and most importantly God.

Healing the wounds of separation and abandonment requires great courage as deep wells of pain surface. Many incarnated in this lifetime to heal the original separation wound; this is no small task. So go forth with humble courage and grace, knowing that this is so much bigger than you and that you are so deeply held and supported by the divine.

When it comes to our emotions, we must embrace the negative emotions as they arise. Get curious about them rather than suppressing them, but do not let them consume you. That's the key: not allowing these emotions to take control of us. We feel them and use them for the valuable information they provide, yet do not dwell in them. Through the release comes liberation.

The intention is to put ourselves back in a position of personal power, where we are impacting and informing our experience of reality. This takes work. Things typically don't transform overnight. Breakthroughs are possible and things can shift quickly; especially right now as time speeds up due to the incoming light energy pouring into the planet. It's not just helping us to do the shadow work and release the densities, old patterns, and emotions; it's almost forcing us.

Everything is here to support us in this process. It's not an easy choice to show up and do the inner excavation; it is a constant choice we must make every moment. Ultimately, it is the easier choice because the more we resist and stay in stagnancy, the louder the sirens grow, the greater the crises become, and ultimately, the universe will deliver our lessons over and over until we get the message and pass the test.

Resistance is a key feeling state to focus on. It shows up as a refusal to accept a certain situation, pushing forward when the signs say to slow down or stop or the need to control. Resistance keeps us stuck dwelling, festering in the lower, heavier, denser emotional states. Resistance arises to show us what and where we are still holding on to, or even clinging to, the past. Resistance calls us to surrender, let go, and trust. In that moment of release, we open ourselves to something new, something better, and more aligned on our soul path.

On the other side of resistance through the portal of surrender lies the pure magic of expansion.

Ultimately, we have no choice but to look within, but it's up to us to choose how long or difficult our journey will be. Our soul chose certain major experiences in advance as points of initiation, however it is up to us how we move through these initiations and integrate the wisdom.

Each day, we have abundant opportunities to practice. How will we respond to that person who cut us off in traffic, that grumpy sales clerk, or that rude server? We can respond by taking it personally and believing they're a bad person, or we can take a step back, have a little compassion, and say, *I don't know what that person is going through right now, so I'm not going to take it personally. I won't react in a way that doesn't support my highest good and personal wellbeing.*

What about that friend or loved one projecting all their stuff onto us? When we haven't done the healing ourselves, we do take it personally. I did for so long. After stepping onto this path, I have been tested numerous times and in sometimes insidious ways. When

I finally reclaimed my health and power and began finding my voice and staking my boundaries, I would stand up for myself and call them out. Yet in the process of creating boundaries and speaking up, certain energies reacted to their own reflection and projected blame onto me for my reaction to their miserable behavior. I had been stuck in a karmic loop of attracting people with narcissistic tendencies who saw me as an easy target.

Part of my journey was releasing the people-pleasing victim mentality that kept allowing these energies into my life. I finally learned that my energy field actually acts as a mirror and reflects and even amplifies other people's energy, and a huge part of my journey has been recognizing what is my own energy and what has come from others, and to clear out the latter. That path of reclamation was rife with challenges and oftentimes quite painful as I placed my trust in the wrong people. But I learned to walk away and take my power, dignity, and worth along with me.

We can choose to take the higher road of being the living light. We can take a deep breath, step back, and remove that energy from ourselves, recognizing that it's not ours and it's not up to anyone else to make us feel how we desire to feel. It's up to us to protect and cultivate our own energy fields by choosing to respond with love, forgiveness, and compassion, even if they don't really 'deserve' it. Forgiveness is for ourselves. We can forgive and walk away. One of the hardest lessons is that no one can make us feel anything without giving them the power to.

It's not about fairness, it is ultimately about choosing how we want to experience life. Do you want to experience life in this lower vibrational state, always being angry and placing responsibility outside yourself? Anger, frustration, and blame generate a victim mentality that renders you helpless, hopeless, and powerless. Sometimes life deals us harsh blows, but we must flip the script and take our power back. I began to see it like the slingshot being pulled so far back the tension was at its peak, so that when it was released I'd go higher and farther than I'd previously imagined. Perhaps within the breakdown lies the greatest gift. You have the power to claim it.

One of the worst states to be in is to feel powerless over your circumstances, your life, and the outcome of a situation. While we may not be able to control every aspect of our external reality, the more we empower our ability to respond and regulate our emotions or feeling states, the more it will impact our external physical reality.

This is the inside job. Again, our thoughts, emotions, and feelings create our reality. They create our experience of reality because they dictate how we perceive and respond to our reality. Accepting responsibility for all of it shifts the flow in the other direction.

As we start to release and take responsibility and see the conditioning and patterns that inform how we respond and show up, our entire life begins to change. We focus on our desired outcomes and, eventually, with confidence, take the aligned actions that allow the manifestations to flow to us. The more aligned our internal becomes with our vision, the faster it materializes. The larger the manifestation, the more of a time delay there may be. But if we keep trusting and taking steps in the direction of our soul aligned destiny, what is meant for us will come.

Taking responsibility puts us in a position of personal power and also allows our relationships to flourish. Once we choose to respond with love, compassion, and understanding and bring awareness to our triggers, our interpersonal interactions and relationships become far more respectful and harmonious.

Rather than reacting in anger or victimhood, when we pause and ask ourselves—*why did that person trigger me? Why did that person make me angry? Why did that interaction make me feel worthless?*—we begin to unpack the layers of deeper wounds of rejection, unworthiness, and not feeling seen and heard; the deeper wounds that constitute the dark seed, as one of my mentors calls it. What is the underlying dark seed? What is the root of this trigger, this uncomfortable feeling?

According to a theory on the wounded self,[49] there are five core soul wounds that give rise to our inner demons: rejection, abandonment, humiliation, betrayal, and injustice. These wounds arise not necessarily from real life experience but our perception and interpretation of the experience. People adopt ego masks as a form of protection to endure the underlying pain, however they serve to perpetuate the underlying wounds. Mask personality traits include control, dependence, rigidity, withdrawal, and masochism which can become 'personality' types. The deeper the wound, the more rigid the mask.

Whatever the trigger is, whatever the experience you're having about that particular situation, typically, there's a deeper root that goes way back, and you realize your feelings are not even about this person or situation. Or you might begin to see that how a person treats you isn't necessarily about *you* but about them and their own inner wounding or unresolved inner strife. Consider what this person is mirroring back to you. What is the lesson here to teach you? Conflicts can be resolved much more peacefully and respectfully or avoided altogether when we can pause and embody compassion, understanding that we are all walking each other home to the truth of love.

Once our inner relationship shifts, our interpersonal relationships shift through conscious communication, and that has a ripple effect into our communities, our societies, our cultures, and eventually the whole world. This is how we create world peace—by cultivating inner peace.

Awareness is the first step in taking personal responsibility for how we show up and for doing this difficult inner work. Healing ourselves helps to heal the planet. There's so much baggage that we need to shed, so many shadows to transmute. This is the time of shadow work, the time of shedding all the layers that no longer serve our ultimate good, our highest potential, or our extraordinary capacity for love.

Showing up and taking responsibility for your choices in every moment is about choosing love, joy, life, and light. Making choices aligned with your deeper purpose, passions, joy, and love is choosing the light. Every time you make a choice for your highest, most aligned good—which you get from connecting with your gut instincts, heart wisdom, and intuition—it has a ripple effect out into the world through the grid of energetic consciousness that connects us all.

Connecting with your divine essence and making choices aligned with that inner divinity is what will ultimately empower your path, empowering your ability to fulfill your potential so that you can serve and create in your highest capacity as a vessel for higher consciousness.

Every time you make that choice, you are serving the light. Every time you make a choice aligned with your highest good, you also build trust in yourself and trust in your journey which is of paramount importance. The way to build trust in life is to build trust in yourself, which requires tuning in, tapping in, and making those mind-body-soul aligned decisions.

Every moment we face a choice point: are we going to choose joy? Are we going to choose love? Are we going to choose light? Are we going to choose life?

We are here on Earth to have an embodied human experience and to live our life fully, and to live fully requires that we choose the light with every opportunity life provides.

Chapter Seven

The Enlightened Heart

The Life-Changing Power of Gratitude

"Gratitude unlocks the fullness of life. It turns what we have into enough, and more. It turns denial into acceptance, chaos to order, confusion to clarity." ~ Melody Beattie

Gratitude is powerful because it is a simple practice that can shift our entire state. As I've mentioned numerous times throughout this book, the shift into gratitude elevates us into the vibration of the light. Gratitude is the threshold between constriction and expansion, and it opens our field to be in the energy of receiving.

We just looked at the importance of taking responsibility for how we show up and respond to life. Again, it's a choice: dwell in the lower, denser, heavier emotions, or empower ourselves by taking responsibility for our emotional state, triggers, and reactions and bringing the power back within to respond rather than react to our situation.

Gratitude is transformative in its ability to bring power back within. It shifts our entire perspective on personal situations and life circumstances and builds appreciation for what we do have. We can see our triggers as teachers and feel grateful for the lessons and opportunities for growth they provide. Sometimes it is through total loss we remember that we have the most important thing of all: life. And throughout all eternity, we always have love.

When we're in the depths of a crisis, trauma, or tragedy, when the world is in chaos, it is not easy to cultivate gratitude. With complete compassion, I acknowledge that. I went through cancer. I've experienced multiple big T traumas. Heartbreak, financial loss through scams and theft, deep betrayal by people I thought were friends, fraudulent healers, impossible bosses, belittlement, rejection, abandonment, and undermining by others. I've experienced unfair judgment based on false perceptions. I've been called crazy and had horrible lies spread behind my back publicly. I've been canceled, gaslit, targeted, manipulated, psychic attacked, and siphoned from. I understand it's not easy.

I know what it feels like to be sobbing on your knees in the bathroom or flat on your bedroom floor because things feel so heavy, and you can't see how they will improve. But I also know that we all can come out on the other side, no matter how alone or deep in the depths of darkness we might feel. Many stories are far more dire than mine, where people rise to incredible success to leave a legacy of inspiration, empowerment, and love. We are far more resilient than we have been led to believe.

Surrender, trust, and keep going. Remember how miraculous and how powerful you really are. God (Source, Higher Power, your Angels, your guides, your ancestors, whoever you connect with most deeply) has got your back, always.

Dig deep, and start small. Keep going. Be grateful for your body, your life, and your next breath. If you are reading this, you have much to be thankful for.

The Science of Gratitude

A great deal of research has been conducted on the power of gratitude.[50] Researchers have studied the effects of gratitude on over 80 areas of life. Studies have confirmed gratitude's impact on improving personal relationships, physical health, career, and success.

When deep in the shadows, gratitude can help transmute them and lift us out of the darkness.

Remember that facing the shadows and going through the darkness is what it takes for most of us to wake up to the fact that we can reclaim our agency and inner power, take personal responsibility, and choose something better. It's the crisis, trauma, and tragedy that typically wakes us up. Most of us need to hit rock bottom before we can rise back up and beyond.

The darkness is a crucible. Like the caterpillar in the cocoon, we need that sacred pause in the darkness where we dissolve into goo so that our old form can be alchemized into a higher expression and emerge more beautiful and brilliant than we ever imagined possible—so that the caterpillar can find its wings and soar. The caterpillar doesn't know what's coming but trusts its natural process and goes within.

Like the snake shedding its skin, we need to release the old so we have room to grow. Like the phoenix rising from the ashes, we must burn away the dull old form to rise with golden wings. Like the butterfly, the snake, and the phoenix, we become more beautiful, powerful, and brilliant.

Gratitude helps us stay the course when hope seems a distant mirage and the light in the distance seems to fade or disappear. It helps restore us to the present moment and reminds us that we are lucky to be breathing no matter what our external reality reflects. It helps to restore hope and faith.

Gratitude engenders a state of contentment. We have more motivation and energy and feel more creative, connected, and productive. A more profound sense of inner wellbeing emerges, along with a more rooted feeling of peace with where we are and what we're experiencing in life, even if it's not all rainbows and sunshine. Again, the more we cultivate this inner state of authentic joy, the more it reflects in our external.

The process of transformation and change isn't linear. It is cyclical. Rather than going around in circles, though, the mission is to generate an upward spiral. If we do the work, we will continue to face our shadows as we go deeper and deeper into the layers, but each time we come out of it stronger, more resilient, one more level up the spiral with the wisdom of a more intricately nuanced perspective. We emerge with a deeper understanding of ourselves, fresh wisdom about our truth and what lights us up, and insight into how we can improve and grow. Each time, we bounce back faster and rise ever higher.

Life brings us circumstances to catalyze and facilitate our growth. Life tests us—have you learned this lesson? How will you respond this time around? If we choose the higher path, we emerge more powerful, refined, and brilliant than before.

Gratitude is a foundational practice that helps us shine our light with brilliance. A gratitude practice is simple and can be implemented at zero cost and with little effort. Kindness and compassion for ourselves and others is a game changer.

We're more appreciative of others as we become more aware of the little things they do for us and how they show up. Be grateful for the grocery clerk or server who was kind, for the postal service, and for the service they provide day in and day out. Consider how many people's services are taken entirely for granted. If we think about it, it's pretty awesome that most of us don't have to go somewhere to pick up our mail and that it just gets delivered to us nearly every day, even in inclement weather. Imagine how much nicer our world would be if we all showed more gratitude and appreciation for each other.

If we begin to tune in to all the little things that are done for us in our lives and start to embrace that notion of gratitude for all the ways that strangers make our lives better, especially those who are typically in the background, feeling and showing gratitude can shift our perspective on so much. Consider the farmers who grow the food we buy at the stores and the truckers who transport the food to the stores; there's so much we take for granted that broadening our perspective can bring much more gratitude into our lives and help us form stronger bonds. Cultivating gratitude before each meal—for the fertile earth, those who grew it, those who transported it, those who sold it, and the light of the sun that makes all life possible—can bring the energy of devotion and reverence into our life as we broaden our perspective on the level of privilege we already enjoy.

Studies have shown that expressing more gratitude in relationships can improve marriages. Makes sense. Imagine if more of us applied gratitude to our relationships—consider how much the divorce rate could drop or how much less contentious they could be.

Gratitude has also been shown to improve sleep. For me, that was a huge one. I had debilitating insomnia for several years—we're talking as little as two hours many nights; no matter how exhausted I was, I couldn't sleep. It began before my diagnosis but continued well beyond the treatment ended. That was a massive struggle for me. Now, I can sleep as much as ten hours if needed, and I average close to eight. Deeper layers of adrenal fatigue were at play in my case, so there was more to the healing than just gratitude. However, it most certainly played a role in helping to heal my sleep cycles.

Gratitude also reduces anxiety. Anxiety and sleeplessness are significant issues in society; the physical and mental health impacts are straightforward and very profound. In times of stress, having a gratitude practice becomes even more beneficial.

Gratitude has also been shown to improve self-esteem. Boosted confidence and reduced stress in social situations strengthen our ability to connect with others so that we feel less alone. The sense of loneliness and isolation has been amplified in the last several years, further impacting our immune system. Even if it's just connecting with people online, having the confidence to reach out to others and get the support you need is paramount. Connecting with like-minded individuals online through social media can significantly boost our happiness and positivity. Most crave real-life human connection; however, remote is better than nothing. Confidence in ourselves is essential not just personally but also professionally. The more confident we are, the more likely we are to go after opportunities to boost our success in multiple ways, generating that upward spiral.

Stress reduction goes hand-in-hand with improved sleep and anxiety reduction. Many studies have shown that gratitude has a direct impact on reducing stress. It helps us cope better with stress and to better manage stressful situations. Not all stress is bad, but in our frenetic modern-day society, we do tend to fall into patterns of chronic stress related to situations which, by and large, have little impact on our immediate survival, which was why the stress response evolved the way it did—to face life-threatening situations.

Moments of acute stress that help us be more vigilant and alert in a way that improves our performance are genuine and often beneficial, such as in a test situation. People can use stress for motivation and to enhance performance when framed in a certain way. It's known as eustress.[51]

However, we face a modern crisis of chronic stress that is debilitating to our immune systems.[52] The vast majority of us experience detrimental levels of stress. A gratitude practice can support us when we inevitably fall into worries, fears, and uncertainties.

Humans don't like uncertainty. But there's no truth in security and safety when it comes from without; we must build that within. That's where the gratitude practice comes in. A study showed that participants' brains showed significantly decreased activity with just a five-minute practice. A calm mind is a clear mind.

Gratitude can help bring us into a state of increased ease and grace with life, like finding the silver linings, no matter what. When I was in the depths of cancer treatment, I would compare my situation to stories and situations that were worse than mine. I knew I was lucky to wake up each day and was fortunate for each breath I took. Sometimes, you have to focus on the nitty-gritty bare-bones truth that if you are reading this right now, if you wake up in the morning, you're better off than somebody else.

Downward comparisons may feel odd at first, but the focus is meant to be on every little blessing in your own life, and overarching comparisons may help more than you might imagine. No matter what, there is *always* something we can be grateful for, regardless of our external circumstances. It's not easy. I'm not pretending it is. If you are struggling right now, know I'm sending so much compassion to each person who finds this little book—I wrote this for you. And this is a gentle reminder that if you are reading this, you are holding tools in your hands and are better off than somebody else out there.

You had the connection to find this, the ability to purchase or receive it. Hopefully, there are some nuggets here that resonate with you. Or use this as a reminder of any other resources or experiences that provided you benefit, solace, joy, love, fun, or support. No matter where you are, there's something that you can find to be grateful for.

What I like to do is an evening or a morning gratitude practice, or both. To end the day with gratitude, especially if you're dealing with sleep issues, is helpful because it can help you refocus on the beauty and magic before drifting off into dreamland. What good things happened during the day for which you can be grateful? What else in your life overall can you be thankful for right now? To start your day with gratitude also sets the tone for more positivity and appreciation. You'll begin to see that you can find more and more to be grateful for.

Once we shift our perspective, it's easier to see how much we have to be grateful for. Many of us have so much abundance that we take for granted. One of the plagues of our society is never being satisfied. Gratitude sparks an enhanced awareness of all we have, expanding our capacity to receive more that aligns with us.

To return to the biology of emotional frequency states, gratitude is the threshold between the lower, denser emotions and the higher vibrational emotional states. This shift brings more abundance, joy, and love into our lives. Cultivating the habit of a gratitude practice and living in gratitude and appreciation for what we have creates a vibrational frequency that attracts more goodness into our lives.

Abundance of all things flows to us with ease and grace, and we become magnets for manifestation. We are better able to manifest everything we desire once we are in that higher vibrational state because we are a frequency match for it. Gratitude is the gateway, the threshold to those higher states where we manifest more efficiently and, crucially, keep those manifestations.

This is something that happened to me a lot. When I was in the process of up-leveling, I would more easily manifest, but the manifestations wouldn't always stick. I would get something, and then the shoe would drop on the other end. I would receive what I asked for, but because I hadn't fully anchored in the embodied belief that I was worthy of *having* and *keeping* what I received, some form of energetic self-sabotage would happen to detract from the beauty of the manifestation. I would lose something or have a strange interaction with someone that left an uncomfortable imprint, or in the case of financial abundance, I would receive money, and then unexpected costs like car repairs would arise.

Another key is trust. In truth, I can look back now and recognize that each time the proverbial shoe dropped, it was another test from the Universe—*do you trust?* It also spotlighted the areas that still needed deeper work, highlighting the worthiness gaps that needed bridging.

The more consistently we remain in those higher states, the more easily and readily we can create the life we desire and manifest and attract abundance. Gratitude helps to usher us through the gateway into the higher vibrational states so that we can more steadily experience joy, love, gratitude, appreciation, and bliss and eventually ascend into a state of unity and wholeness where infinite possibilities exist. Co-creation of Heaven on Earth becomes effortless.

The Spiral Journey

Ascension is a concept many in the spiritual community are familiar with. Some may associate it with the Ascension story of the Bible; however, more accurately, it is the ascension of frequency and consciousness. It's the process I've been discussing in this book, because it is a journey of deep embodiment.

While ascension evokes the conception of going up, the real work is about going within. One of my guides calls it 'incension.' Some call it descension, as we anchor higher frequencies from the spiritual realm down into the physical realm. The term I prefer is Embodied Ascension, which means we ascend our frequency through the physical vessel that is our body temple.

As we live in a dense realm of matter, we inevitably come up against tests or roadblocks as we purify our physical vessels to hold these expanded states of consciousness. Ascension is not a linear path but a spiral journey as we move through the process of raising our frequency.

We can reflect on where we are on our journeys and consider whether we are going in circles or are moving in an upward spiral. Even if you feel as if you're on the backside of the spiral, don't despair. It's part of the journey of shedding, purging, and healing. We are meant to go deeper and deeper to shed as much as possible, to shed those dense emotions so that we can ascend our frequency even higher, like peeling back the layers of an onion.

If you fall back into triggered states, trust that it's all part of the process. Return to a state of trust, awareness, and appreciation for what is happening so that you can reflect on why this is happening, learn from it, grow, and continue on that upward spiral. Awareness of the trigger is a sign of progress; most in the unawakened state are entirely unaware of what triggers them when it is happening, much less the deeper root reason why. The same patterns tend to show up for us until we learn the lesson, but also to help us anchor and embody the lesson, even once we feel like we've learned it.

When we feel like we've processed and integrated, the Universe often offers another test reminiscent of that old trigger. Have you genuinely shed this layer of unworthiness, lack, or scarcity, or is there still a little left to process? Are you ready? Are you there? Have you fully integrated? It's an ongoing journey, but I believe there are particular thresholds along the way as we level up in the game. Our resilience also increases, so the bounce back becomes faster and smoother. This is why gratitude and meditation are crucial—they anchor us and accelerate the bounce back.

Each time we go through these cycles, we become stronger than before and continue on the upward spiral. These situations can only bring us back down if we allow them to, and perceive them to hold power over us.

When the muck hits the fan, life is trying to get your attention. There's a lesson there. Pay attention to what that lesson could be. Remember, when in doubt, when in fear, when in the depths of despair, there's always something to be grateful for. Gratitude is the key to unlock the treasure chest of wisdom held within.

Chapter Eight

Out of the Head, Into the Heart

How to Connect with the Light and Live a Heart-Centered Life

"And now here is my secret, a very simple secret: It is only with the heart that one can see rightly; what is essential is invisible to the eye." ~ Antoine de Saint-Exupéry

"Begin with the heart, which is the noblest part of the body. It lies in the center of the body from which point it bestows life on the whole body. For the spring of life arises in the heart and has an effect like heaven." ~ Meister Eckhart

Out of the Head, Into the Heart: Living a Heart-Centered Life

The hegemony of Mind as the Master of our body and reality is a recent phenomenon. For millennia, our ancestors viewed the heart as the true master organ of the body—the center of thought, emotion, memory, and personality. It turns out, they were not wrong as research begins to unravel the mysteries of the Holy Grail within.

Ultimately, this quest is one of returning to our hearts and living a life guided by heart and soul rather than a logic-minded head alone. Heart-centered living is about connecting with our inner heart wisdom that brings us peace. Living in a heart-centered space allows what brings us a sense of love, compassion, and a deeper connection to guide our lives. Coming back to the heart is crucial to enhancing a sense of connection in all ways.

As a society we have prioritized mind over matter, celebrating mental logic and linear, rational mental models to create our society. The heart has been deemed irrational and blinded by emotions. The Cartesian dichotomy perpetuated a model of dualism that claims mind and body are separate and ontologically distinct entities. This theoretical split pervades modern thinking and is the foundation upon which many current systems have been built. The well-known Placebo effect debunks the theory, proving the power of belief to affect physiological change.[53]

Functional medicine has also shown the profound link between the health of our gut and mental function. The gut-brain connection elucidates how mental health, attention, and mental clarity are profoundly influenced by microbiome imbalances in the gut.[54] We also now recognize the role of the enteric nervous system and how much information is processed by our body's nervous system before it even arrives at the brain to be processed. The majority of information is filtered out by the subconscious.

Heart coherence is a biologically based way of understanding the flow state and heart-centered living, defined by the HeartMath Institute as the state when the heart, mind, and emotions are in energetic alignment and cooperation. Coherence builds resiliency, leaving more energy for manifesting our true desires and creating more harmonious outcomes.

Being in these higher frequency states tremendously impacts every aspect of our lives, including longevity. We want to be in a state of love. Love over fear, always, yet humans have been living lives directed by fear for so long. The shift into heart-centered living is about returning to love no matter what, returning to a state of compassion for ourselves and other people.

Fascinatingly, nascent research is finding the heart has its own intelligence.[55] It is not just a pump, but also a sophisticated information processor as well as endocrine gland. Its intrinsic nervous system contains roughly 40,000 neurons that exhibit both short-term and long-term memory and facilitates memory transfer. Fascinating case studies show that after heart transplant surgeries, the patient can suddenly find their tastes and preferences change, and may even recall key memories of the donor's life.

Surprising to many, it also functions as an endocrine gland that produces its own hormones, including cardiac natriuretic peptide, which affects blood vessels, the adrenal glands, the kidneys, and regulatory regions of the brain. Intrinsic cardiac adrenergic cells release dopamine and noradrenaline. Perhaps less surprising is that the heart secretes its own oxytocin, the feel-good bonding hormone, with concentrations as high as the brain. Makes sense. Research is catching up.

One of the key roles of this 'heart brain' is to facilitate communication between the body and the brain. It detects changes in hormones and other chemicals in the body and translates the language of the body—emotions—into the language of the brain—electrical impulses.[56] The vagus nerve acts as a bidirectional information highway linking the two.[57]

Growing evidence suggests profound risk correlations between the heart and mental disorders. In a longitudinal Danish study, adults with congenital heart disease had a 60% higher rate of dementia compared to the general population, which increased to 160% in people younger than 65. Negative emotions have been correlated with increased risk of heart disease, while heart attack is associated with increased rates of subsequent depression, generating a three-fold increase in rise of death. Grief also impacts our health. After the loss of a spouse, people are more likely to incur sleep disturbances making them more vulnerable to inflammation, raising their risk of disease and even death.

Interestingly, the leading cause of death in those with schizophrenia is coronary artery disease. Cardiologists believe this could be due to a number of lifestyle factors that escalate risk.

The heart itself is an electrical system, so it stands to reason that intense emotional experiences such as grief, anger, stress, and anxiety can disrupt cardiac function by changing the flow of the electrical current. Electricity is energy and emotions are energy in motion. Again, makes sense.

Finally, research has uncovered that 80% of the information flow between the travels from the heart to the brain, and only 20% of the information flow comes from the brain down. The vagus nerve is 80% afferent, meaning it carries information from the heart and surrounding organs to the brain.[58] This literally flips the paradigm of brain over body on its head, pointing to a true intelligence contained within the body temple, centered within the heart.

The Heart is not just a pump; it is a source of energy, intelligence, and life, generating electricity that ignites the spark of life that fuels the light of our soul. The more we nurture the temple in which it resides and heal the wounds that dim our joy, the more we allow it to grow brighter and shine out into the world.

A true heart intelligence resides within, awaiting our full embrace as we liberate ourselves from the confines of our mind and the shackles of pain that keep it from blossoming open to reveal the wisdom of the cosmos contained within.

Lighten Up: How to Connect with the Light

Many in the spiritual community preach love and light from a state of disembodiment. Choosing the light is not simply focusing on light and love and pretending everything is wonderful. That's spiritual bypassing. One will certainly not reach enlightenment or truly embody the love of Christ consciousness that way. Facing the shadows is a crucial part of the journey, and we cannot pretend that the shadows don't exist.

That said, we need to be connected to Source light to be protected doing the deeper work. And when it comes to facing the collective shadows, it's *so* much easier to face the darkness that exists in the world when we have already become anchored in the light.

Having a foundation of practices not only can help you elevate your frequency and stay focused on the light at the end of the tunnel, to have hope and faith, but it also helps us stay protected as we open up to higher realms and frequencies. This chapter will look at practical ways to generate and ground down these higher-frequency states.

The tricky thing about the spiritual awakening journey is that if you hastily dive into practices that elevate your frequency, it's possible to raise your vibration too high to the point where your body can't handle it, as your nervous system does not yet have the capacity to hold the frequencies of expansion. This is a classic case of spiritual bypassing (often unintentional due to lack of awareness) that can cause us to detach from reality, go deeper into a cocoon, have a nervous system meltdown, or in rare cases cause a state of psychosis where one operates in total delusion. The total nervous system meltdown happened to me while in a high-level coaching container as I was more fully opening up to spirituality and was left to fend for myself without knowing what was happening, so trust me when I say it's essential to lay the foundation and stay grounded.

We are humans having an embodied experience in the physical reality; embodiment is the key to our expansion. Right now, we're going deeper into the practicalities of generating that higher vibrational state within yourself and, crucially, anchoring it down into your body.

Gratitude practice. Connect with a sense of gratitude and appreciation day in and day out, no matter where you are in life. When I was going through cancer, sometimes I would go to the level of, 'Well, at least I have a decent prognosis. At least I'm young. At least I went into this with a strong body. At least I know a lot about mindset.' There's always a silver lining. At least you're breathing. At least you woke up alive.

Connect. Connect with your friends, family, loved ones, and others who support your growth. Crucially, you want to surround yourself with people who support your growth and who support your wellbeing, your vision, and your progress. Connect with people who uplift you, inspire you, and nourish your soul.

Second-degree connections, such as listening to an inspiring podcast or watching an inspirational YouTube video, can help us feel less alone. That's certainly not where I would recommend most of your connection energy goes. However, the positive aspects of social platforms include finding people with similar viewpoints and creating a sense of community if you don't feel supported by people in your immediate life right now. Because so many are still unawakened or just beginning their journey, it can feel lonely as old relationships slip away due to the vibrational mismatch. They might meet you on the path, but we all awaken in our own timing.

Re-evaluate. This is also a beautiful opportunity to get clear on your values and relationships and who is supporting and uplifting you, nurturing those who are, and letting go of the ones who are no longer nourishing you.

Disconnect to reconnect: Earthing and Grounding. Disconnecting from technology and devices helps us to remember that we are part of something much greater: the Earth. The Earth and the sky have so much to offer us—grounding, healing, wisdom, light, and life. Connecting with nature is crucial for our wellbeing, always. Being disconnected from nature is to be disconnected from life itself. Yet the inverse is true: to be connected with nature is to be connected with life in its purest essence and form. Its natural rhythms nurture and guide our own. During the pandemic, leaders and talking heads encouraged us to stay inside to 'stay safe' and 'protect' ourselves, yet this advice is the opposite of what we need to stay healthy.

Many research studies show that nature heals.[59] Connecting with nature directly, physically, like putting your feet in the grass or sand or gardening with bare hands, allows you to connect with the ions in the ground—with the Earth herself, whose surface can be likened to the 'battery' for all planetary life. What do we call the bottoms of our feet? The soles. What does that sound like? Soul. Grounding and Earthing, the term for directly connecting with the Earth through bare skin or simple cotton, is highly beneficial to your health, and it is no wonder when considering the soles of our feet help anchor our soul to the Earth. Rubber soles on shoes remove this connection almost entirely.

Forest bathing is a Japanese practice ('shinrin-yoku') of immersing yourself in the atmosphere of the woods. This simple yet profoundly beneficial practice calls you to connect with the air and the Earth, the trees and the sunshine that sparkles through the leaves above by taking deep breaths and entering a meditative state of connection with the environment. Studies show benefits for mind-body-spirit wellbeing.[60]

Electrons on the surface of the Earth have a physical healing impact on the body, and those electrons can change our physical state. Bodies of water, whether a lake, a stream, a river, or the ocean, hold profound mind-body-soul healing potential. Water carries consciousness and flows within our bodies, so immersing ourselves in water profoundly nourishes, heals, and rejuvenates our essence.

Looking up at the sky inspires a sense of wonder and awe. The vastness, the soothing blue hues, the ever-changing clouds, fiery sunsets, promising pastel-hued dawns, the mysterious moon, the infinite starry night sky, and, of course, the sun, beaming life-giving rainbow frequency rays of golden light onto every molecule on the surface of our beautiful planet.

Sunshine. The key to life and biological health. Sunshine is our source of light. The most critical and literal way to connect with the light is to go outside and soak up the sun.[61] Staying inside prevents us from receiving these abundant rays of light and activating the healing Vitamin D created in our skin. We've been taught to fear the sun, which means we've been taught to fear the source of life.

Go outside, get some sunshine on your face, let it penetrate your skin. To fully absorb the rays, wait to put sunblock on for at least 10-20 minutes; adjust accordingly depending on the time of day and strength of the sun where you live. Be smart and practical about the time of day and intensity of the sun where you live. As a general rule, though, fifteen to twenty minutes per day of sunblock-free sunlight will generate sufficient vitamin D, and a healthy body with a low toxicity load should not generate a sunburn. If you have fair skin, carefully build up your tolerance by going out early in the morning and later in the day. When you do need it, use natural or organic sunblock.

Vitamin D is crucial for our immune system. Research studies measuring cancer patients' vitamin D levels found that across the board, cancer patients have low levels of vitamin D, and, in many cases, are clinically deficient. I learned that my levels were deficient during my diagnostic process. Coming out of winter in NYC, perhaps this wasn't terribly shocking. So, I did the research myself and found the studies. Naturally, I immediately began sunbathing as much as my fair skin could tolerate and further supplemented with a liquid dropper. By the time treatment began, my body was cleansed, my skin was golden, my vitamin D levels were high, and the treatment was smooth and immediately effective.

Interestingly, they found the exact correlation with Covid patients: low vitamin D levels were highly correlated with illness.[62] This understanding reveals a great deal about the state of health and disease in our body and society as work days spent under fluorescent lights and in front of blue-lit screens have replaced tilling the fields. The more we prevent ourselves from receiving sunshine and fresh air, the more we directly reduce our optimal health and wellbeing by limiting optimal immune functioning, specifically as it relates to vitamin D, which has in fact been shown to reduce severity of coronavirus symptoms.[63]

Connecting with sunshine doesn't just impact our physical health but our mental and emotional states as well. I often playfully use the phrase 'sunshine state of mind.' When we're in the sun, we feel lighter, freer, and more joyful. Soaking up the sun is both practical and soul-nourishing.

Self-Connection. As I've intimated throughout these pages, cultivating a connection with yourself is essential. Nothing will ever fill the hole of loneliness if we feel disconnected from ourselves. A good indicator of how much we feel connected to ourselves is how we feel about spending time alone. Introverted by nature, I love my alone time. As a Virgo hermit, I like to retreat to my cave and often prefer to be alone. We all have different energetic needs and means to regenerate, but extroverts, too, need time to connect within. If we don't carve out time to be with ourselves, connecting with our inner guidance and intuition will be much more difficult. Deepening that connection and learning how to trust ourselves and tap into our inner wisdom generates more and more trust in yourself.

Meditation is a powerful way to rekindle that sense of inner connection. Known for its beneficial impact on calming our minds, releasing stress, and improving physical health,[64] meditation also helps to raise our frequency. Meditation can calm the sympathetic nervous system response—aka fight-or-flight. It can decrease emotional reactivity and strengthen regions of the brain associated with learning, cognition, memory, attention, and self-awareness. It helps us connect with our intuition and inner wisdom as well as our higher self and higher consciousness. Tuning in enables us to know ourselves and connect to God, Source, creative consciousness, whatever term resonates with you. Meditation is a beautiful way to nurture and strengthen that connection. During treatment, I would complete my meditations with a gratitude prayer, often followed by visualizing myself being healthy and happy, laughing and dancing at my sister's wedding, which was five weeks after treatment ended and just three days after my remission scan—sure enough I was healthy, happy, and dancing at her wedding and the whole family could fully relax and truly celebrate.

Nurturing a connection with a higher power helps us to feel supported and loved regardless of our external circumstances or human relationships. This connection keeps us grounded in faith so that we can keep going no matter what. We are not alone, ever.

Meditation helps to calm the mind. Our monkey mind thoughts interrupt the connection, so coming into a sense of stillness soothes the body, calms the mind, and clears the pathway for our soul to connect with our higher self and higher consciousness—or the source of light itself.

Movement. Moving your body helps to shift and move the energy in a literal way. Movement doesn't have to be physical exercise where you're winded or dripping sweat. Sweating is extremely healthy as it helps to detox many of the chemicals and toxins held in the skin and lymphatic system. Sauna is also highly beneficial.[65] However, movement can also look like a walk in nature, which incorporates a number of the elements we've discussed so far, rebounding (bouncing on a mini trampoline, both fun and invigorating!), cycling, swimming, rollerblading, stretching, and of course dancing—my favorite way to move my body.

Dancing immediately raises my vibration; when I put on a song I love, my body naturally wants to move to the beat, sway to the rhythm, and hum along to the melody. It feels delicious, and there's so much room for self-expression. Put on a song that pumps you up and moves your body in any way that feels good. Feel the music and let your body move you—let loose without judgment. Bouncing side to side, swirling your hips, swaying your arms through the air—it all moves stagnation. Dancing both moves and generates energy, so go ahead and shake it off.

That's what movement is all about: allowing the stagnant energy in your body to move, flow, and release. So many of us now live sedentary lifestyles, and the energy in our bodies gets stagnant from sitting down all day. We must consciously prioritize getting up and moving our bodies, which makes us feel better. Take the stairs. Park across the parking lot so you have further to walk. Even doing simple stretches in your chair can help release tension.

Cultivate Joy. Have fun! Live in joy as much as you can. Your soul is meant to express itself through joy. The heart is the seat of the soul so joy elevates us and allows our soul's essence to blossom as our hearts open. Reconnect with the things that bring you pleasure, that you find fun and exhilarating, and that bring you joy. Think about when you were a kid; what was your favorite activity? What do you like to do on your days off? Try to bring as much of that into your daily life as possible because we lack fun and joy in our modern society. Celebrate the simple things in life, watch silly Romcoms, put on music and dance, get creative, eat your favorite dessert, do your favorite activity, or go to your favorite place in nature. Travel, change things up, do anything that brings you joy and lets you have fun.

Be in the flow. Any creative outlet helps us enter this state, whether it be writing, art, playing music, or dancing—anything that puts you in the zone where you are fully absorbed in what you're doing, fully in the moment and connected to the flow of creative energy. If you love your career and it brings you joy, you might understand that feeling of being so absorbed in that state that you lose the sense of time and feel one with whatever you're doing. Being in that state of flow—which some refer to as being in the zone—can raise our energy in its own way. Writing does this for me: it opens my channel.

Give. In a culture that often celebrates hedonistic and individualistic values, there is a swelling undercurrent of generosity. Giving is not just good for our soul, but also our physical health.[66] It opens our heart and helps us to remember our connection to the greater global commUnity. Your brain secretes the 'feel good' chemicals including dopamine, serotonin, and oxytocin. When we help others, we feel a greater sense of purpose. Biologically, we are in truth wired for altruism.[67] Generosity can lower blood pressure (with benefits measured to be as effective as diet and exercise) while studies have shown that people who volunteer live longer than those who don't.[68]

Acts of service can be more meaningful and impactful than donations, so don't make it about the money or feel as if you have nothing to give if your funds are limited. Help the elderly, walk your neighbor's dog, carry someone's groceries, hold the door, and even just smile and say hi to your neighbors and strangers. Smile at the homeless rather than avoiding eye contact as you walk by. Stopping and speaking to them even briefly, even if you have little to give, can bring light into a dark existence.

Here is a brief recap of practical ways to connect with the light:

Cultivate a gratitude practice

Connect with yourself

Connect with your body through movement

Connect with your heart

Connect with people in your life, find your tribe

Connect with nature

Connect with your intuition

Connect with your higher self

Connect with source consciousness, God, a higher power, whatever resonates

Connect with your creativity and self-expression

Connect with the essence of life by having fun and living in joy as much as possible

Connect with the sun, the source of light itself.

Connecting with the light means connecting with everything in your life in a deeper, more profound, and more heart-centered way.

Additional Resources

Clear to Connect: Access my free Energy Cleanse meditation and my free Higher Self Activation on my website or inside my Free Community.

For deeper practices on energetic cleansing and protection, head to my website, where I share a complete list of programs, courses, and free resources to assist you.

Chapter Nine

Light in the Darkness

Preparing for the Descent into the Underworld

"There is no light without shadow and no psychic wholeness without imperfection." - Carl Jung

Inner Alchemy is the Path to Mastery

Light needs darkness to exist. Without the dark, there couldn't be any light to shine. It's time to delve deeper into duality, polarity, separation, and shadow work. Now begins our descent into the dark side.

Tremendous amounts of light codes and frequencies have recently been pouring into the planet through solar flares and coronal mass ejections. From a scientific perspective, our planet has been bombarded by light frequencies.

When the light shines brilliantly, it illuminates the shadows and purges and purifies the density and toxicity that does not vibrationally align with the light.

The shadows of humanity are coming to light; our collective demons, the proverbial and literal skeletons in the closet; the light is forcing us to look at the darkness and excavate the closets. Light frequencies are forcing the shadows to surface as shadow energies cannot coexist with higher frequencies that pierce through the darkness to illuminate truth. This is what is happening on the collective and personal levels.

Collectively, we are moving through the dark night of the soul to allow the false foundations to crumble. Illusion and deception are being illuminated and purged. Individually, the dark night helps us to embody the light more fully. This is the process of alchemy. We transmute the shadows into light and become more powerful as we embody our wholeness. The dense wounds become the gold of our soul as the coal compresses to become pure and refined radiant diamond light.

As humans having this third dimensional human experience, most of us still require difficult times to wake us from our slumber and allow our beautiful dreams to become reality. We can't embrace, integrate, or release the shadows without going through the darkness. We are here to transcend this duality and polarity, but to do so, part of our job is to journey through the darkness and fully experience duality so that we can more completely appreciate and integrate the light.

What are duality and polarity?

Duality is separation and opposition: light and dark, good and evil, black and white, yin and yang, life and death; anything opposite.

The Chinese symbol of yin and yang is a beautiful representation of creating harmony from the duality. The circle with black and white in perfect balance represents integration to create a perfect whole, each holding an aspect of the other within to create a beautiful harmony. The dots represent the seed of light in the dark and the seed of dark in the light; the unification creates a perfect whole—unity from wholeness and the cyclical union of life. After death comes rebirth, and each time we are reborn, a more whole and integrated version of self.

If we didn't experience fear, anger, or despair, we wouldn't be able to have the full experience of love, joy, and serenity. As humans living this dense Earthly experience, we must experience duality to appreciate, understand, and embody the light, the higher, freer, more expansive ways of being. Going deep and exploring what lurks within, becoming aware of the shadow, examining it, looking at it, embracing it, integrating it—this is what allows us to reach our full potential as whole humans having integrated the wisdom of totality. Ignoring our shadow aspects will prevent us from self-actualizing. To grow, ascend in consciousness, and return to truth, we must face and embrace the shadows.

The human experience is one of duality and polarity. We all have freedom of choice in how we respond to life and all it brings. However, the human experience is here to help us transcend these notions by going through the dark night of the soul. While we are here to transcend duality, most of us carry enough wounds and conditioning that keep us blocked and asleep, so we typically need a rude awakening, which often comes as a crisis.

The duality of man refers to the separation of the body and the soul. In modern society, we have separated the two. Just like mind and body have been separated, body and soul have been separated. In our understanding, we perceive the soul from a higher level, separate from the body, as having this human experience. We understand existence through the body, our physical reality, and the material world.

Many on the spiritual path fall into the trap of only wanting to live in love and light while avoiding—or bypassing—the shadow work. This is disembodied spirituality preached by those not operating in integrity. They do not want to face the shadows because it feels uncomfortable or think focusing on the darkness will attract or create more of it.

In truth, they are afraid of the dark and of facing the shadows of shame within, or worse, false light operating in service to the forces of darkness by misdirecting people on the path. The irony is that avoiding the dark prevents us from fully accessing and embodying the light. The beauty is that once we become aware of these truths and examine our shadows, it becomes increasingly possible to experience that desired 'quantum leap.' Either way, the shadows must be faced and embraced.

Understand that awakening to the dark and experiencing the dark night is part of the human journey that compels us to transcend the shadows and raise our vibrational frequency. Collectively, in the 2020s, we have been given an incredible opportunity to face those shadows head-on and shed our limiting beliefs so that humanity can evolve into love.

The truth with a capital T is that separation, duality, and polarity are illusions when we see beyond the third-dimensional human experience. Separation of mind and body is also an illusion. Once humanity collectively evolves into our next era, we will not need to grow through pain, struggle, and suffering. Rather, we will learn to remember the fullness of love through joy, play, and expansion.

We are here to integrate mind, body, and soul to tap into our inner knowing and tune in to our heart wisdom because this is where our spirit resides. Our task is to come back into alignment with our soul's truth. Separation is an illusion and the shadow work helps to pierce through the veil of illusion, the layers of programming and conditioning of our ego identity that prevent us from feeling connected at the soul level.

Everything blossoms once we come back into alignment and feel connected at the soul level. We align with our true nature, with states of love, unity, oneness, abundance, and joy, and instant manifestation happens. We must integrate our shadows for manifestation to actualize and to harness the power of creation.

What is the shadow? The Psychology of the Psyche

The shadow constitutes the parts of ourselves that we disown, which then become relegated to the unconscious mind. The shadow is the dark side of our ego self, which strives for power or gives way to greed, envy, anger, lust, and so on. It's the proverbial devil that leads us down the road to hell, which is really just the illusion that we are separate from divinity, unworthy of love and grace.

The shadow is formed in childhood by rejecting or disowning those parts of ourselves that were deemed 'bad,' such as anger, selfishness, and greed. This correlates directly to our needs being met by our childhood environment. A child's behaviors are not necessarily greedy, selfish, or 'shameful' as they are learning to navigate the world as they grow. However if a conflict threatened our basic needs such as physiological needs, safety and security, or belonging, we learned to suppress our needs and the shame that accompanied the accompanying sense of disapproval.

Our most repressed shadow aspects are revealed to us through what irritates, frustrates, and triggers us most. Others mirror to us what we have suppressed in ourselves. This often causes us to project onto others, blaming them for being the problem when it's really an aspect of ourselves we have not yet been ready to recognize.

Ignoring the shadow can cause us to feel anxious or depressed, engage in self-sabotage or self-loathing, do or say things we later regret, act self-absorbed, have low self-esteem, struggle in relationships, and even swing from a sense of grandiosity to insecurity (ego inflation to ego deflation).

Doing shadow work is necessary if we want to reach our true potential. We all have shadows, a dark side. Repressing the darkness of shame blocks many from experiencing the joy of life waiting for us all. We believe we should suppress the emotions we don't feel comfortable experiencing because it's not 'good' to experience them. If we do, it makes us wrong, weak, or sinful. We're told to have a stiff upper lip, keep calm and carry on about life's most challenging circumstances. If we aim to transcend difficult emotions and elevate our emotional and life experiences, we must examine the shadows.

Ignoring and suppressing these darker, uncomfortable emotions manifests in mental illness and physical disease. Dis-ease in the mind can result in physical disease in the body. It can result in addiction, a scarcity mindset, and low self-esteem. Depression, panic attacks, sudden onset of eczema, autoimmune disorders—dare I say even cancer. With statistics indicating that a whopping one in three will now develop cancer, we must critically examine our perception of where it comes from. 'Bad genes' ain't gonna cut it; that's clearly not the whole story.

Part of the collective shadow is ignoring dramatic rises in health conditions across all age groups in recent history. Obesity, autoimmune conditions, ADHD, autism, allergies, cancer, mental health, and pathologized neural divergence are all on the rise.[69] Sweeping everything under the rug, ignoring the skeletons in the closet, and not looking at the demons and shadows within us only perpetuate and exacerbate the darkness that fractures our being and manifests as illness and disease.

Ignoring the darkness can also be labeled 'toxic positivity'—a pop psychology phrase for pretending everything's okay, pushing through, and not examining the deeper layers of your emotional experience is both toxic positivity and spiritual bypassing. It's the ubiquitous 'I'm fine!' or 'I'm good' in response to a 'how are you?' when really deep down your are suffering in unspoken agony. Focusing on a positive mindset alone doesn't work because we'll keep falling back to ground zero without integrating our deeper emotions and subconscious beliefs.

Ignoring the shadow will keep us in the shadow even longer. Often, it will manifest in an experience worse than what we've already experienced because our bodies and souls are trying to get our attention. *Oh, so you're going to continue to push through the stress and disregard the whispers we've been giving you; you're going to try to outperform the underlying trauma, adrenal fatigue, and gut issues and keep suppressing your soul's calling? Okay, let's see if cancer will get your attention.*

I was unaware of the issues festering within—the adrenal fatigue, gut issues, and trauma still *stuck in my body*. I had done talk therapy, which helped to a degree, but I ended it when, intuitively, I felt it wasn't moving the needle any further. I kept thinking once my external life circumstances would finally shift (the hope), I would finally feel better. The adrenal fatigue and gut issues? Neither are recognized or adequately addressed by Western medicine to this day. Nor does the DSM or our medical system adequately address trauma:[70] every single cancer survivor I have spoken with has indicated they experienced significant stress prior to diagnosis and typically had a history of trauma as well. This may—as I have long intuitively hypothesized—also contribute to relapse, recurrence, or chronic conditions.

Suppressing emotions can indeed cause them to get stuck in the body. This is often what happens with trauma: when somebody's system goes into freeze mode, which causes them to feel stuck in place, the chemicals released during that fight or flight response get frozen in their cellular memory. The freeze response kicks in when the body doesn't think you can fight or flee. Signs include a sense of dread and feeling stiff, numb, cold, or heavy, pale skin, and a loud, pounding heart and decreasing heart rate.

A fawn response will cause a person's system to collapse fully; in the face of fear or danger, someone who has experienced past trauma may get stuck in a freeze response or fall into fawn rather than fight or flee. Signs of a fawn response include being overly helpful, over-agreement, and placing others' needs over your own, as it typically occurs in those who grew up in abusive families or situations. Similar situations or events down the road may trigger this cellular memory to the surface, causing a vasovagal syncope episode[71]—often manifesting as a fainting episode, and sometimes may appear with seizure-like symptoms as the body seizes up while entering the collapsed state.

I experienced several of these vaso-vagal responses during my diagnostic process; the first major episode occurred after one of my big T traumas several years prior. They all connected to having my blood drawn or an IV. The most severe episode was after my bone marrow biopsy—the procedure itself was smooth and successful; after the fact, however, I apparently lost consciousness, seized up, and stopped breathing, and my face turned deep purple. I woke up to an oxygen mask on my face with 13 doctors and nurses surrounding my bed. As I finally came to, I felt like my brain short-circuited a dozen times; I felt like I kept fainting, but it seems I just lost consciousness momentarily each time. Eventful day at the oncologist's office. Apart from two fainting episodes in 2020 and 2021 under extenuating circumstances, since I have done the ongoing deeper trauma work and nervous system regulation, I haven't had any further episodes.

My personal view on health and healing—one held by increasing numbers of professionals and laypeople living the experience—is that trauma and suppressed emotions are underlying the vast majority of chronic diseases, as well as cancer.[72] Facing the triggers and traumas and dealing with the suppressed emotions isn't just so we can live a high vibe rainbows and sunshine spiritual mermaid fairy lifestyle.

Doing this inner work is crucial to our physical and mental wellbeing in a very tangible, grounded way. We don't want to get depressed. We don't want to get cancer. We want to raise healthy future generations.

So, if we become proactive about resolving underlying traumas and emotional wounds, we have a much lower chance of experiencing such conditions or of them perpetuating or returning. I have come to all of these understandings because of my personal experience going through cancer and the ensuing healing journey that brought me deeper than I ever imagined possible. On this journey, I've met countless others who have traveled similar paths and come to the same conclusions. This work is essential not just for our personal health but for that of the collective.

Doing this shadow work can be daunting, yet without going through the dark, we cannot fully appreciate the light, and we won't have the same depth or texture of life's wisdom woven into our souls. We're mired in the density and heaviness of fear and duality. The journey of healing and process of integration is unique to each of us because we have personal shadows to confront and our own soul journey to travel. Yet the human condition is universal, and the hero's journey is our path forward. What opens on the other side is beautiful: the blossoming of our experience of life itself. Transcending the duality helps us transcend the human experience of fear and embody love and possibility.

Jungian Psychology and Shadow Work

Shadow work is anchored in psychology. Jungian psychology, a theory of the human psyche that focuses on the unconscious mind, sees the shadow as all the conscious personality perceives as negative.[73] The ego personality resists the shadow, and as we discussed earlier, resistance only perpetuates and prolongs the patterns. What we resist persists. Again, it's all energy. Resistance feeds precisely what we don't want to experience with potent energy. We are always manifesting; we simply aren't always conscious of how we are doing so, and we always manifest at the level of our energy field. If we operate more frequently in the unconscious shadow self, our life will reflect this.

From the psychological perspective, one of the core tenets of Jungian psychology is that when one's authentic self is blocked, mental health issues can form and grow into depression, addiction, anxiety, and more. It gets to the root—the core wound that typically stems from childhood trauma.

Facing—rather than shaming—our shadows is what will ultimately give us that inner strength and resilience to move forward. Shadow work is an introspective, psychological practice. As challenging as it is, it is worth it because once you get through, the light shines even brighter and more beautiful, and life becomes magical. The light shines ever brighter into the darkness, and we rise higher and higher.

The Better it Gets, The Better it Gets

Grappling with the darkness isn't easy. Fear, anxiety, hurt, disappointment, frustration, anger, grief—literally every emotion has come up for most people during these turbulent times as we reach the solar maximum. The turbulence is shaking them loose so they can come to the surface to be reconciled and integrated. Face and embrace the shadows. Now is the time.

Of course, there are infinite degrees and varieties of the dark night of the soul. But I can say that if you are willing to show up and do the work, to do the shadow work, to do the work of shedding, the light begins to shine brighter.

Tell yourself: I'm ready for something better. I'm ready to be the greatest version of myself. I'm ready for magic. I'm ready for abundance. I'm ready for love. I'm worthy of it all.

Once you're fully in that space, embodied in that new version of self, everything unfolds, synchronicities flow into your life, and things begin to align. The shadows will start to release. You'll start to shed the limiting beliefs, the heaviness, the density that's been holding you down and keeping you back. And your life will begin to blossom in the most beautiful and unexpected ways right before your eyes.

The better it gets, the better it gets.

Engage with the Shadow

Actively engaging with the shadow emotions such as anger, jealousy, fear, resentment, bitterness, hopelessness, guilt, shame, and so on is what helps us to transmute and alchemize our inner demons. There are multiple ways to engage in shadow work, so try different methods and find what resonates with you. Use your intuition to guide you; you may find a creative way to work through the emotions that is unique to you.

The first step is awareness, and the second is Integration—essentially making it a part of you as you reclaim these disowned aspects of self to return to a state of wholeness.

Journaling, self-inquiry, self-reflection, and meditation are potent ways to allow awareness to rise to the surface. Keeping a trigger journey can help you to excavate the root of what angers or upsets you.

Breathwork, movement, and somatics are potent ways to move and release stuck energy. Ritual release and rage ceremonies can assist with catharsis and release. Yell into a pillow or at an empty chair. Smash a watermelon on the ground. Write a letter to the ones who you felt wronged by.

Write a letter to yourself about your emotions or simply free-write and allow your uncensored thoughts to come through. Creative pursuits can facilitate the expression of such feelings. It's no secret that some of the most extraordinary art and music have been birthed from deep pain and anguish.

Consider this a brief overview of shadow work; in the next chapter we will dive deeper into the processes themselves.

Chapter Ten

THE BRAVE HEART

Alchemizing the Shadows

"Your task is not to seek for love, but merely to seek and find all the barriers within yourself that you have built against it." ~ Rumi

We live in a world of duality during a time of unprecedented upheaval. We have been forced to face our shadows hidden in the deepest, darkest corners of our souls and society. We are here in this physical form to experience it all. With the light also comes the dark. From the dark, the light emerges. It is the nature of life. Life is born in the darkness of the void, the Womb of creation.

This path takes courage. The bravest souls signed up for this time on Earth.

Finding the courage to face the shadows comes from tuning in yourself and determining what is truly important to you. Am I willing to do this? Am I willing to move forward and face what I've been avoiding? Am I willing to face the shadows?

We are cultivating the courage of a Brave Heart forged through the fires of alchemy.

Like a snake shedding its skin, we have been thrust into the crucible of transformation to shed what's no longer serving us, what's keeping us small. The snake must first shed its skin to grow into the next version of itself and rise in its full power. Once our energy unblocks, it can rise up like the snake on the caduceus—the Kundalini energy rising up the spine to activate and awaken our soul.

Yet, this process of transformation can bring us to our knees.

The butterfly doesn't emerge from the cocoon with ease. Its case sticks to it. After the laborious journey of the caterpillar losing all form and turning into literal goo in the darkness of the void of the unknown, it finally comes into form, only to be encased in a sticky shell that still keeps it stuck and small. Having gone through the arduous process of transformation, the caterpillar then has to break out of the cocoon to finally spread its wings and fly.

Facing the shadows and doing the deep inner healing work is a challenging process. It does take courage. For most of us, it takes life thrusting us into a crisis and crashing down to rock bottom to be cracked open and finally willing to do the work. Even then, many refuse to answer the call and cling to their old life, climbing out of the depths only to return to the patterns that were not serving them, continuing to suffer in fear and anxiety and wondering why life is so unfair.

But we can also choose to face the shadows before life forces us to do that work through crisis. Then we are one step ahead of the game and—if we're lucky—might just be able to avoid full-on breakdown or winding up back in the same position we were before because we didn't learn the lesson.

Ignoring and suppressing our limiting beliefs, shadows, darkness, fears, and traumas deeply wound around our DNA will attract crisis, disease, and dark nights, which is life calling us to step up and do the work.

This isn't an easy call to answer. The inner work is the hardest work we can do in our lives. And yet, it leads us down a path of increasing ease, flow, magic, and abundance. Cheers to your brave heart for being here right now.

So, how do we find the courage to show up in the first place and start to examine the shadows? We have to get honest with ourselves about our life and our circumstances and ask: Is this what I want, the life that I'm living, the experience that I'm having, the day in the day out, my daily grind, is this everything there is for me? *Is this as good as it gets?*

The truth is we live in an ever-expanding universe of infinite possibilities, so no matter where we are in life, there is always something better available to us. We are always meant to grow and expand. It's the law of the Universe, the creation of the Creator.

If you don't want to move forward, that's a choice you can make. But remember, it is your choice to stay where you are. If you're feeling stuck, if you're feeling stagnant, if you're feeling resigned, if you're feeling like throwing in the towel and giving up, giving in, and doing nothing, then you have to be honest with yourself and say, okay, yes, I choose to do nothing to change my situation or how I feel about it. And I choose this, even though it's uncomfortable. It's what I know, and I'm just going to stay here in the comfort zone that isn't actually very comfortable, but at least I know what I'm facing.

That is a choice.

Procrastination is a choice as well. It is a pattern often rooted in deeper trauma, but if we find ourselves constantly starting projects and not finishing or allowing minor urgencies to take precedence over our larger goals and dreams, it might be a signal of underlying trauma or subconscious beliefs based in wounding that we must face and address. We often say we want things to change and then do nothing about it. We create excuses as to why we could not do x or y that day. The excuses continue and nothing changes, day after day. I know from experience it can be hard to recognize when we are still playing the victim and getting the courage to admit it. Sometimes our trauma keeps us stuck and looping even if we can acknowledge the pattern, so nervous system regulation should be a priority for anyone who has experienced trauma or chronic stress.

It's hard to stay complacent once we are that honest with ourselves. A lot of us don't even want to face the fact that we do have the capacity to change our reality. It's not easy.

But be honest—are you comfortable inside that little box?

Stepping outside of the known requires courage. If we are not happy where we are and can admit that we are not comfortable in the little box that has been created for us (or that we created for ourselves), then we are finally in a position to get clear about what our priorities are in this lifetime. Are we here to experience stagnation, just living a humdrum life or carefully curated existence to meet societal expectations and keep up with the Joneses, or are we here to step into possibility and blossom into our most whole, most expansive expression?

From that space of belief in something better, we may have the courage to face the shadows that create the illusory shackles of limitation.

The Choice

So, how do we develop a brave heart? Where do we find that courage? We find that courage by deciding that we choose better. That we are worth better. It is a daily choice.

Courage comes from being willing to show up and face the fear, and from that spark and belief that there's something better waiting for you to show up and claim it as your own.

The courage comes from within. It comes from the inner knowing that this is not all there is; there is more and better. If you can envision it, you can create it. If you can dream it, you can manifest it. It comes from faith in something greater and trust in your worthiness to receive and capacity to have it. Committed courage builds confidence, and that confidence snowballs into conviction and success.

Rebuilding self-trust after facing incredibly difficult situations with people who did not have my best interest at heart was a significant challenge for me. The most insidious aspect of narcissistic abuse, gaslighting, and deep betrayal is the loss of self-trust that occurs when you place your trust in the wrong person or situation. Self-blame and shame are pernicious monsters that can keep us in the dungeons of despair if we allow them to fester and capture our psyche. So give yourself a lot of grace and compassion if you've faced circumstances that caused you to doubt yourself, your worthiness, or your capacity to create a beautiful life. But pick yourself up as many times as it takes, and take small steps to rebuild self-trust and inner peace. You are worth it.

Think about what you want for your life. What are your visions, your dreams, your greatest aspirations that arise from your true heart's desires? However silly they may seem to you. What's one small step closer you can take to creating that? Maybe it's creating that side hustle to make some extra income or changing your physical environment. Perhaps it's buying a new dress that makes you feel like a queen, a new pair of sneakers, or a new notebook to write your inspiring thoughts. Taking that class. Investing in that program. Moving your body in a new way. Meeting someone for coffee. Emailing that person. Sharing that post. Can you find a way to create that one small thing for yourself in the immediate future?

Stepping into your vision and claiming your birthright as a powerful, masterful manifesting creator starts with small baby steps: what's one little thing you can do to create a small change? Build trust in yourself and in the divine plan of your life. Build your manifestation muscle bit by bit, one baby step at a time. Build your capacity to receive. See it, believe it, and put your energy into the state of it already being done. Then, take the aligned actions. Reframe failure as feedback to get you closer to what is right for you.

Release self-judgement and embrace forgiveness. Forgiveness is for yourself, always, and sometimes its ourself we need to forgive most for betraying our own needs. Forgiveness unlocks possibility.

From there, grow your vision and your idea of what is possible for you now.

Again, what many people don't realize is that we are *always* manifesting—it is usually subconscious and at the level of our vibration. We often manifest things we don't want because we are focused on them (fear) and are a vibrational match for that thing (are you going in endless loops?).

Here's the key: *deciding* to break the cycle and rise *up* the spiral. This requires us to do the shadow work and clear our body temple of energies not aligned with our highest potential. If we don't face those shadows, those limiting beliefs that keep us stuck in the first place, we will keep falling back into the same pattern. To shift the pattern, we must shift the beliefs, clear out the old emotions, heal the old wounds, release the guilt, grief, shame, and self-doubt, and face our demons—the repressed emotions and traumas from our past that keep us stuck in these loops. Trauma can keep our nervous system stuck in patterns of response and reaction. So we must bring awareness to our triggers and thought patterns: where am I stuck in a rut? Awareness is key.

Remember, there's zero blame. There's zero judgment and zero shame. Go into this with a clean slate. This isn't easy. Have so much compassion for yourself that you overflow with self-love, self-care, and grace. Cultivating unconditional self-love, compassion, and acceptance is key to shifting our reality.

As you go through this process, please leave judgment at the door. When you sit down to do this work, stuff will come up, and it may feel like too much for you to handle on your own, so give yourself space and create a support system: a therapist, a community, a coach, a mentor, a friend—somebody who can hold the space for you without judgment.

Keys for Shadow Work

Patience, Trust, Surrender, A Safe Space.

Having a safe container to do the deep inner work is essential. It allows us to open up Pandora's box and examine the pieces of us we've been scared to face. Without a safe space to process, release, and integrate, it can become too overwhelming and we may slam the lid back shut and shove it into an even darker corner.

Have that safe container and a support system in place. This includes your physical environment, mentors, programs, and tools. You may find that that container grows. You may figure it out as you go along. What might that support look like for you? Transformation is both a process and a journey, not a one-shot, one-week, or even one-month deal. The work is ongoing, but you feel lighter and lighter and freer as you ascend.

You will evolve. You will transform as you do this work and shed the layers of your old identity. You will grow, and you will have to shed again. You will grow even more, and you will have to shed once again. Have compassion for where you are now, have compassion for yourself throughout this process, and get that support system in place. And also, be patient. Quantum leaps are possible, but they usually come after deep inner work. It doesn't have to take a long time, but you must be willing to go there and get super honest with yourself.

Patience is far more powerful than most realize because patience essentially tells the Universe, your higher self, and God Source that you trust. Patience, at its core, is a powerful sense of trust. Trust that all will come when the time is right, the divine timing for your life. Release the sense of control, or grasping, of forcing, and trust that in divine timing, everything you envision will fall into place, that what you desire will come to you.

That, or something even better. We often cling to a specific vision or method. Let go of the how and allow the Universe to bring you the magic. Often, usually (maybe even always?), it's far better than anything you could have allowed yourself to believe possible. Surrender and see what kind of magic is possible. Trust is key, and patience is a sign of trust. So have patience with yourself, and have patience with the process. That moment of surrender often creates the quantum leap, and our patience and faith are rewarded far more rapidly than we could have hoped. What we resist persists. But when we let go, we allow the blessings to flow.

The Body is the Key: Nervous System Regulation

Before we even dive into the self-inquiry and internal processes associated with shadow work, we must remember that the key is to anchor this work in through the body. The body holds the both the trauma and the wisdom; the body is the key.

Nervous system regulation helps to maintain a balance between the sympathetic (fight-or-flight) and parasympathetic (rest-and-digest) responses. A regulated system is not necessarily a calm state, but a system that is flexible and can fluidly move between different states of arousal while maintaining a sense of safety and trust.

The nervous system essentially controls every other system through communication and integration of complex electrochemical signals, so a system that is imbalanced can result in poor decision making, problem solving, and social engagement in addition to a host of physical symptoms.

Physiological responses of the parasympathetic nervous system are involuntary, however we can bring conscious awareness to these processes—such as breathing – and harness them to bring our body into a balanced state.

Building conscious awareness of our internal bodily sensations can help guide our responses. Hunger, heart rate, pain, and emotions can all point to areas we can proactively improve our state. Sleep hygiene provides a simple example—how do you feel after a night of insomnia? What can you do to improve this? Perhaps you can turn off devices and blue light an hour earlier, drink herbal tea, or write in your gratitude journal.

Controlled breathwork is a powerful practice for nervous system health, one that has been a game-changer for me. Yoga, exercise, lifestyle changes to reduce stress, gut health, and improved sleep hygiene will all facilitate nervous system regulation.

How to do Shadow Work

Now that we're sufficiently primed as to the what's and why's of shadow work... *how* do we do the shadow work? What does it even look like?

A simple way to begin is to journal. While it might sound basic, journaling is a powerful process. Journaling allows us to take what's intangible—what's floating around in the crowded chaos of our minds—and bring it into the physical reality for the purpose of processing and dot-connecting, creating space for the Aha moments. On the positive side, journaling affirmations and writing your vision into reality is powerful because it's taking your vision and bringing it into tangible reality for the purpose of creation.

Words are powerful; they create our reality, so with conscious intention, we can use the power of our words to shape the world around us.

Similarly, when it comes to processing our darker shadow side, journaling allows us to organize our thoughts, bring awareness to them, and get clear on the root of our beliefs because without bringing them out into the tangible reality, we're not fully conscious of the thousands of thoughts swirling through our minds.

Day in and day out, we have countless thoughts. One essential step in doing shadow work is getting crystal clear on your stories and thought patterns and bringing that into the tangible so that you can rewrite your story and re-create your reality with clarity on where you are and what's *not* working. We are clearing the space to create something new for ourselves.

Record your thoughts, record your feelings, record your emotions. Like a food journal, you might like to maintain a journal that tracks your thoughts, feelings, and triggers because what we bring awareness to can begin to shift.

Awareness is key. So, bringing mindfulness into the equation is a large part of the shadow work process. Mindful awareness is powerful because if we don't understand where our thoughts, emotions, and feelings are, we'll never be able to shift those patterns and the habitual way we show up day in and day out.

Determine whether your thoughts are primarily optimistic or pessimistic, positive or negative, or, as I prefer, helpful or unhelpful. This shift goes beyond the reductionist labeling of positive and negative: are they beneficial to your growth and wellbeing, or not? Are they critical or supportive? Are they growth-oriented, or are they fixed?

A growth mindset[74] focuses on lessons learned and how to improve, whereas a fixed mindset makes universal conclusions about the self based on circumstances, such as *I'm a failure, I'm bad at math*, or *I'm stupid*. I AM is a powerful statement—anything that follows becomes your identity, and the Universe will respond with situations and circumstances to mirror your beliefs. Unfortunately, the Universe doesn't have a sense of humor either, so mind what you say, even if you say it jokingly.

A growth mindset is empowering because it can quickly shift the narrative from failure to feedback, from obstacle to challenge. Those with a fixed mindset have a harder time seeing the possibility and are much more likely to fall into a victim mentality where you are powerless to control your reality. Seeking a savior—whether it's a doctor, the government, or Jesus—is very typical in the matrix, as this is how we have been programmed and conditioned. But it is time to break free from the mental matrix that causes you to give your power away to external circumstances and feel helpless about them. So reflect on this: Do you have a sense of autonomy, or do you tend to feel like everything is happening *to* you and out of your control?

Please leave judgment at the door. This is a time to get curious about who you are being right now so that you can shift into the energy of who you are becoming. Being in a state of victimhood is very disempowering—we feel like we don't have control over our reality and that things are happening *to* us. Do you feel empowered by your thoughts, feelings, and emotions, or disempowered by your thoughts, feelings, and emotions? Without judgment, get curious and bring awareness to these notions.

With that awareness in place, you can then take a step back. What if this isn't happening *to* you but *for* you? What if it is all serving your highest growth and expansion by forcing you to go deeper within and discover the light that was always there?

Over time, you will start to see recurrent patterns. Once you have this awareness, you can interrupt the unhelpful thoughts in the moment and begin to shift your internal dialogue. You can start to rewire your brain by changing the conversation you're having with yourself in your mind. Change your internal dialogue so that instead of your own worst critic, you're your own cheerleader, best friend, and lover.

Trigger Warning

Okay, let's get into the juicy stuff—triggers! People often preface deep shares or potentially controversial topics with 'trigger warning.' But what is a trigger?

In the context of mental health, a trigger is anything that stimulates a strong adverse emotional reaction or awakens a painful or traumatic memory, feeling, or symptom.[75] It can bring on or worsen symptoms someone is already experiencing, typically rooted in a traumatic event or circumstance. It can cause overwhelm and distress or even elicit an angry outburst, usually an entirely unconscious reaction.

When it comes to inner healing, shadow work, and personal growth and development, recognizing your triggers, bringing awareness to when you are being triggered, and eventually catching yourself before you enter into full-blown trigger mode is a crucial part of the process. People often project their shadow qualities onto others without this awareness and self-reflection. Projection is an unconscious process, as it is the qualities we deny or bury within ourselves that we tend to 'see' in others. Projections distort our perception of reality by creating a filter of self-perception.

It's typically in the things that irritate you most about others where your shadow work resides. Your biggest pet peeves. You can't stand people in their spiritual ego or who lack self-awareness? Well, that's probably because you have a fair amount of work to do on those shadows yourself but haven't yet been ready to look in the mirror. If you get irritated when people are rude, it's probably because you still haven't owned the shadow of rudeness within.

Projection is a self-defense mechanism rooted in past pain and trauma, often from childhood. Patterns may have been perpetuated through the lineage, and this is where the expression 'hurt people hurt people' derives. However, the inverse is also true: 'Healed people heal people.'

Having the tools to process and release emotions and energy is also crucial. This is the work. This is a straightforward way to create shifts: responding versus reacting. Pause, take a deep breath to calm your system, and calmly respond. Remember that someone else's triggered reaction is usually not (basically never) about you anyway. Bring compassion to the other person and yourself in the process. This is how to move through life with grace.

This inner inquiry and self-reflection is the most challenging but most rewarding work there is.

As you notice your triggers—whether a minor annoyance or something that triggers a massive outburst—dive deeper and get curious. What *really* triggered you? Was it really because the gardener was cutting the bushes too short, somebody asked you what brand your dress was, somebody cut you off on the highway, or because the server was rude when they gave you your coffee?

Was that actually the reason you had a massive outburst? Probably not. There was probably something much deeper underlying the triggered reaction—a sense of being disrespected, of not being able to take up space, not being seen, heard, feeling unworthy, feeling undeserving; there are multiple layers that can fester underneath, and sometimes it's wild to realize the tiniest circumstance triggered something buried deep within. Dig down and examine: what is this genuinely bringing up for you?

It's not a fun process, but once you start to pick them apart, you bring increasing levels of awareness, and you can catch yourself before you react from a space of being triggered the next time. Little enlightening Aha moments arise, you begin to unravel the confusion and weave into harmony the threads of your life, and thread by thread, you feel increasingly in tune with the wholeness of who you are.

It's not a one-and-done process. You will get triggered over and over, and different patterns will unfold. The same trigger will come up many times. And that's okay. Just keep going.

When we're deep in the process of 'doing the work,' sometimes we can feel like a failure if we notice we are getting triggered yet again. It's not that we're failing at the process; it's something we can celebrate because we're bringing awareness to it more quickly. Catching ourselves in the reaction before we respond is the goal.

It's not that we won't react. It's about taking a step back before we respond. That's the ultimate goal. Before lashing out, we can pause, breathe, think, and say, okay, what is this really about? Have compassion for yourself and the others in the situation. Respond with clarity and boundaries in place; this is not about excusing poor or abusive behavior.

Allow yourself to feel the emotion. Pause before expressing it, but allow yourself to feel emotions as they come up and express yourself in a way that doesn't harm or project your pain onto another. It's bubbling up for a reason: it needs to be released. If you suppress it again, it will bubble up even more powerfully later or, over time, will get buried deeper and deeper and potentially manifest in disease. Anger is often a cover for grief and pain so the outburst may be a burst dam ripe for release. Let go and let it flow, and you will feel relief, space, and peace you didn't even realize was possible.

Feel it. Examine it. Process it. Release it. Integrate it. And if you need support, find it.

When these intense feelings bubble up, they're ready to be examined. Triggers are a catalyst for our emotional healing and growth, and situations arise so that we can release these deeper wounds. Honestly, a lot of us reach boiling points without really understanding why. This process is about understanding ourselves—coming to a space of inner knowing.

Ultimately, it's a journey of self-mastery.

Those triggers lead us to the pot of gold that lies within—our power, our truth, our treasure chest of wisdom.

Eventually, you may arrive at a funny place where you get excited about your triggers, like, 'Awesome, this is an opportunity for me to grow!' This is another opportunity for me to learn more about myself, to shed another layer, to heal and integrate the underlying root, and to bring life back into the empty voids within.

Let It Burn

Burning rituals comin in hot! *(Sorry, not sorry, I couldn't resist that terrible joke ;).* When we are ready to face the old patterns and beliefs and release them, we can create a ritual or ceremony for ourselves to write it all out on paper to get it out of us and then tear it up or burn it in a bonfire (safely, of course!). Fire represents the power of purification through alchemical transformation, and watching the words that defined our past burn away is beautiful and powerful.

After the majority of my hair from my first round of chemotherapy fell, I didn't dispose of it immediately. Two days after it started falling, I had a photo shoot—for my hair. It was a unique color, a fiery strawberry blond version of red, and long. I had heard hair often didn't grow back the same after chemo, possibly not the same color. My whole life people had commented on my hair, so in an attempt at self-preservation, I decided to schedule a photoshoot. That morning, I made the mistake of washing it, and in the shower, it began falling in clumps, and I wound up with a giant mess of a matte. I sobbed as I desperately tried to comb it out and salvage what I could, with more clumps filling the sink as I pulled with the comb.

A neighborhood acquaintance miraculously happened to knock on the door to say hi at that moment, and helped me cut out the matte, curl what was left, and do my makeup. She even ran home to get a clip-in extension that was serendipitously a close match to mine as she had died her hair red. I had texted the photographer, and he said of course let's do it anyway and capture something real.

The extensions were falling out by the time I made it to the photoshoot. My hair wasn't strong enough to hold it. The photos were real and raw, and it was probably one of the best things that could have happened since I was going to lose it no matter what. A few days prior a friend had come over and captured other shots of my hair. So I wound up with images of both my hair in the natural and the stark contrast of loss in the studio.

The upshot was I had a pile of my old hair that, for some reason, I wasn't letting go of. Of course, I was holding on to the past. I knew that, but I felt the right moment would come. That moment came when I went on a rock climbing trip for young adult cancer survivors in the Colorado mountains, which included bonfire on the itinerary. I knew I had to bring it and burn it there. It felt powerfully symbolic and extra special to do it ceremoniously with witnesses who could truly understand the journey as they'd been walking it themselves. My hair was growing back, still short, and yes, a different color entirely. It was time to release the old and embrace the new. And it was right around the solar eclipse of August 2017. Little did I know the extent of the new journey that lay ahead.

To be most effective, a physical release and embodiment process should accompany these rituals. Rage ceremonies or rituals can be a powerful way to fully feel and release your anger, rage, bitterness, and resentment without actually harming anyone else in the process. Going out into a quiet spot in nature and yelling, hitting the ground with a baseball bat, smashing a watermelon onto concrete, beating a pillow, or screaming into it are all surprisingly effective catharsis. If tears come, allow them to fully flow. You are ready to release, and that is a beautiful thing. Underlying rage is grief, and once you bring the rage up to the surface for release, the dam breaks and the waters of purification follow.

Tears hold memory through water consciousness, so when we allow ourselves to fully feel the pain and let the tears of past pain flow, they literally carry the pain, trauma, and stuck emotions out of our body. This is the biological underpinning of cathartic release.

To bring the story full circle, just this year—8 years later—that friend who now lives across the country 3,000 miles away messaged me 'out of the blue.' She wished to share with me what had actually happened that morning. She hadn't come over to bring my dad leftovers. That was her excuse. She had had a dream about me and woke up with a sense of urgency, knowing that she had to go over and help me, right then. We were little more than neighborhood acquaintances at that point. She grabbed the food and ran out the door. My dad answered her knock and asked her if she could help me. Without his awareness, she had already known that was why she was there, so she walked right in and up the stairs. She was my angel, and our angels conspired for her to be there when I needed her most. Naturally, we formed a strong bond after that. In her dream, I was pregnant and going into labor; it turns out, I was in the process of rebirthing myself.

Eight years later, interestingly, I went through another unexpected shedding. After a period of stress followed by an intense fever that reached 105 and lasted five days, after which I also had a psychic attack on my crown, my hair suddenly began to shed once again. Needless to say, it triggered traumatic memories to the surface. Exactly eight years prior, I had been bald, and now that it had finally grown long enough to touch the small of my back, it began falling. In an attempt to monitor the hair fall, I kept the clumps that came out of my brush. After a few weeks, I had an alarmingly large pile; my long hair bulked it up, but it was quite upsetting.

Once again, I took the hair and burned it in the fire pit. It was time to shed and fully release the past and the trauma and pain of this recent cycle as well as all separation wounds that had arisen in my consciousness. Wrapped in a piece of paper where I had written all the emotions and energies I was ready to leave behind as well as my intentions for the new life I was prepared to claim, I lit it and watched it all burn til all that was left was ashes and memories that would no longer haunt me but empower my path forward, like the phoenix rising with golden wings.

Shift Your Perspective

Rewriting the narrative of painful moments from the past can be a powerful form of alchemy. We can shift the meaning we make out of it or even go back and rewrite the outcome of the experience as the empowered victor, the version of ourselves that has boundaries and a strong sense of self-worth. When it comes to shifting thoughts and beliefs that are not helpful or supportive, if we can find a shred of evidence to the contrary, we can shift our perspective on our situation. And little by little, we can move forward and shed these limiting beliefs. We can begin to see possibility and then develop that more profound sense of faith, inner strength, and courage.

When you believe in a sense of possibility and your ability to create that possibility, you begin to step into a place of personal power with utter self-conviction. Unshakeable self-belief is unstoppable. Getting to that embodied state is challenging for most, but it is doable for everyone.

Empower yourself by challenging your own beliefs. Is it true that things will never get better? Is it true that that was the only job for you, or that was the only person for you? Is it true that no one or nothing else is out there? Is it true that there will be no other opportunity for happiness for the rest of your life? Is it true that that's all there was for you, ever? Is it true that nobody loves you and you are completely alone?

Curiosity is what will move us forward. Resist the inclination to dwell on the emotions of hopelessness and helplessness. The more we stew in anger and resentment, the more we dwell in the darkness of despair and depression, the harder it is to break through that inertia and build the energy to shift. But remember, emotion is E-motion, energy in motion. So if you're experiencing those heavier energies,and emotions, remember you have the power to shift those experiences by generating a different emotional experience through motion.

Get up and move your body; get up and dance; get up and put your favorite upbeat, high-vibe song on and dance; belt it out and shake your booty.

Shake it off, literally. There is a reason dance is healing. There is a reason animals in nature shake their bodies after trauma: they shake to release. Dance, shake, and feel super silly. Or super sensual and intimate. Surrender to the flow. Allow your body to guide you deeper into connection with what it needs at this moment. Shut yourself alone in your room if you need to, and shake, move, twist, flow, feel the emotion out, and express it through your body.

When releasing trauma and engaging in deep inner emotional healing, verbal expression is also essential. Journaling is powerful, but speaking it out loud is crucial because it activates the throat chakra. Even if you're talking to a chair across the room, imagine the person you're saying these things to sitting there, listening to the things you wish you said, all that was left unsaid. Scream it out if you need to. Yell. Cry. Get Angry. Fully express it. I guarantee you'll feel a lot better. And you may not feel the need to confront that person in person. This exercise may be necessary and especially powerful when you cannot face that person in real life.

If, for whatever reason, you can't face that person, whether they've passed on, they're in a different state or country, you don't have their contact information, or perhaps for safety reasons, you can't or shouldn't face them in person, it's a powerful practice. Yell it out, have a conversation, cry, tell them how their behavior made you feel, and explain why it was so hurtful. Get it out, and dance out the rest.

Interpretative or expressive dance may feel awkward for some because we've repressed the emotions of shame so deeply, along with fear of judgment and rejection. Dancing alone in our room can help shift these patterns on many levels.

Dancing is healing because it allows us to move our bodies more fluidly and intuitively. It helps us to get out of our heads and into our bodies. A primal force takes over when we fully allow the body to move us rather than our mind. Moving with the rhythm and the beat activates and channels something deep, primal, and innate. Trauma gets buried deep within our tissues and cells, and the vibration and intuitive movement of dance is a potent way to release the stuck energies at a cellular level. Movement and dance are potent healing modalities for many reasons.

We can even add affirmations as we dance to help anchor the energies into our cells. I am powerful, I am beautiful, I am strong, I am loved. Whatever resonates and will shift the energy. I am healthy. I am full of vitality. I am abundant. I flow with the divine. Just move your body and allow the feelings to guide you.

Little by little, step by step, we keep moving forward, dancing with the flow of life. As we do this work, eventually, we will find that golden nugget buried deep within. Beauty and magic will blossom and unfold when we water and nurture the golden seed within.

Blossoming is an ongoing process, but the more you commit and allow the process to unfold, the lighter and brighter you feel. Eventually, the diamond at the center will be revealed, illuminating the pure brilliance of your being. I promise you're worth it.

Forgiveness

Forgiveness is simple in theory, powerful in practice, and incredibly challenging for so many of us to do. Forgiveness does not require reconciliation. It is not about enabling abuse or sweeping an offense under the table. Forgiveness is for you.

To forgive means to cease feeling resentment toward. Resentment is a bitter poison that erodes our hearts, so, as unfair as the circumstance may be, it only hurts us to hold on to the wrong. Forgive, let go, and let God.

The Hawaiian Ho'oponopono prayer is a simple yet powerful forgiveness practice to forgive both yourself and others:

I'm Sorry. Please Forgive Me. Thank You. I Love You.

CHAPTER ELEVEN

THE LONG SHADOW OF LIMITING BELIEFS

DECONDITIONING AND UNLEARNING TO RECONSTRUCT YOUR REALITY

"The mind is its own place, it can make a heaven of hell, a hell of heaven."
- John Milton

Limiting beliefs cast a long shadow. We carry our beliefs for our entire lives, only questioning them once confronted with alternative viewpoints. Most of us are unaware that our worldview is primarily formed not by fact but by belief, much less where they come from. We take beliefs for granted as fact or Truth, and that's largely an illusion.

Beliefs are just that, no matter how widely accepted or deeply ingrained they may be. Everyone in your circle holding the same belief still does not make the belief necessarily accurate. Religion is a perfect example: many people believe their religion or faith is the only 'true' way. They can't all be 'true.' Beliefs inform perception and perspective, resulting in a widely accepted notion that we each experience our version of reality, our own Truth.

Beliefs are not inherently *bad*. They create a mental architecture for distilling and interpreting the complexity of the world around us. They help us to categorize information and act as internal commands, and in their absence people feel disempowered. However, the task is to be able to discern the origin and validity of our beliefs and have the capacity to change them in the face of new, disconfirming information.

While there is undoubtedly Truth in the notion that we all create our own experience of reality and, therefore, coexist in the intersection of billions of overlapping realities, I do believe there exists a higher Truth that permeates our reality, whispering to our soul to guide us back home to the heart. This is the hero's journey we're all called to embark on eventually—returning home to the heart of Truth.

Beliefs are inherently limiting. Therefore, ego identity-based beliefs keep us firmly in the realm of separation. They block our ability to see beyond our box, to see what else might be possible. They often keep us closed in, not open to hearing other perspectives and seeing alternative options. Questioning our beliefs is the first step in shifting them.

Often, when presented with opportunities to see something differently, we dig our heels in even more deeply. This is an ego trap that keeps us in duality and separation.

Questioning our beliefs confronts us with two very uncomfortable prospects: that we may be wrong and that our entire understanding of the world and reality itself may be false. Beliefs become part of our identity, so if we are confronted by the notion that our belief may not be as universally accepted or valid as we initially believed, we are now faced with an identity crisis: our ego clings on because it doesn't want to be wrong. Ego death brings us to our knees, but ultimately, it liberates us. The ego doesn't truly die, but the false walls and boundaries in our perception of reality dissolve to allow our expanded self to infuse our sense of self with a higher guiding intelligence.

Unless we bring awareness to and shift our beliefs, we operate from the energetics of the beliefs that keep us stuck for our entire lives. Or we can examine our beliefs, question them, and say, 'Is that true? Does it have to be true? Does it have to be true *for me*?' Then, we can start to pick them apart and reconstruct an expansive belief system, a set of beliefs for yourself that supports your growth and expansion and achieving your potential, and moves you toward abundance, love, and joy.

Where do our beliefs come from?

Most of us are unaware of how beliefs are formed. Many consider the formation of beliefs to be programming or conditioning. Our brains are sponges for the first seven years of our lives,[76] and this is the timeframe during which most of our fundamental beliefs are formed. Our brains are in a theta state, absorbing everything from the environment. Filters are virtually nonexistent, and we are sponges for the stimuli in our environment. This spongelike quality allows us to develop language rapidly and to form an understanding of the world. However, our spongelike nature does not discriminate—it includes ideas and behaviors in our environment that are not consciously given to us, but we absorb them anyway. It includes emotions, how we respond to them, and energy. Just like toddlers repeating curse words without knowing what they mean, we unconsciously absorb and model patterns of behavior displayed by those around us.

When we are tiny, we have no concept of the quality of what we're learning, of what's true and what's not true. But if it comes from mommy or daddy or our primary caregivers, we will trust it because we trust them with our lives. Whatever they say or do, we take it as Truth. If they respond to a situation with fear, we learn that fear. We take on a belief of fear related to that situation. If they react angrily toward a problem, we likewise learn to react in anger. Our environment programs conditioned responses, wiring them into our being.

Even as adults, we as a society are largely unaware that this is how our children become programmed, nor are we fully conscious of how we program them in every moment. Cultivating this level of awareness isn't just vital for ourselves but also for the people in our lives, especially if we have little ones in our circle. Becoming aware of beliefs and where they come from is incredibly important. They come from our culture, from our society, from our community. They come from any exposure that we have, especially in those first seven years. Our brains develop critical thinking skills after those first seven years, and we act with more autonomy. However, in those first seven years, most of our beliefs form.

It's quite wild to consider from that perspective: our belief systems come from our fragile childhood, shaping our entire world into adulthood.

Then, the task is to zoom out and begin to ask questions. Does this belief apply to me and my current circumstances? Where does my money mindset come from? Does my mom's belief that money doesn't grow on trees serve my abundance? Such phrases are rooted in scarcity. Does that belief that making money is difficult, requires lots of hard work, or is hard to come by *have* to be true?

The task then is to start digging in, diving deep, and questioning the beliefs that we've taken on without any judgment, shame, regret, or blame. We only know what we know and don't know what we don't know. Learning new information allows us to question what's in the highest good for ourselves and others.

From there, we have the power of choice; from there, we can grow. Now is the time. Every present moment is an opportunity for you to shift in the direction of your dreams, goals, and most brilliant expression. Simply get curious. About your beliefs, about this whole journey called life, about the way the world really works. Anytime a situation comes up where you're feeling limited or blocked, take a step back. *'Why am I feeling this way? Why am I feeling 'not good enough'? Why am I feeling unworthy?'*

Let's examine another common one: 'I'm bad at math.' I used to be a math tutor, and in the industry, we found that test performance was often rooted in more profound performance anxiety based on limited beliefs. This particular belief was widespread in young girls. Where does this belief come from? It usually stems from this societal bias that girls are not as good at math as boys. Such widespread cultural beliefs are damaging because not only are such grandiose generalizations simply not true for the whole population, but they also create glass ceilings. Unfortunately, the education system churns out teachers who solidify these beliefs rather than nurture a growth mindset in their students.

Often, these limited self-perceptions become ingrained in our internal belief system from one bad test grade or one lousy teacher. We identify with the story, and that story becomes our reality. This one belief can unfold into a belief set related to a lack of confidence, a sense of not being good enough, and performance anxiety that can follow someone through life. So, it's imperative to discover the root of our beliefs or to clear the energetic essence of the pattern. Sometimes, we'll even discover that the root of the belief is a perceived 'random' situation that arose in childhood, like a parent making an off-the-cuff remark that we deeply internalized. We don't have to dredge up every painful memory, only those our soul requires for wisdom and closure.

There may have been a time when we got injured or felt ill, and our parents didn't initially recognize the severity of the situation. *'Oh, it looks like you're okay.'* Then it turned out it was in fact more serious. At that moment, we didn't feel properly seen or heard. Often these situations were not intentional or devastating, but the emotional impact of their responses—or lack thereof—stayed with us because it created a sense of not feeling seen or heard, or even a sense of abandonment as our needs were not adequately met.

Perhaps your caregiver didn't show up at the proper time to pick you up from school one day, and you felt utterly alone. Or a teacher made an off-the-cuff remark about your behavior, making you feel wrong or inherently 'bad.' While the situations may seem insignificant in the grand scheme of things, the emotional impact can run deep, especially if these situations compounded into repeated response patterns on the part of the parent or caregiver. None of it should be disregarded or discarded. Examining how we felt about the situation is of primary importance. The excavation process is not easy, but it is essential. Once we see it, its grip loosens, and it becomes quite easy to transmute the wound connected to the belief.

When you start to pinpoint some of your limiting beliefs, look for the root of that issue. Is it a worthiness issue, or not feeling good enough? Did you feel rejected? Usually, the belief is rooted in five core wounds, sometimes called the wounds of the soul: abandonment, betrayal, rejection, humiliation, and injustice. Beliefs rooted in these wounds limit us and our growth and expansion. Throughout my progression, there was a pervasive, ongoing belief of *'I'm not there yet. I don't feel ready yet.'* This is actually rooted in: *'I don't feel worthy of doing this thing because I don't feel good enough. Who am I to do this?'*

The root of unworthiness could be rejection, though I personally see unworthiness as an encompassing wound that could be humanity's primary core wound. The root of the issue will open up the possibility of shifting the energetic pattern in our system. When we find a belief, we can shift it by finding evidence to the contrary and negating it. From there, we can rewrite our story and create a new belief that is the opposite or more supportive.

The belief *'I'm not good enough,'* based in a fixed mindset, can be replaced with, *'I'm working hard and getting better every day.'* Affirmations can be potent when accompanied by shadow work to release and integrate the stuck energy and embodiment practices to anchor in the new beliefs. Belief transformation doesn't happen overnight, but once you commit to it, it's a powerful process, and it's entirely possible to completely rewire your belief system into your brain and body.

The People You Surround Yourself With

Another crucial aspect to consider is the people in our lives. We can always find people to support us in our limiting beliefs. Commiserating and complaining with friends—about your boss, job, ex, frenemy, stubborn illness, or any 'disease' with which you now entirely identify and defines your life—perpetuates the loop of dissatisfaction.

It's validating to feel like people understand where you are; there can certainly be value in that. We all want to feel understood; to feel seen and heard. However, the value it provides is limited if the nature of the conversation keeps us stuck in a low-vibrational loop.

Zoom out and get curious about the conversations you're having with people day in and day out. Are they the same conversations every time? Is there a specific energy pattern underlying the conversations? Then get clear: *is this somebody supporting my growth or keeping me in the loop?* Are you stuck in a box? Do you feel uplifted or heavier after speaking with them?

Try shifting the direction of the conversation with that person the next time you see them. If they don't pick up on it and continue to fall back into the pattern, you may want to reconsider how much time you spend with them. Surrounding ourselves with people who support our growth, inspire us, and stretch us to believe more in the possibility that there can be more is one of the most important gifts we can give ourselves.

You don't necessarily have to cut people out of your life but take stock of who you are giving your energy to. Where your attention goes, your energy flows. Is this the direction in which you want your energy to flow? You can always be the one to shift the relationship entirely. Be the person to change the energy and stand for your friend or your loved one's highest good. You can be that person. If the person isn't responding to your gentle nudges, then perhaps scale back on time and energy spent with them.

Not everyone can come with us on this journey. Not everyone moves at the same pace. The Truth is relationships often do fall away once you embark on your hero's journey. But your life becomes filled with something so much greater than the life of limitation you are leaving behind, and new, uplifting relationships aligned with your new identity fill the space. Taking space or walking away entirely is okay if someone is an energy drain or operating fully from their wounds. Some people are here just for a season or serve a purpose as a mirror to reflect where we need to grow or to mirror that we have, in fact, already grown. While challenging, it's okay to be the one to move on from a friendship or relationship that is no longer serving your highest good with as much grace as possible. And you never know; by forging ahead on your path, you may inspire others from a distance, and they may eventually walk right back into your life, curious to know more about how you got where you are.

Media and Culture

The Media also plays a large role in shaping collective beliefs, particularly around politics. Celebrity and influencer culture ingrains certain beliefs more deeply as people identify with the 'stars' as they pull on desire to fit in. Unfortunately, the majority of legacy media is biased, and by default any for-profit corporation should be examined. The News has become less about reporting than it is projection and shaping a perception of reality. Upon deeper examination, many have come to recognize that the mainstream media channels have been taken over by propaganda that perpetuates divisive rhetoric while Mark Zuckerberg admitted that Biden administration pressured his company to censor information that did not align with their preferred narrative. People are creating their beliefs based on a carefully curated and crafted biased reality, especially as it pertains to politics. The algorithm serves you more of what you like, creating a distortion that everybody perceives reality the way you do, and those that don't are the fringe minority.

Belief Shift Recap

Bring awareness to your beliefs, then start examining and changing them. Consciously choose your environments and surroundings because they create feedback loops that strengthen neural connections. It's incredibly empowering to take back control of your thoughts and beliefs because, from there, we can harness the power of our emotions and energy.

Essentially, we create rules for ourselves and how our lives can or should look. Beliefs become mini dictators of our lives. Examine your top three limiting beliefs. I'm not good with money. I'm not worthy of love. I am never going to be successful. What are they? What are the limiting beliefs that are holding you back? I attract the wrong people. I don't deserve abundance. I'm not worthy of having what I truly desire.

Recognizing our innermost thoughts can be incredibly confronting, bringing up painful memories. But ultimately, this process is liberating. So get clear with yourself and ask if that is true. What validity does this hold in my life? Does it *have* to be true? Do I *want* that belief to be my reality? Or do I want something bigger and better? Can I shift this for myself? It's a choice. We always have a choice.

Remember that these beliefs are typically not even yours. Most of our beliefs didn't even come from our own experiences. We did not choose them; we absorbed them from our parents and childhood environments, our caregivers, and our communities. Perhaps one minor experience that most would have written off profoundly impacted us because we felt rejected. We felt unseen, unheard, or unworthy.

We are all being called to shed outdated systems, modes, and beliefs that aren't even ours so we can collectively shift our reality and create a better world for everyone.

You can choose a different reality and a different vision for yourself. Your past doesn't have to be your future. Your past is not your Truth. Choose a different way of being and show up differently for yourself and the people in your life.

What are your values? What do you want your legacy to be in this lifetime? Are your beliefs important enough to stop you from achieving your dreams? Are they important enough to prevent you from pursuing your goals?

It's always a choice, but life always calls on us to expand. Life is about expansion. When we are not growing, life will often force us to grow, but in the form of a crisis or a disease. Life will force us to examine our beliefs and our values. It is our choice whether we pay attention to those signs and signals that our body is proffering, that our life is providing, and that the universe is bequeathing. Once we start to trust those signs, pay attention, and follow the breadcrumbs, life begins to unfold and blossom into beauty and magic.

Individually, we are being called to step into the heart of darkness and face the shadows, but this also occurs on the collective level. Healing the collective begins within.

Focusing on the higher vibrational states of being and deliberately choosing emotional and feeling states where your vibration is elevated—states of joy, gratitude, love, and appreciation—generates a state of expansion.

If you fall into the drama, fear, and stress, which keep us tense and constricted, make the choice not to remain in these lower vibrational states. Denser emotions keep us stuck in patterns of all we want to leave behind, and our beliefs perpetuate these energetic states.

Awareness is the first step, and then we must be deliberate about where we put our energy and the circumstances we find ourselves in. This awareness provides an opportunity to cleanse, release, and let go of emotions of past trauma and behavioral patterns that do not serve. Reevaluate where you are in life and examine what is serving you and what is not so you can upgrade your beliefs, identity, and life experience.

Chapter Twelve

THE GOLDEN GREAT RESET

The Deeper You Dive, The Higher You Rise

"We are immortal until our work on Earth is done." ~ George Whitfield

Humanity is in the midst of a Great Reset, one of alchemizing the grit into gold, and we must leave behind all the old ways of being. Physical, emotional, and mental cleansing help us to release the past, reset our body temple, and recalibrate to the new frequencies. Because, to put it simply, we can't take it with us. The second half of this chapter discusses practical methods to reset your physical vessel and your life.

The Deeper You Dive, The Higher You Rise

Remember, we are living in the Greatest Show in the Universe, the Great Reset versus the Great Awakening. The plot of this drama began to thicken in January 2020 with the outbreak of Covid.

At the start of the show, before I perceived what was going on behind the scenes, I was shown what was not working for me so I could finally begin to let go of that old version of myself. Like peeling back the layers of an onion, it has been an ongoing process of ever-deepening personal evolution.

I could see clearly, though, that I'd been subconsciously choosing the smaller version of myself for years because I wasn't ready to step into the empowered version of myself that is my fullest expression. 2020 served up one whopper of a lesson after another. I experienced loss. I went through grief. I endured several intense situations that magnified the energetics of playing small, allowing my boundaries to be trampled and allowing myself to be disrespected.

I was also blessed with the gift of freedom. I walked away from those situations that weren't aligned with my highest good so that I could deepen into the heroine's journey of self-exploration I was oh so clearly being guided on.

Along my journey, I've experienced the full spectrum of emotions. As I've confronted my own shadows, I've shed many tears and experienced deep pain. Each time these deep, repressed emotions rise to the surface, they present a powerful opportunity for release.

It should be evident by now I'm not sitting here high on my throne saying, Hey guys, this is easy. Just be light and love, and it's all gonna be hunky-dory, rainbows, magic, and sunshine. No, no, no, no. To raise our frequencies, we must go deep into our shadows to face them, integrate them, and release them.

True spirituality is about facing reality head-on. I've gone through the wringer myself, over and over and over again. We all have different soul lessons and soul journeys. Some of us came here to transmute and alchemize for the lineage, which means it may feel like we took on a more considerable burden than others. No role is better or worse, more special or less critical. From a nuanced soul-level perspective, we should not compare ourselves to others, especially if it seems so much easier for them.

This also touches on the realm of spiritual warfare—there are forces and energies in our fear-based matrix of enslavement that do not want us to be empowered or liberated. Frequency fences and dark forces exist. This is a deeper subject for another time, or even a book perhaps; however, I would be remiss not to touch upon it at all. The Great Reset is an agenda of global control, yet we can claim the higher timeline and use this time of destruction of the old to Reset our lives and step into the Great Awakening. As Pluto completes his journey through Capricorn and moves into Aquarius, we are also completing a 250 year cycle since the last time Pluto made this transition, right at the time of the American Revolution.[77] This time, the revolution is catalyzing the evolution of humanity. The shadows do not want the liberation of humanity to happen.

We need to protect ourselves and understand the multidimensional layers of energetic protection and clearing necessary for many of us to ascend as we've been hooked into and siphoned from through the wounds and weaknesses in our energetic fields. For those here on specific spiritual missions, this journey is not a walk in the park.

However, I can say with utter conviction that the light at the end of the tunnel is there. It is there to guide you; it is available for you as long as you keep doing the work. Keep choosing it step-by-step and trusting the process. Keep trusting your journey. Stay focused on what feels true for you, and you will get to where you are meant to be.

And yes, at a certain point, it does *get to be easy*. Because we are still mired in the paradigm of polarity and, in some cases, battling literal demons along the way, it is not easy for most of us to extract ourselves from the realm of suffering and struggle; simultaneously, ease and flow are available to us. Ease and flow are what we all desire, regardless of what that might look like on a practical level. It can happen quickly, depending on your soul journey, and when our soul is ready, we can choose the higher timeline and let it be done with ease.

My journey has been particularly long and arduous, so I could make all the mistakes, integrate and transcend them, and bring this wisdom together to guide others more efficiently, which is how my school and this book were born. Your journey prepares you for your specific path and purpose. We must individually follow the path; however, I was guided to create a system that streamlines the process and provides a framework to bring others to that alignment more efficiently and effectively. This is part of my personal mission and purpose in this lifetime. You have one unique to you.

A Galactic Perspective

If we take a step back, it's clear that the past several years have been some of the most dramatic in history, like every movie ever made all playing out at once. Humans are truly putting on an endlessly climactic show. From a big-picture perspective, this is all meant to come up to the surface for humanity's evolution into higher consciousness. What we're going through collectively is one component of a much broader metamorphosis from a universal galactic viewpoint. As part of the universal body, Earth is ascending into a higher dimensional plane of existence. After a grand experiment playing with free will, we are returning to the organic Edenic blueprint to live in alignment with divine will and cosmic law.

As complex, daunting, or even unsettling as this may seem to some, all it really means is Earth and her human inhabitants are ascending in vibrational frequency, and we are anchoring the blueprint to create a paradisiacal reality here on Earth. We've been living in the third-dimensional realm where matter is dense, time is linear, and mental logic reigns supreme. The third dimension is dense. It's matter. It's material. It's the physical. And it's utterly antithetical to our soul's boundless nature.

There is much misunderstanding when discussing Ascension: we're not leaving the physical world. Many in the New Age speak of 5D, a higher vibrational frequency that operates in a different reality of perception through a lightness of being, but in Truth, that false timeline of 5D Ascension is behind us. The split, the flash, the aliens are coming, Jesus is returning—these narratives all serve to perpetuate polarity and separation and place our power outside of ourselves. For many, they become a distraction and an endless waiting game that keeps them complacent and out of their purpose. We are now anchoring in frequencies of 12D and higher, which is truly incredible.

However, I caution against attaching to any specific narratives. Focus on Love and your relationship with the divine above all. Focus on your own path of personal mastery and righteousness. The second coming of Christ comes from within as we follow the footsteps of his teachings and resurrect the blueprint of divinity within. Mind-based rationale, carbon, and lead are being alchemized into heart-centered intuition, diamonds, and gold. We are shifting from a paradigm of doing into one of pure being.

Ascension is the process of Earth and its inhabitants raising our vibration into a higher-dimensional frequency of existence. Higher dimensions hold a higher vibrational frequency, so raising our emotional frequency, feeling states, and energetic states is the key, as this is the precise mechanism to unlock the gates to that reality. The more you focus on doing the work of inner alchemy, the more available you are to receive the light and the more manageable the Ascension process will be.

The body is the key. You are the key.

The less stuff you have stuck in you—the old patterns that don't serve you, the lower vibrational programs, the toxins—the easier Ascension will be. Planetary Ascension of this magnitude has never happened anywhere in the universe before. What Earth is going through right now is incredibly special, and this is precisely why we are the center of attention, acting out the Greatest Show in the Universe.

Before we incarnated here on Earth, we all chose to be here for the big show, this Great Awakening and Ascension. There are eight billion of us on the planet right now. We chose to be here for the climax in the battle between light and, dark, good versus evil that is underway. Those who are struggling, those who don't understand the bigger picture perspective, also chose to be here. As humans, we forget our soul's consciousness, but each lifetime is chosen before we arrive. It's a balance of karma and free will. The dark forces have gone too far, so certain covenants have been enacted to protect humanity and ensure our collective Ascension. However, each soul must choose the path. The light always wins, we just have to remember this eternal truth and surrender to trust and faith in the face of the external chaos.

According to some, we are the lucky ones, the chosen ones who were allowed to incarnate during this time of great challenge and upheaval because we've been through enough lifetimes, incarnations, and soul lessons to handle what's happening on the planet. Starseeds and lightworkers are here to awaken and anchor these codes for the Earth and collective humanity.

I know many people are not fully awake to it yet, but more and more are beginning to see the bigger picture. Welcome to the Great Awakening. We're collectively waking up to the Truth of our nature and what's been happening on the planet.

We are in the midst of the battle of the dark versus the light, but in Truth, the light has in fact already won. We wouldn't be ascending if it hadn't. The Ascension is already happening and I've seen numerous signs of completion and victory. The light always wins, as in every fiction and sci-fi movie, which all hold kernels of Truth, more so than many realize. Dark forces exist, and they are grasping at every straw to prevent this from happening to maintain their tight grip on control. The battle for the soul of humanity is reaching a pinnacle, and each one of us is both a target and the Soulution, and every one of us must make the choice: fear or love.

This is why we've witnessed such dramatic attempts to control society by the corrupt puppets we call politicians, as well as the unelected 'elite' running the lettered global governance bodies and hypocritical billionaire 'philanthropists.' The intention is to propagate and perpetuate fear because fear is a lower vibration in which our perception of possibility becomes extremely limited, and we are much more susceptible to control and manipulation. Fear keeps us small, and it keeps us stuck. A demoralized person cannot assess accurate information, thus the perpetual propaganda and insidious censorship.

Our interdimensional galactic families are waiting to see what happens with the humans on Earth. Will we successfully transcend the chaos and dysfunction as the false matrix crumbles? Are we going to successfully ascend as a collective? It is an individual choice; collectively, we must come together. We need to support each other. We need to lift each other and embody light and love. Now is the time to shed, do the shadow work, and release the past so that we can step into our higher vibrational, fully empowered, fully embodied, fully expressed versions of ourselves because that's what humanity needs right now: for more of us to step into our power and radiate our light. You are light. You are love. We got this.

You Can't Take It With You

There is a sign on the side of the highway heading north leaving Tulum: You can't take it with you. Having spent about a year there, I've driven past that sign dozens of times. Every single time, it hits me as a poignant reminder. Every. Single. Time.

It's one of the truthiest truths. You can't take the baggage of the past with you if you want to manifest a beautiful new reality. We can't take the broken systems and structures of the old if we're going to create a new golden era of Heaven on Earth.

The actual Great Reset we need is this journey: detoxing on every level—physical, mental, emotional, and energetic—and doing shadow work, shedding, purging, clearing, cleansing. We are in the midst of a major collective transformation that begins with individual inner alchemy. We are being given an opportunity to look back and reflect on our life and then look forward and consider what we want to create, to get crystal clear on what isn't working for us, what isn't serving us any longer, and let it all go.

Detox all that's clogging you on every level of your being—physical, mental, emotional, energetic, and spiritual—to step more fully into your power. We've discussed the mental, emotional, and energetic clearing in-depth, but this also extends to the physical. We want our vessel and surroundings to be as clean and clear as possible. Release as much old, dense, toxic, negative energy as possible. Clear the clutter from every area of your life. Fully clear, aligned, and integrated, we have room to create something new, a version of reality that works.

The Physical Reset

The unfortunate reality is we live in a highly toxic world, and we must be proactive and vigilant to mitigate our toxin consumption. Chemicals come through the air we breathe, the water we drink, the food we eat, pesticides, herbicides, antibiotics, cosmetics, body products, cleaning products, plastics, perfumes, air fresheners, scented candles, grocery receipts, non-stick pans, sunscreen, bug spray, pharmaceutical drugs we take to be 'healthy,' lions and tigers and bears, oh my!

Estimates say the average person is exposed to hundreds or even thousands of the over 87,000 chemicals currently used in the US per day.[78] Of those, only a scant fraction—just over one thousand—have been formally examined and graded for their carcinogenic potential. Alarmingly, a full half of those tested have been graded on a precautionary scale. A survey by the Environmental Working Group (EWG) found that women expose themselves to 168 chemicals per day, on average, about twice as many as men. Many of these chemicals are classified as endocrine disruptors, which disrupt hormonal balance often by mimicking hormones, influencing brain health and the development of certain cancers.[79]

The impact of such chemicals on our hormonal health and overall health—including that of our gene expression—is vast and downright alarming. Phew, it's exhausting to try to keep up. However, rather than diving deep into the rabbit hole, we can focus on purchasing and using products that are natural, organic, and free of such chemicals.

Maintaining energetic hygiene means we must detox toxic and unnatural chemicals from our lives as much as possible, and this includes physically cleansing and releasing the toxins that have built up in our bodies over the years to the best of our ability. This also includes parasites and old pathogens that lay dormant in our system and heavy metals that fill our blood. It includes fluoride and chloride. Fluoride itself has been found to be a neurotoxin[80] that in excess quantities can lead to a lower IQ.[81] Our bodies are powerful, but against an onslaught of toxicity, they need our love and support. Once we embody a certain frequency, our body can more readily transmute lower densities and toxins.

Inflammation is one of the key drivers of disease,[82] so curtailing anything that could contribute to inflammation within the body is one of the primary considerations when healing and optimizing vitality.

There are so many layers and factors that it is impossible to address them all in one chapter, but I will endeavor to address the most important factors.[83]

I do not believe there is a one-size-fits-all diet. Our diet may evolve and shift through different phases of our lives and healing journeys.

Generally speaking, however, eating natural, organic, and locally grown food as much as possible is the way to go. Given that the majority of Americans still live on the SAD diet, this alone will generate dramatic shifts for most. Focus on eating living high-vibrational plants like fruits and vegetables and nutrient-dense foods. Minimize products more likely to be highly processed or tampered with, like gluten and dairy.[84] However, this is more about quality and source than absolute avoidance. It has been suggested that gluten content has risen in GMO crops, so one cup of wheat now contains multiple times the amount of gluten it used to before the crops were modified. Glyphosate is another undeniable major issue for wheat and oat crops (amongst many other products derived from these crops, like pasta).[85] For some, gluten sensitivity and other gut issues may be connected to glyphosate levels in the crop. This is why so many people can go to Italy and France, eat all the bread and pasta they want, and return home having lost weight.

A similar situation holds true for dairy: many mass-market dairy products come from cows raised in squalid conditions and fed unnatural diets of corn and soy. They are treated with hormones and antibiotics and produce unhealthy, contaminated milk that is then pasteurized, further removing most of the beneficial enzymes that help humans properly digest dairy and receive actual nutritional benefits.

Avoid anything processed or with chemical additives, added sugars, seed oils, GMOs, antibiotics, hormones, pesticides—anything unnatural. A good rule of thumb is to avoid it if you can't pronounce it or recognize it as real food. Steer as clear as possible from the junk. Eliminate or limit alcohol—especially if you are in a healing state—as it is a known contributor to many diseases[86] and keeps us in a low vibrational state and can open us up to entities (there's a reason alcohol is also called 'spirits'), and endeavor to consume as little caffeine as possible (coffee and dark chocolate are my two 'vices' so play around with limiting your intake levels ;).

For someone in an actual healing 'crisis,' I would personally suggest considering removing all foods that would tax the system unnecessarily or cause excessive stimulation, such as caffeine; the correlate to 'fight-or-flight' is 'rest-and-digest;' we must be in a relaxed state to properly digest and process our food and to heal. The gut is directly connected to a vast range of chronic diseases,[87] so the better we digest and absorb our food, the more optimal our health becomes. The health of our microbiome is intimately connected to skin issues, mental conditions, and even cancer, so cleansing and rebalancing our gut should be a top priority for most everyone who has not yet addressed their gut health.

That said, we are all human beings living in a highly toxic and polluted world that's become increasingly complicated to navigate, so in general, once rebalanced, I don't endorse being overly rigid either because, honestly, that can serve to add stress and tension to our lives, perpetuating the exact states we're trying to heal and can even morph into a form of disordered eating called Orthorexia. You can do your best to plan ahead while traveling and pack prepared food, for example. However, there is only so much you can do. I've relaxed into flexitarianism, especially if someone has prepared food and invited me to dine with them. Food made with love and shared with love holds a much higher frequency.

I still love my morning cuppa after I drink my daily warm lemon water. Making my healthy mocha is a comforting ritual for me. To keep it as healthy as possible, I sometimes switch it out with ground-up dandelion root with zero caffeine or acidity, organic decaf, or straight organic cacao. I add some organic chocolate-flavored low-sugar plant-based protein powder. This may sound bizarre to many, but it adds a creaminess to the coffee, making it more like a mocha and adding an extra protein boost to my diet. A spoonful of cacao, a sprinkle of cinnamon, and a dash of milk, and I've got the most delicious healthy mocha to start my day. Sometimes, I'll enhance it further with adaptogen powders.

My morning mocha fix is a small example of finding balance in a complex and chaotic world and choosing healthier, nourishing alternatives to the deadening options we have been conditioned to accept. The overarching point is to be mindful and discerning of what you're putting into your body at a physical level.

Fasting, Detoxing, and Parasite Cleansing

Entire books are written about fasting, diet, food, and healing. Of course, I am only providing a superficial overview of these subjects so you can dig deeper into what feels aligned for your body and discover your path.[88] But I will touch on cleansing and fasting as these methods can provide a powerful reset for the body.

Immediately after learning I had a grapefruit-sized growth inside my chest, I treated it like the worst-case scenario: cancer. I pulled up Google and started researching natural methods to heal cancer so I could do whatever I possibly could to begin healing while waiting for the following scan.

Juicing was one of the first DIY methods I came across, so I found a juice shop in the middle of Edmond, Oklahoma, where I was for my uncle's funeral, and drove out of my way to get it.

As a vegetarian who had already avoided fast and fried foods, I did my best to eat fruits and vegetables that weekend. I went deeper into the research and found information on carrot juicing to heal cancer, so when I returned home, I started doing that daily. I kept researching and found promising anecdotes and evidence suggesting that cleansing and eating a raw diet improved patient outcomes, some claiming to heal. So I put myself on a no sugar, no dairy, no gluten, nearly keto raw vegan diet. There was no sugar aside from berries and carrot juice, protein through nuts and seeds boosted by some organic vegan protein powder, and fats in the form of avocados and spoonfuls of raw almond butter. No chocolate, no coffee, and lots of sunshine and carrot juice.

I got a colonic several weeks after shifting my diet to clear out my colon properly, and by the time I was ready to start treatment, people said I already looked better. My skin had cleared up and looked brighter, and I genuinely felt pretty good. After my first round of treatment, I experienced minimal side effects, and people were shocked at how good I looked after having gone through 100 hours of consecutive chemotherapy over about 4.5 days.

At some point in the diagnostic journey, I found a functional medicine nutritionist with whom I started working. While she applauded my efforts to cleanse my body pre-treatment, because I had blood cancer, she suggested more protein and blood builders as my body and digestive system could handle.

So I took the advice and added pasture-raised eggs, and—astonishingly to those who'd known me as a vegetarian for over eight years and who hated hamburgers growing up—I started eating meatballs. Half organic grass-fed beef, half pasture-raised turkey mixed with gluten-free bread crumbs, nutritional yeast, and a hefty dose of minced veggies, a recipe modified but inspired by my friend's Italian mother.

At varying points in my healing journey, my diet shifted from plant-based and high-juicing to moderate amounts of animal protein. I had to heal my gut, then my hormones due to adrenal fatigue, and then rebuild my muscles. My body tends to prefer a predominantly plant-heavy diet; however, I remain a flexitarian.

As I have researched healing more and more, I've learned that we all have parasites and heavy metals that can contribute to chronic inflammation and chronic conditions.[89] Most of us consume too much sugar and processed food. We are dehydrated and depleted of essential nutrients, especially Magnesium. We have overburdened livers that cannot keep up with the toxic onslaught of our modern environment.

What I later learned about carrot juice is that beta-carotene helps to optimize liver function. When we don't consume enough beta carotene, the liver doesn't have a proper supply of resources to perform its waste processing functions at optimal levels. Furthermore, I learned that cleaning out the colon and digestive tract is also essential for the liver to perform its duties optimally, as we need a clear passage for the toxic waste to be eliminated. If our digestive tract is blocked or sluggish, toxins released from the liver will fester and create detox symptoms as the toxicity is reabsorbed.

The lymphatic system is the unsung hero often neglected in the wider picture of health; I learned this the hard way with a diagnosis of non-Hodgkin's Lymphoma. It is a circulatory system that is also part of the immune system and includes the lymph nodes, lymph vessels which carry white blood cells and lymph, thymus, tonsils, spleen, bone marrow, and adenoids. It protects us from disease and infection and helps to maintain a healthy balance of fluids while facilitating the excretion of waste and abnormal cells from our tissues. It also promotes the absorption of fat soluble nutrients. Exercise, deep breathing, and dry brushing all help to optimize lymphatic health as it facilitates the the flow of lymph through the body. Stagnant lymph can become too toxic for the body to manage.

In my case, in spite of regular hot power yoga, a naturopath told me that my body had become so overloaded that my lymphatic system was doing an excellent job protecting my vital organs but had gotten overwhelmed. Quite an interesting lens to view cancer through. Compounded emotional trauma and nervous system dysregulation created an invisible perfect storm of internal toxicity. It made sense.

There are multiple types and methods of detoxification, which I cannot comprehensively cover here, but a general overview and approach of the essential detoxification steps for optimal results and vitality follows:[90]

1. Follow a gentle elimination diet to cleanse your colon and digestive system. Consider a professional colonic or at-home enema after cleansing for at least a week.

2. Next, if you feel called, do a complete liver cleanse. Find a protocol or practitioner to guide you through this step.

3. Then, do a parasite cleanse and a heavy metal detox. As mentioned above, find a protocol or practitioner that aligns with you. There are many different protocols, but they will include supplements to support this detoxification step. This step should come *after* you have already completed the first two steps.

4. Implement any long-term dietary shifts you feel would support your vitality, especially those that bring you in the direction of more natural, organic, and local.

5. Consider regular cleanses, such as seasonally or yearly.

6. When your body has adjusted, consider occasional water fasts.

Always use guidance and discretion and pay attention to how your body responds, especially if you eventually embark on a water fast. Do not plan to operate heavy machinery or engage in heavy physical activity during fasts.

For additional support to get you started, download my free, gentle whole foods Refresh Cleanse Guide, which includes several simple recipes, available on my website.

Nourishing the Mind, Body, and Soul

Discernment about what we feed ourselves also pertains to our mental, emotional, and social spheres. What are you allowing in, and what are you nourishing? Are you nourishing that which serves your highest good, or are you feeding the beast? Release all the junk from your body; release all the junk programs in your mind.

Think about a computer when it starts to run out of space: if the hard drive is full, it doesn't operate as well. We, in our human vessels, are very similar. If we're jam-packed with old, outdated programs, we won't function well. We need to clear the space for upgrades so we can operate at higher levels.

What do you need to let go of? What do you need to release to create space for something new? Reflect, journal, meditate, and consider what you must let go of. Letting go is not easy, but tuning in and bringing awareness to these provides the clarity you need to move forward, empowered, freer, and lighter. Once you release all the old baggage, you're available for more and ready for the new.

Consider where you might be blocked, uncomfortable, or uneasy. If a situation feels heavy or bothersome, it might be a sign that it is time to upgrade or release it.

Ask yourself: where do you feel stuck? Where do you feel heavy and dense? What brings your vibe down? Start to tune in with these inquiries. The past few years have been a doozy for many of us, and lessons can always be learned from a crisis or challenge. Determine what you are feeding your mind, heart, and soul, day in and day out. What is the programming running your daily show?

Self-Reflection and Celebration

Part of the human experience is growing and transforming. Consider where you are now compared to where you were a year ago and the lessons you've learned. Collectively, we have been through so much. Personally, it's no different.

What insights have you gained? What personal wins have you experienced? Celebrate yourself as much as possible in this process, and appreciate the progress you have made. Maybe you're not where you want to be. But perhaps right now, you are in a different place than you were a year ago, whether professionally, physically, emotionally, socially, mentally, or even spiritually. That's something to celebrate.

Even if it feels like you've taken a step back, with a little awareness of the pattern, you might just be on the backend of an upward spiral. Or the slingshot has been pulled back even further, ready to propel you farther and higher.

Even if you are on a downward spiral, you're here now, paying attention so you can shift the trajectory. And that's amazing. Celebrate being here right now. We must go through our dark night of the soul to fully emerge into the light. When we hit rock bottom, we can only go up.

Celebrate wherever you are and give yourself heaps of compassion and love. Self-love is crucial. Shower yourself with love and practice self-care that feels good for you.

Tune into your heart, listen to the wisdom held within, and allow your soul to speak. What is your soul calling for more of? What is your soul nudging you to do right now or how to *Be*? Maybe you don't have all the answers. Building trust in ourselves is a journey. Start small. Stepping into our soul's purpose, calling, or mission can be intimidating. We don't have to jump to that level immediately.

But what is your soul telling you right now? It could be telling you to rest. To relax. To surrender.

It may be telling you to reflect. Maybe it's telling you *You are worthy*.

Just tune in and listen. It's a practice. Learning how to tune in and trust your intuition takes time. Quiet your mind, breathe deep, and tune in. It's quite calming. I can almost guarantee that you will feel totally different even five minutes later once you sit down and allow yourself to be still—just five minutes.

It's not always easy, but I have been through the wringer myself, and I can tell you it is so worth it. The pot of gold on the other side of the rainbow is there—it exists. Keep going, keep trusting, and keep following the path back home. Reflect on the past and what you have learned from it. What knowledge and wisdom have you gained? From that space, what can you create next?

Where can you go from here? Where do you *want* to go? Don't limit yourself with thoughts like 'That's not realistic.' Such thoughts are a relic of the logical, linear paradigm of limitation that has kept us stuck and separated from our true potential, which will soon fade into a distant memory.

Dream big, dream bold, and feel the frequency of the magic of possibility.

Chapter Thirteen

Confronting the Collective Shadow

Challenging the Status Quo

"You must always be willing to truly consider evidence that contradicts your beliefs, and admit the possibility that you may be wrong. Intelligence isn't knowing everything, it's the ability to challenge everything you know."
~ Unknown

Truth is stranger than fiction. We are in the midst of a real-life battle of the Dark versus the Light. The ascension energies have been relentlessly purging and purifying the planet over the past several years, pulling out the demons lurking in the shadows. Each month brings multiple opportunities to go deeper into our shadows and rise higher than before. This time has been preparing us for the Ascension into a higher-frequency state of being.

In the New Earth we are entering, there is no room for fear, pain, suffering, or scarcity. Those lower emotional states are not a vibrational match for the burgeoning Golden Era of Light and Love. The baggage must be left behind. Because the old structures and systems based on separation and control cannot come with us either, we are seeing the world apart around us, the old systems and structures of enslavement collapsing.

Zooming out, it's time to face the collective demons—the fallen system and its layers of corruption, deception, greed, control, and perversion. We live in a paradigm that has pushed profit and hedonistic pleasure over peace and collective prosperity, and we are now witnessing the fall of the profiteers and false prophets.

Collective shadows are challenging to confront. All that is swept under the rug and considered taboo or politically incorrect must be addressed. The depths of Evil can be a shock to the system when it first comes to Light. The Truth behind the issues that get people 'canceled' and cancel culture itself must be reconciled, as 'canceled' is a cloaked term for censorship.

We cannot heal what we cannot see. We cannot heal what we cannot face. True for both the individual and for the collective. The influx of light frequencies is shining a light into the collective shadows into the darkness, illuminating what's been hidden and exposing the demons hiding in plain sight. A great deal of shocking and disquieting information has been surfacing, and the darker forces have been trying to sweep it all under the rug and keep it hidden to preserve their fragile hold on control because once the Truth is revealed, the whole game is up.

Many prefer to deny, turn a blind eye, or cry 'conspiracy theory' rather than question what's going on behind the curtains because the ugly Truth utterly destroys our understanding of reality.

We are now being forced to confront the fact that our beliefs and understanding of the world may be based on deception and lies; all we thought was true is far from it. It's a shattering of reality that can cause many to enter a dark night of the soul. Confronting the dark, twisted shadows of Evil is a disquieting and painful process for most, yet facing the truth head-on is essential. The cognitive dissonance is too much for many to handle. It is much easier to first anchor into the Light and the spiritual reality available to us as we begin the personal shadow work, or to at least have this knowledge and these tools while grappling with the collective darkness.

To move forward united as a collective and heal the false mind viruses that have created the ills that plague society, we must acknowledge what's actually happening behind the scenes to begin to fix it. The reality is that if we can't see the bigger picture or acknowledge it, then we can't actually fix or heal it. Stay with me here, because what follows may be triggering for some. Once you get through these next couple chapters, however, the light of hope and possibility will shine oh so bright.

The Inverted Matrix

We could dedicate multiple books to structures and systems built in accordance with the inverted matrix of illusion—in fact, numerous such books already exist—but let's begin with the foundation of the faulty system.

Whatever your perception of reality, we can all acknowledge that the system hasn't been working for us. Our healthcare system is a sick care system; our education system is one of indoctrination rather than critical thinking; and our political system is one of dogmatic separation and insidious greed, hypocrisy, and nepotism. The media is manipulated to control our minds. Liberty and justice for all have long been left behind. Even entertainment is a tool the system uses to program and control us.

This is a war on consciousness, spirituality, Truth, and freedom, as the Truth is we are all sovereign beings. The game has been rigged to keep us blind to the Truth and, therefore, complacent, disempowered, and more easily manipulated and controlled. Humanity has been enslaved.

If it sounds dark, it's because it is. Mind control has kept us entrapped in a mental prison while our hearts have been locked inside fortresses of pain. Unfortunately, this has been happening for hundreds of years. Thousands even. Poverty, suffering, death, and destruction have plagued humanity for millennia. The Truth has been withheld from you.

A very dark agenda guides the actions of the proverbial 'elite.' Some refer to this ruling class using terms that begin with C and I that would dub them conspiracy theorists. Most people at the top, the ones we think are in control—who we are told are in control—are puppets. They're chess pieces played by people in the shadows who hold the true power.

This corrupt group has kept the True knowledge to itself for the purposes of control and manipulation. It has known about the coming Awakening and has been doing its best to keep the Truth in the shadows by all means possible. It sounds outlandish to many that such a small group of individuals could control humanity, but if you follow the money and understand how the hierarchy of pyramid schemes enables the trickle-down of filtered information on a need-to-know basis, it becomes not just plausible but evident that this is precisely how the system has been manipulated.

Many accounts on social media platforms have been removed; many have been shadow-banned. Those who share about organic Ascension and spirituality have dropped in the algorithm. Followers and subscribers removed. Many who speak out against the agenda have been silenced or 'canceled.' This is censorship in its rawest form, yet people have blindly gone along with it because of the insidious indoctrination, obfuscation, manipulation, and outright gaslighting of the public. This phenomenon has heightened in the past couple of years. However, it has been going on for decades, even in the so-called land of the free. Media spouts controlled narratives, dictating our world perception and molding our beliefs—until we break free from the matrix programming. Propaganda abounds in our false democracy.

Politics and the narratives spun by the media are what woke me up fully in 2020, but this isn't about politics: it is so much bigger. I am not interested in politics so much as shifting the systems and structures that construct our reality to truly enable a thriving society based on Life, Liberty, and the Pursuit of Happiness. My political stance is anti-corruption, and pro Truth, Liberty, and Justice for all.

Beyond the shadows of Evil, what they're keeping hidden in the shadows is not just their evil agenda but also the Truth of the Light and our connection to Eternal God Source. The Truth of our potential. Of our cosmic origins. Of who we truly are and how powerful we are. The Truth of how we heal and how we create abundance. The Truth of our divine birthright—that we are all worthy of love and innately abundant. Each and every one of us is a living, breathing, walking, talking miracle.

So, we must illuminate the Truth because it is so bright.

You Are What You Eat

Let's start from the ground up: our food system. Our food supply is poisoned. It is so far from nature, yet most of us don't even realize how completely brainwashed we've become to believe what we've been told is food is entirely fake.

Roundup. Glyphosate. Hormones. Antibiotics. Chemicals. Additives. Blue number 2. High fructose corn syrup. Soy lecithin. Corn and soy are the two most genetically modified crops out there,[91] and derivatives of these two crops sneak their way into nearly every processed and packaged food on the shelves. Non-organic oats are covered in glyphosate, a known carcinogen implicated in many forms of lymphoma, including mine.

Monsanto has already paid out roughly 11 billion in lawsuits[92] after a study found that exposure to glyphosate increased an individual's risk for non-Hodgkin's lymphoma by 41%.[93] Yet their glyphosate-containing pesticide Roundup is still sprayed in vast amounts all over crops across the country. How is this allowed?

Where is the government in this crime against humanity?

Now consider that Bayer—a German pharmaceutical company—merged with Monstanto, an American agrochemical company. This constitutes the largest merger ever, one between a company that makes cancer drugs, including for non-Hodgkin's lymphoma, and a company that makes products that cause said cancer. *Come again?* Problem–Reaction–Solution at its most perfidious apex.

It's not just one conglomerate, it's all Big Food. Kellogg's—a multinational food company known for making cereals, especially those for children—has come under fire lately for failing to uphold health standards for its American consumers, who are largely children. The same cereal in the UK and Canada, for example, has far fewer ingredients with limited chemical additives while the American version of the same cereal is highly processed and riddled with high levels of added sugars, artificial food dyes, and preservatives, many of them known carcinogens. After failing to take action to remove them, a grassroots movement is boycotting the conglomerate.

The sick truth is that the government sanctions a great deal of atrocities when it comes to food and pharmaceuticals. FDA approval means jack—the so-called regulators are complicit in the crimes. Glyphosate, the key chemical in Roundup, which Monsanto manufactures, is still all over our crops. Immense levels of glyphosate have been detected in non-organic oats—with more than 95% of oat-based foods containing the herbicide—corn, and soybeans, from which corn syrup, soy lecithin, and multiple other additives are derived. One study by the EWG found that Cheerios and Nature Valley products were the most glyphosate-contaminated products.

This chemical is a known carcinogen, yet it is still found all over our food, including food marketed toward children. *How* is this possible? *How* is this legal?

Glyphosate damages the gut microbiome, and accumulating research links a compromised and imbalanced gut with the majority of diseases, including cancer and mental health.[94] Antibiotics contribute to gut imbalances, and just two rounds within a year can cause a 65% increased chance of a major depressive episode in women within the year.[95] Doctors liberally prescribe antibiotics as a panacea when, in Truth, they trigger a silent chain reaction.

Clearly, we cannot the FDA if this is allowed. They also cleared a Pfizer booster for the Omicron variant for EUA with exactly zero safety data. Zero.[96] For a pandemic that by that point didn't exist, for people that barely suffer. They fought with fury to demonize Ivermectin while virtually nothing has been done to curtail the fentanyl epidemic, which, with a potency 50 to 100 times that of heroin and 505 times that of morphine[97] has been allowed to destroy millions of lives. Substances deemed too dangerous for household products are claimed to be perfectly safe vaccine ingredients. Follow the money, and you'll find answers.

Now, after people were censored for sharing this low-cost remedy, research has found Ivermectin to be an effective Covid antidote[98] with anecdotal affirmation mounting. Not only that, recent reports reveal that decades of research has found promising evidence that Ivermectin could be a powerful cancer treatment.[99] Ivermectin is an anti-parasite. Interesting.

Meanwhile, after decades of research, the FDA has just denied the approval of MDMA as a treatment for post-traumatic stress disorder, citing that they desire further research to prove it is 'safe and effective.'[100] Thus far, it has proven to be highly effective for veterans, a population experiencing a dramatic rise in suicide.[101] Meanwhile, the FDA pushed through untested and unproven Covid vaccines for the entire population, touting them as 'safe and effective' with zero conclusive, longitudinal evidence to back it up. Mind you, alternative panaceas were readily available yet suppressed.

Make it make sense. Well, it actually does, when you finally recognize and acknowledge the system as the parasitic beast that it is.

You can't profit off of a healthy population. Is it a stretch to consider that the pharmaceutical, medical, and food industries have been deliberately set up to keep the population alive but unwell? Perpetual patients of the profit-based system?

This is why we must trust ourselves first.

Our soil has become depleted due to GMO use,[102] poor crop management, and subsidies granted to the corrupted industries and crops that keep us unwell. An apple today contains a fraction of its nutrients 60 years ago.[103]

Hidden in blind sight, food and pharma have been slowly stripping away our natural ecosystem while poisoning the population for decades.

Sugar. Corrupted crops. Poisoned dairy. Tainted meat. The wrongful demonization of fat and salt only to replace them with excess added sugars and chemicals.

We know for a fact that added sugars are harmful to us. Diabetes is directly linked to excessive sugar consumption, and Alzheimer's is now colloquially referred to as diabetes three. Researchers have linked Alzheimer's directly to a diet very high in sugars and the ability to process sugars.[104] Although not fully embraced and acknowledged by the medical community, many scientific studies have indicated that sugar consumption directly impacts cancer cell metabolic activity as well.[105]

Aside from that, we know that excessive sugar consumption results in inflammation, a known driver of many diseases and conditions in the body. So we know sugar isn't good. And yet sugar has been subsidized by the government.[106] Dairy has also been subsidized, yet the industry is controlled and riddled with issues.[107] Factory farming involves copious amounts of hormones and antibiotics, and all of these substances are getting absorbed into our bodies, in addition to the pesticides and GMOs the animals consume, on top of the fact that dairy-farm cows consume corn and soy instead of grass. This holds true in the meat, pork, and poultry industries, while documentaries have shown the appalling conditions in which the animals are kept. Beyond unnatural substances, we also consume the stress of the animals and even fecal matter that pollutes their surroundings.

Six billion pounds of pesticides are sprayed on our food each year, an invisible and tasteless poison that is toxic to our cellular biology. It's not just sprayed all over our food, but our lawns, parks, and playgrounds too. These pesticides act as estrogen receptor agonists, meaning they can mimic hormones by binding to the hormone receptors that activate the function of endocrine glands, impacting hormone levels. Breast cancer, for example, is an estrogen born illness which now affects one in eight women. Where is the rise in risk coming from? Perhaps we need look no further than our poisoned food. Here's a harrowing statistic to consider: self-poisoning by pesticides accounts for somewhere between 14-20% of global suicides. Yet we are told they're safe.

There is no one-size-fits-all diet. By all means, eat the way your body asks you to. Feel better with a bit of meat? Go for it. But go for organic grass-fed pasture-raised animals. Go as natural and minimally processed as possible. I love fruit which contains natural sugars and treats like dark chocolate. We are humans having an embodied experience, and one of the things that we are meant to experience in this life is pleasure. Food, when consumed mindfully and with gratitude, is part of that.

These food groups are not inherently bad, but our agricultural system corrupts the products and is not designed for our wellbeing. Minimal nutrients are available from the soil because crops have been mismanaged, the soil has been depleted, a massive amount of pesticides are being used, and GMO crops have taken over. An enormous amount of antibiotics and hormones are injected into the animals we consume.[108] Beyond all this, our perception of a balanced diet has been very skewed. The sugar industry paid off the government to say fat was bad[109] when good fats are crucial for brain health and cholesterol is one of the most critical components of the cellular membrane. Additives, chemicals, and processed foods make up a good chunk of our diet, removing us further from nature.

Unfortunately, fake food is also cheaper. Organic, healthy food is (paradoxically) more expensive, so it's not as accessible, and as a society, we've been conditioned to choose the cheaper option when it comes to food. At the same time, we're spending more on insurance and healthcare,[110] which is backward. A much larger percentage of our paychecks used to go to food several decades ago. Going back a couple of thousand years, the father of medicine, Hippocrates, said, 'Let food be thy medicine.' Yet now we go for the cheap fake food and the expensive unnatural remedies. We have become so disconnected from food as medicine. If we consider governmental funding, subsidies, and how the whole system operates, we can begin to see that the system is not considering our best interests when it comes to diet, nutrition, and food consumption.

So, let's look at the healthcare system next since it is directly linked.

The Sick Care System

Our healthcare system is not a healthcare system. It is a sick care system based on profit-driven symptom care designed to keep us stuck in the matrix of disease. Medication isn't for healing; it is designed to get us hooked on pharmaceuticals. This approach is a fundamental disconnect from nature, as nature is medicine. In just the last century, we have been conditioned to believe that popping pills and taking chemical-based medications is the best way to help us move forward when we experience symptoms or are diagnosed with an illness or condition. People are catching on.

A study published in the summer of 2024 found that public trust in medicine has fallen from nearly 80% in early 2020 to just 40% four years later, one of the most rapid declines in history.[111] Meanwhile, it was just revealed in October 2024 that Big Pharma paid $1.06 billion to reviewers at top medical journals. Of the nearly 2,000 reviewers analyzed, over half received at least one payment from the industry between 2020 and 2022.[112] This comes as no surprise, simply affirmation, to those who saw medical professionals who spoke up get imprisoned, censored, or lose their licenses. No wonder public trust is eroding. Crimes against humanity are coming to light.

Do people still believe these pills or potions will actually *heal* or *cure* them? I don't know, but newsflash: they won't because pharmaceuticals are designed to manage symptoms, not the root cause. This is not to disparage doctors because most enter with benevolent intentions of wanting to help people heal, but as intelligent as they are, medical school is set up, deliberately by design, to keep practitioners in their silos of specialty. Medical schools are essentially devoid of education on nutrition, and as students are corralled through and driven toward increasing specialty, they lose sight of the whole and become indoctrinated into pharmaceutical care.

Medical school is pharmaceutical indoctrination, and what medical students learn is pharmaceutical intervention through the allopathic model enforced on institutions through the Flexner Report in 1910.[113] Consequently, the system has become disconnected from true health and healing, and more physicians are beginning to recognize this. They enter with the noblest intentions and exit with profit-driven tools that neglect the Hippocratic oath and, at a more fundamental level, biology 101.

It's quite astonishing to me to zoom out on the healthcare system because I used to be a biology nerd myself. Biology 101 is left at the door in medical practice. Medical students receive, on average, five hours of nutrition at best. That one fact alone is mind-boggling and eye-opening for many people; it was for me. Remember, nutrients fuel our cells and are the building blocks of which the molecules in our body are made.

To be sure, specialization enables the life-saving miracles heart and brain surgeons perform and for obstetricians to save the lives of mothers and babies who may not have been so lucky in another day and age. I'm not suggesting all the life-saving medical advances should be walked away from. Absolutely not.

There remains, however, an interesting conundrum within the hyper-specialization of the modern medical system: doctors are capable of performing modern-day miracles due to their laser-focused ability to pull on intricate technical knowledge. However, this often comes at the expense of a holistic way of viewing the body, health, and healing where everything is integrated.

From another perspective, we wouldn't expect our physicians to be experts in other fields within medicine; we wouldn't ask our dermatologist for specific advice on healing cancer. Likewise, we wouldn't ask our oncologist for advice on ObGyn issues. So, from that perspective, why do we expect our oncologists to be nutrition experts?

This inquiry brings up both sides of the issue, however. First, we shouldn't turn to oncologists for nutrition advice, nor should they presume to tell patients what they should and shouldn't eat during treatment. However, the more fundamental issue at hand is the original disconnect between oncology and nutrition because cancer and other chronic conditions inherently connect with the overall wellbeing of an individual, and the simple fact that we are what we eat. Nutrition should not be seen as separate from the healing of any disease, particularly not one that ravages the body through inflammation and immune dysfunction as cancer does.

With practicing doctors receiving little to no nutrition education in medical school, despite the fact that diet-related diseases are the number one cause of death in the US,[114] you, dear reader, may very well know more about nutrition than an oncologist. That's a very massive generalization, of course. Many doctors read and research independently but tend to focus more on research related to their discipline. And there exists the well-known psychological phenomenon called confirmation bias: people tend to gravitate toward sources and articles that support their current knowledge and understanding.

After undergoing many years of expensive training and education and being told that you were chosen because you are the best of the best and are on track to be experts and specialists, you can hardly blame somebody for believing that they do know best and that anything that supports their current paradigm of knowledge is valid and anything else that is counter to that is less valid. That's the unfortunate Truth: experts are just as fallible due to mental biases and their egos—if not more so when their entire sense of identity rides on their title and educational achievement.

To be sure there are many doctors who are simply doing their best in a broken system, remaining silent in order to keep their licenses and offering a more compassionate, human-centered experience to their patients, as it should be. May heart-centered compassion and the Hippocratic oath be the guiding ethos for all once more.

Confirmation bias exists in the world of publishing as well. Research that gets funding in the first place and ultimately published as articles in top medical journals dictates the continued direction of medical research and establishes science 'fact' and 'truth,' which in part derives from aggregate acceptance and consensus. Agendas and red tape often dictate what sees the light of day in our lauded science journals, which themselves are profit-driven. And if it's not published in a top journal or runs counter to the accepted narrative of the current paradigm, it's often rejected or outright ridiculed. Let's not forget that many of the 'safety' studies are conducted by the pharmaceutical companies themselves, the very definition of conflict of interest.

Science is only as good as those conducting it. As much as we revere science as the path to ascertaining Truth, our current understandings are still limited by cognitive bias and basic human psychology. Our paradigm is also limited by our tools: scientific studies fail to capture the myriad nuances of complexity in the human body and the realm of healing. Our tools have been created to measure a world of matter, yet we live in a world of energy. Quantum science has proven that everything is energy, yet our systems and structures are still stuck in the world of matter and have yet to embrace this fundamental understanding. Just as Copernicus created a revolution mired in controversy, our experts and systems have yet to fully embrace this new understanding, and we are still grappling with the controversy of belief in how our world works. This resistance exists in no small part because a great deal of money is tied into the old paradigm. The ivory towers churn out not just PhDs but finely polished egos with a tight grip on a sterilized perception of reality.

With this zoomed-out understanding, though we have just barely scratched the surface, we can begin to see the extent to which money comes into play through the agendas of people pulling the strings behind the scenes. Regarding our understanding of 'science' and 'medicine,' the ugly Truth is that funding and profit play a significant role in pushing forward the agendas of those with vested interests.

Before we move on, let's briefly touch this touchy vaccine subject head on: anti-Vax is a pejorative term put on those who question vaccine safety, people who expect scientific rigor to uphold through tests and trials of solutions injected into tiny newborns and developing young children. The National Childhood Vaccine Injury Act of 1986 established a governmental compensation program that did not hold manufacturers liable for vaccine injury. In other words, pharmaceutical companies cannot be sued in the case of vaccine injury. Since then, the Childhood Vaccine schedule has increased from inoculations against four diseases in the early 1980s to fifteen today, while the schedule itself has increased from 10 vaccines to as many as 90 in 2024. Children receive 27 shots before the age of two.[115]

Now, all I will ask is for you to consider the rising rates of chronic disease, ADHD, autism, allergies, obesity, diabetes, and so on. In 1980, the rate of chronic disease in children was 2%, a doubling from the 1960s rate of 1%. Today, more than 40% of school-aged children have a chronic health condition. Then, read the inserts that include ingredients.

I'm not necessarily saying *all* vaccines are bad, or that the technology itself is altogether ineffective. But does the data suggest that this increase has improved the health of the global population? Could a little investigation and further independent third-party safety trials perhaps be warranted?

The Education System of Indoctrination

Now, we come to the education system as a whole. It is clearly not designed to optimize creativity or critical thinking. Where does funding get cut first? Arts, physical education, and home economics. We take children who are meant to learn by playing and exploring the world through their bodies and force them to sit still at uncomfortable desks in concrete box buildings that resemble prisons to learn a core curriculum that has little bearing on real-life skills, and we then blame them for not paying attention and say something is wrong with them. We feed children unnatural diets and remove them from their natural state and wonder why behavioral issues and diagnoses of ADHD are becoming increasingly prevalent.[116]

Authorities consider it acting up when children want to run around and play, to speak up or sing, but the system is essentially set up to suppress their natural urges to express themselves and to learn by interacting with their environment. Current models are failing our children and our society at large because they run counter to our natural inclinations and instinctual modes of learning.

The saga continues well beyond grade school. If the system hasn't thoroughly indoctrinated us and we don't fit into the perfectly molded box of good grades and a well-rounded resume, we're cast to the sidelines and made to feel less than, unworthy, or like failures. Those that do succeed often do so through masking and suppression of their innate desires.

At face value, the idea that everybody should be able to go to college sounds beautiful, like a great equalizer when it comes to accessing higher education, achieving success, and becoming anything you set your mind to. Everybody should be able to access the training and education they feel called to. However, college isn't for everyone, and it's pushed as the lauded ideal, made accessible to many by outlandish loans that handcuff so many of those graduates to a corporate system of lifetime enslavement, giving their valuable time, energy, and prime years to be a cog in the wheel. That is—if they can get a 'real' job in the first place, even with a degree or two under their belt. This isn't the case for every single college graduate, but the cracks in the system are evident to so many and are only growing wider.

A college degree shouldn't be made out to be the end-all-be-all goal for everyone because people have different gifts that should be developed and celebrated. Beyond that, lauded college degrees often leave graduates entirely underprepared for the real world and saddled with mountains of debt. Having received both undergraduate and Master's degrees from top global institutions, I can attest to my utter lack of preparedness for entrepreneurship. It's an entirely different skill set than what the core curriculum or my psychology courses prepared me for. I've basically received a PhD's worth of continued education through courses and training and going through the trials and tribulations of starting my own business, from the practical levels of marketing and sales to the more nuanced layers of mindset and self-motivation.

While I'm immensely grateful for the solid foundation I received in psychology and research through my formal degrees and for having had the opportunity to have the college experience at a time when social media was at its naissance and smartphones were just beginning to hit the market, the skills I've gained through ad-hoc trainings and hands-on self-teaching are more practical and applicable to our modern economy.

Beyond education, consider what it takes to be a successful adult. Rather than calculus and American History for the eighth time, a valuable core curriculum might include communication, marketing, and personal finance 101. What about emotional intelligence? Mindset? Basic tech? Video editing? These days, marketing 101 and public speaking should be embedded into our high school education before students even move on to college. Let's only talk about college when someone knows they desire to pursue a more specialized discipline. Let's promote gap years and young adults taking time to explore the self, the world, and different paths before expecting them to commit to a path and potentially hundreds of thousands of dollars of debt before they even enter the workplace. Better yet, let's start from scratch and rebuild the entire education system based on a holistic model of self-development.

I believe in celebrating critical, independent thinking. I believe in encouraging reading novels that inspire imaginations and books that promote self-growth. I believe in cultivating curiosity and an innate desire to learn and grow through nurturing a growth mindset. I support education that expands our sense of possibility and sets students up to succeed in their endeavors, whatever path they may choose, whether creative or technical.

Progress, innovation, and invention come from a beautiful blending of the two, from thinking outside the box and merging and melding ideas.

Politics and the Corporatocracy

Let's briefly delve into the delightful realm of politics, a deep, dark rabbit hole that could take us down never-ending twisted tunnels. Campaign finance and lobbying have fundamentally corrupted and distorted the political system, while public perception of candidates is manipulated through controlled media. The revolving door between business and government serves the special interests of the elite, perpetuating a corporatocracy that benefits the politicians in the pockets of the CEOs and those who own said corporations.

Over the last several years, there has been an overt and distinct move toward censorship and suppression of so-called 'alternative' voices such that any supporter of democratic ideals, regardless of political viewpoint or values, should be outraged. If this comes as new to you, Mark Zuckerberg, the CEO of Meta issued a statement indicating that the Biden administration pressured the tech giant to censor Covid-19 content.[117] Many people have been shadow-banned, had posts flagged or removed, and even de-platformed for sharing information not just pertaining to covid but anything inconvenient to the official narrative. This suppression of opposition and alternative voices is the very hallmark of fascism.

We must also consider the blatant hypocrisy of the majority of the politicians and pundits. They profess to care about women's rights while propping up industries that directly poison women and undermine their fundamental right to health. While crying we must save democracy, they promote censorship and suggest that our fundamental right to free speech must be re-examined.

This Pandora's box is the subject of other books, but a simple consideration of campaign finance and special interests makes it painfully evident that manipulation runs deep. Our elections are not as unbiased or fair as they would have us believe.

As with anything that gives off the faintest whiff of deception or hidden agendas, follow the money. Trace it back, and you will see how things are not as they seem. Politics is rife with corruption, but here's the thing: once you go deeper, you begin to see that most politicians are not calling the shots. It's all a show. Go back to who controls the money: the very, very, very wealthy elite of the world who largely remain hidden in the shadows, unknown to the vast majority. The cadre that controls the money and, in essence, runs the world operates mainly in the shadows, with elected puppets and visible global 'leaders' doing their bidding. Moreover, we should be concerned with the unelected leaders running the global governance acronym agencies such as WEF, the WHO, the CDC, the UN, NATO, the IMF, and the FDA.

The Military Industrial Complex is a beast I won't touch (though I got a glimpse into its murky underworld while interning for the NGO in London during its investigation into corruption within the defense industry), nor will I attempt to unravel the complex web of global control that works through the three independent districts that are the Vatican, The City of London, and Washington, D.C, but it should seem self-evident that any industry that profits off of death and destruction might have an interest in perpetuating death and destruction. Likewise, any entity that benefits from power and control would only want to centralize power and control further.

Peace and health are not desirable for industries that profit off of death and illness. Prosperity and sovereignty are not desirable for entities that profit off of control.

The Financial System

Now, the money. We need a fundamental overhaul of not just our financial system but our perception of money, currency, value, and worth. One of the core mind viruses controlling humanity is poverty consciousness. Our innate energetic signature is that of abundance and expansion—we are here to grow and experience the fullness of our existence. Earth is regenerative and inherently abundant, and we are part of the Earth. Clean and cheap fuel sources exists, however the technology has been suppressed. Tesla discovered how to harness free energy, however this too has been suppressed. Why?

We could call it the oligarchy, the corporatocracy, the big business banking monopoly that is propped up by big government special interests kept in control through the military industrial complex that profits off of death and destruction.

The Federal Reserve was founded in 1913, with the IRS founded in 1862 during the Civil War. Both institutions are, apparently, set up as private institutions[118]—although the IRS would, of course, like to argue otherwise.[119] The Federal Reserve is a privately owned central bank that acts as an independent agency with no accountability, and no governmental agency can overrule the actions taken by the institution. Throughout the world we have national central banks, then the international central banks including the IMF and World Bank, and then the Central Bank of the central banks.

Fractional reserve lending enables banks to loan out up to nine times as much as they have in their vault reserves.[120] The central banks are allowed to determine the amount a bank must legally have on reserve, which in the United States is ten percent. So if you deposit $100,000 into the bank, they hold $10,000 in reserve and loan out the other $90,000 to others. The same money circulates, getting loaned and re-deposited until the initial amount is worth ten times more. The banking system created $900,000 by loaning out your money. Which, in today's digital era, was only ever numbers entered into a computer, no longer backed by gold. So essentially, the bankers make money out of nothing while the rest of the population has to work laboriously to earn a living—to earn their right to live.

And there lies the inversion: Your birthright is to live, you do not have to earn your worth to be alive. They bank—literally—on our ignorance of how the system works.

"It is well enough that people of the nation do not understand our banking and monetary system, for if they did, I believe there would be a revolution before tomorrow morning." ~ Henry Ford, 1922

The system is largely rigged against our capacity to thrive, on every level, but especially financially. In a contemporary form of serfdom, the average citizen has become a debt-slave to the modern day monarchs that are the financial elite hidden under the guise of furthering global Democracy.

Increasing numbers are choosing to exit the game and release the golden handcuffs of corporate salaried life. However the dollar itself is on the brink of potential collapse and our economic future highly uncertain. Acknowledging how the system has been rigged against the masses helps us to develop and embrace solutions for the future. Central bank digital currencies are not the solution, either, as they inherently prop up the centralized system with the added layer of absolute digital control based on social credit scores, a system implemented by China.

Imagine the capacity for them to lock your account and prevent you from purchasing goods with your phone or your card because you said the 'wrong' thing or posted the 'wrong' message online. This is not just a 1984 thought experiment. These wrongthink thoughtcrimes have officially entered the realm of non-fiction and people have already been temporarily denied access to their accounts for supporting the 'wrong' people – in Canada.[121]

Now consider that even property 'owners' pay property taxes; if you don't pay up, the government can swoop in and seize the property you paid for. And they keep increasing the rent, year after year.

'You will own nothing and be happy' is the line straight out of Agenda 2030, the World Economic Forum's grand master plan for the dark agenda's Great Reset of humanity. No, this would not be a happy future, and research backs that up, suggesting it will undermine personhood.[122] Let's face it: communism has never produced happy results.

While many visionaries in the spiritual community foresee a golden age reality independent of the need for currency, that societal evolution must occur organically through a higher level of consciousness with systems and structures already in place to support the expanding abundance and thriving of each human. Top-down dictates based on authoritarian control will never produce a truly sustainable—or happy—future.

This next evolution is one of involution—it is the inside out revolution. Ownership of the self is prioritized over ownership of the material. What is required is a level of collective consciousness that celebrates the autonomous self as part and parcel of a harmonious whole.

The Media and Hellywood

Finally, Satan's playground: the news, celebrity culture and entertainment. News media and entertainment are the means of programming the masses. In psychology, we refer to it as conditioning. The common term for it is brainwashing.

Bereft of a higher power to worship, our materialist culture of celebrity worship has created a cult-like celebration of the false god-like 'Stars' we've placed on pedestals as stand-ins for gods.

Music manipulates the masses both through celebrity influence and through frequency itself. Popular music used to be tuned to 432 Hz, the 'miracle tone' believed to be in harmony with the natural vibrations of the universe. This frequency stimulates the brain's alpha waves, is associated with wakeful relaxation and increased clarity and focus, promotes a sense of calmness, improves sleep quality, reduces stress and anxiety, and stimulates natural healing. Historical accounts on this vary slightly, but in 1939 an international conference recommended tuning the A above middle C to 440 Hz as the pitch standard, a less natural frequency for our systems. In 1955, 440 Hz was adopted as the global tuning frequency and was reaffirmed in 1975 as ISO 16 for worldwide music standards. Research indicates that 432 Hz has measurable benefits on our health, including decreased heart rate and improved focus and sense of satisfaction as compared to music tuned to 440 Hz.[123]

When we zoom out and look at the degradation of pop culture over the past couple of decades in particular, Satanic influences have increased dramatically in pop star performances, music videos, and ensembles, much of it outright grotesque, with hideous, ungodly displays normalized under pain of being accused of being hateful and intolerant if you speak up against it. When the opinion of only a small minority matters, you know a deeper agenda is at play.

Once you zoom out and view TV 'programs' and movies through a discerning lens, it is quite shocking and borderline horrifying to see how they are conditioning us, especially the children. Through the media, they attempt to indoctrinate and brainwash us into believing that specific ideas and ideals are okay. They plant seeds for possible armageddon timelines and dystopian futures as predictive programming, siphoning collective energy into projecting that timeline into our reality. If we create our realities, it is through news, media, and tell-lie-vision that collective realities are constructed. And we innocently watch, oblivious to the agenda underlying the Hollywood glitz and drama.

Meanwhile, the majority of media, including the 'News' is owned by the Big Six—AT&T, CBS, Comcast, Disney, Newscorp, and Viacom—and boast a combined net worth of over $430billion (*based on 2020 data*).[124] These six conglomerates own 90% of the media outlets in America, proffering an illusion of choice and promoting a fantasy of objectivity. During the pandemic, people caught on to the scripting given to news 'reporters' who really are no better than actors. Narratives have become increasingly opinion-based and divisive, promoting intolerance of dissident voices. Mass formation psychosis[125] rose into collective consciousness as people witnessed the majority get swept into an authoritative narrative that effectively steamrolled contradictory data. According to this theory, at some point in the rise of a totalitarian influence, the masses enter a sort of collective hypnosis, unreachable by any logic or argument.

The media is a tool that amplifies the chosen narrative dictated by those holding power and control, facilitating and enabling such an astonishing phenomenon as the mind-capture of an entire society. 'Repeat a lie often enough and it becomes truth;' the infamous law of propaganda. Legacy media has effectively fractured minds, families, and lives, and has a great deal to atone for.

Having studied social psychology, I became familiarized with the notorious conformity and obedience experiments conducted by Milgram and Asch. Milgram's controversial research on obedience to authority found that people will obey out of fear or a desire to be cooperative and go to the extreme of inflicting pain on another when told, even against their own better judgment.[126] Asch conducted a series of experiments on conformity, finding that 75% of participants would conform to the broader consensus even when they know the response was incorrect.[127] Finally, Zimbardo's Stanford Prison experiment revealed the rapid escalation of psychological affects of authority and powerlessness. The experiment was shut down early when prisoners endured dehumanizing abuse—both prisoners and guards were volunteer college students randomly assigned roles.[128]

Pyschological research has found that fear-based appeals are highly effective at influencing attitudes and behaviors. *The KGB and Soviet Disinformation: An Insider's View*, published by Lawrence Martin-Bittsman in 1983, outlines the KGB's use of disinformation and information warfare. Disinformation is defined as a "carefully constructed false message leaked to an opponents's communication system in order to deceive the decision-making elite or the public." They found that if you bombard human subjects with fear messages non-stop, the majority are entirely brainwashed to believe the false message to the point that no amount of information to the contrary can change their mind, even when backed by evidence.

In combination, these studies reveal the fragile nature of our mental and moral fortitude when external pressure is exerted. This inquiry can best be summarized with the following quotation:

> *"First we overlook evil. Then we permit evil. Then we legalize evil. Then we persecute those who call it evil."* ~ Fr. Dwight Longenecker

However, the more one has a strong sense of self and connection to a higher truth, the less easily manipulated one is. Our strongest protection against mental warfare and mind control is a strong sense of self: to truly Know Thyself.

The antidote to Evil is to remember the wholeness of who you are and the divinity within.

The Media and Hellywood are a distraction from ourselves (and from all the other agendas they push through when we are looking the other way). They siphon and loosh our energy so we stay focused on the external and lose our sense of self. The more you come to know thyself, the less interest you'll have in celebrities and Hellywood, and the less you will be able to tolerate even turning on the TV.

EMFs and Technology

EMFs have risen into our collective awareness with the rise of 5G and the pervasive use of technology. EMF stands for Electric and Magnetic Fields of invisible areas of energy (also known as radiation). Electric fields are generated when a device is on, while magnetic fields result when current flows. High frequency EMFs, such as x-rays and gamma rays, are ionizing and can directly cause cell and DNA damage. Low-mid frequency EMFs include power lines, computers, mobile phones, radio, wi-fi, television broadcasts, and microwaves.[129]

Currently, authorities say there is no known harmful effect from the low frequency EMFs. However, a review of thirty years of research suggests otherwise. A comprehensive review of a collection of studied dating from 1990 through October 2024 conducted by Dr. Henry Lai, Professor Emeritus at the University of Washington, Editor Emeritus of the journal, Electromagnetic Biology and Medicine, and an emeritus member of the International Commission of the Biological Effects of EMF stated, "Biological systems are very sensitive to RFR... It is clear that the current RFR exposure guidelines are not valid in the protection of the health detrimental effects of RFR." Radio Frequency (RFR) may be re-classified as 'probably carcinogenic to humans' after being deemed possibly carcinogenic in 2011, while extremely low frequency (ELF) was classified as 'possibly carcinogenic to humans' a decade prior. Many studies in the past decade have found significant evidence that RF causes genotoxicity.[130]

Once again, authorities have sidelined evidence of potential harm to humans for corporate interests. And considering the quantum perspective that everything is energy, this really should not come as any surprise. *The Invisible Rainbow*, by scientist and journalist Arthur Firstenberg, traces a compelling argument of the detrimental effects electrical pollution has had on both the environment and on human health, including major disease of the industrialized civilization, heart disease, diabetes, and cancer.

Much more could also be said about the increased use of technology in our society and its impact on our mental health, behavior, and socialization, but it is clear that the industrialization of our ecosystem and pandering of government to corporate interests cannot continue to go unchecked if we are to create a beautiful and sustainable future for our children, one where they have a chance to live healthy and free.

Climate Change and Weather Warfare

For decades, we have been sold a narrative of Global Warming and Climate Change under the guise of saving our planet but which upon closer examination is more accurately about controlling the masses. While the climate may indeed be changing, we must take a step back and ask why. And, if our concern truly is about the environment, we must ask why the obvious issues of pollution are not adequately addressed. Science shows that periods of global cooling and warming have occurred for millions of years; our planet is not currently the warmest it has ever been. Now, are the changing weather patterns influenced by humans? Yes. But not in the manner most would presume based on the media-spun narratives. Stay with me, because it's time to apply both logic and fact.

If we were truly concerned about the levels of atmospheric carbon, the first step would be to curtail deforestation and burning of our forests, particularly the African and Amazon rainforests, which are the largest carbon sinks in the world. Carbon is food for plants via photosynthesis, and trees consume loads of it, rendering them 'carbon sinks.' When forests are cut down or burned, they release that carbon into the atmosphere, significantly contributing to atmospheric carbon. How often do you hear the climate pundits speak of deforestation and burning? No. Instead, the focus is on cow farts and your capacity to drive to work. Not to mention they fly to global conferences where climate is the priority agenda in private jets while telling us to eat cockroaches and pay emissions tax. Factory farming and fossil fuel pollution may be problematic for the animals and the environment in other ways, but the climate 'experts" solutions are not it.

Regarding the increase in dramatic weather events, humans behavior is likely to blame, but not because of your commute. Between 1890 and 2024, over 200 patents were issued for geo-engineering and weather modification technologies.[131] There is also historical precedent for weather warfare. Through Operation Popeye in the Vietnam War which ran from 1967 to 1972, the United States used weather warfare to increase rainfall over the Ho Chi Minh Trail to make it difficult for North Vietnamese troops and supplies.[132] They utilized existing cloud seeding technology to soften roads to make them impassible, cause landslides, wash out river crossings, saturate soil, provide rain and cloud cover for infiltration, and create acidic rainfall to disrupt enemy radar equipment. Cloud seeding technology was also weaponized against Cuba during the cold war to dry up the sugar crop to demoralize the people and make Cuban communism a failure.[133]

Meanwhile, Dubai is very publicly dabbling with cloud seeding, with potential detrimental effect after extreme flooding in April.[134] While virtually every mainstream outlet carried a similar headline in the days following saying cloud seeding likely did *not* contribute to the flooding, pointing to it not being done on the day of the flooding, what they don't address is that cloud seeding is often done in the days leading up to the weather, to prime the skies so to speak. These articles readily said cloud seeding occurred in the days preceding. Experts decry the notion that we have the capacity to create monster weather events, saying we simply don't have the technology, however there is ample evidence highly effective weather modification technology has been in use for decades. The public is never fully privy to to full extent of the technology available to us; so much technology has been hidden and suppressed.

HAARP, which stands for High Frequency Active Auroral Research Program, is a perfect example. HAARP research, designed to study the ionosphere, the outermost layer of the Earth's atmosphere that keeps out harmful solar and cosmic radiation, has been public knowledge for decades, and since the mid-1990s, critics have been sounding the alarm against its potentially devastating consequences. When the sun's energies hit the ionosphere, the Aurora Borealis, known as the Northern Lights, occurs. Three decades ago, the stated intention of the fully operational station was to transmit extremely powerful blasts of high frequency radio waves into the ionosphere to effectively punch a hole in it, ostensibly for the purposes of communication.

Researchers outside the military, however, see it as a high-tech weapon with global implications. Interestingly, in a document created in 1982 with a forward by Newt Gingrich, one section spoke about the use of radio frequency radiation transmitters to disrupt human thinking, ostensibly to disrupt enemy military troops' mental process and effectively debilitate them. Sounds perfectly safe. Mind you, these discussions were over four decades ago.

How long will we continue to 'trust the experts' when common sense, independent research, and critical thinking suggest alternative conclusions? Is it really such an implausible possibility to conceive that if the technology was advanced as it was in the 1960s, that in the decades since with dozens more patents filed, the technology hasn't improved when smartphones have transformed our world in a mere decade and a half?

While much of the extreme weather may still be attributed to natural causes, it is more likely that the energies flooding the planet through the solar maximum (not humans) is contributing to anomalous weather events, volcanic eruptions, and earthquakes, as the Earth herself is purging the density of the old and undergoing a deep rebirth. She is anchoring the high frequency light codes into her grid, as evidenced through the highly erratic Schumann Resonance readings[135] and her rumblings are part of the purge, much like a human releasing waste during a detoxification process.

Pollution of our waters, skies, and soils is the real problem; species extinction and dramatic reduction in pollinator populations is the problem; pollution of our minds and consciousness is the problem. These issues receive no airtime or concerted focus from the powers that be. Meanwhile, our skies are covered in unnatural chemically created 'clouds' that resemble a tic-tac-toe board. We won't discuss how Western North Carolina skies were covered by dozens of tracks in the days preceding Helene. We won't discuss how every town and city that experiences catastrophic weather events or devastating fires has in the preceding months or years publicly outlined plans to become a fifteen-minute 'Smart' city—Lahaina, Tampa, Jasper, Asheville, Henderson, even Gaza—naturally under the guise of progress.

(But now that I've mentioned it... happy rabbit holing.)

The Truth is Stranger than Fiction

In the so-called Land of the Free, freedom of speech has been under attack. Unless you hold a particular belief system or fit a specific mold, you're ability to speak out or have a voice has been heavily curtailed. You risk being canceled or outright censored and blacklisted for sharing your views if they run counter to the media narrative. Truth is being shut down. It is quite astonishing to witness so many intelligent individuals support the degradation of our First Amendment right: freedom of speech. Every single mainstream news network has had word for word the exact same scripting for specific recent major stories and headlines. It's disturbing.

What a wild time to be alive. Medical freedom has been under threat. Science has been weaponized. Billions have been sent overseas for death and destruction while citizens struggle and suffer. Illegal migrants are receiving handsome welcome packages from the government while the country's cities are succumbing to homelessness, drug abuse, and violence. Hypocrisy is at an all-time high. My body, my choice, has been shouted from the rooftops by the same individuals wanting to enforce medical decisions on others.

As a sovereign being, I would like to maintain my right to determine what goes into my body, especially when there's zero safety, accountability, or legitimate science behind an experimental product, thank you very much.

Fluoride has been pumped into the water system for decades, ostensibly to keep teeth strong,[136] calcifying the pineal gland in the process, reducing melatonin production and contributing to earlier onset of puberty.[137] Calcification of the pineal gland disconnects us from our ability to tune in to our intuition and higher selves. It severs our ability to connect with higher consciousness. In my humble opinion, this is deliberate.

Fluoridation of the public water supply has been done not for the health of our teeth but to keep us from accessing our full power, spiritual gifts, and potential. A calcified pineal gland puts us to sleep spiritually, and it's easier to control people when they are disconnected from the Truth and disempowered through deception. In a state of disempowerment, we are more easily controlled and manipulated. As I was doing my final round of edits, the EPA admitted that Fluoride is neurotoxic in a court case brought against the agency that has gone on for nearly a decade, leading the judge to rule against the agency and force them to take action to regulate the 'unreasonable risk' fluoridation poses.[138] Further proof conspiracy is the reality, not theory.

It's not just fluoride corrupting our water supply; it's bacteria from the pipes, pesticide and herbicide runoff, antibiotics and hormones from medications, and a host of other unsavory chemicals and compounds like Atrazine and Lead that are detrimental to our wellbeing. Environmental Working Group keeps tab of tap water contaminants, how many times above the guidelines they are detected, and their potential effects by zip code. Considering we are water bodies, it's unsettling that our number one necessity for survival after oxygen is completely polluted, to say the least.

We live in an inverted matrix where everything is upside down and backward. The anti-life inorganic matrix keeps us disconnected and separated from Source and Truth. Life is about expansion and growth. Everything right now is designed to keep us controlled and living in tiny little boxes. Hello, 15-minute 'Smart' cities.

Fear has been used to keep us in a disempowered state, which makes us more susceptible to manipulation by 'authorities' in positions of power and control. In previous chapters, I've discussed how fear keeps our energy contracted, disempowered, disconnected, and in a state of victimhood. When we're in fear, we look outside for help. We are disconnected from our sense of empowerment, from our sense of autonomy. Fear is deliberately used as a form of control; it is used as a weapon in psychological warfare.

It's incredibly insidious and quite dark to consider that there are actors deliberately trying to suppress humanity in this modern world of so-called democracy. But if we look back at recorded history, this is simply a continuation of what has always been the status quo: elites suppressing the populace. It's been hidden behind a facade of freedom, democracy, and choice as the population has slowly been dumbed down and made sicker and sicker, distracted through pop culture and social media that sucks our energy and resources through consumerism.

The defense industry has sucked up trillions of dollars, padding the pockets of entities that profit off war, suffering, destruction, and death. More resources have been funneled into building weapons of mass destruction than promoting health and wellbeing for the citizens of the world. Wars are waged to create the need for both control and the industries that further profit off of death. I have no problem with legitimate free market capitalism (which doesn't currently exist) and profiting through the creation of genuine value, but I have a serious problem with greed, deception, and nefarious intention.

We are facing a real-life version of 1984 Orwellian state, Brave New World, Atlas Shrugged, or The Handmaid's Tale. Just like Harry Potter and Star Wars, we've been engaged in a real-life Battle of Light versus Dark. But the Light has already won—even if we can't see it in our external world yet. Dive deep, but focus on the Light.

The astonishing amount of hidden Truth is the subject of another book. It goes unimaginably deep; we've barely scratched the surface of the iceberg.

Yet the even Greater Truth that is being hidden is full of Light, Hope, and Love.

Follow the Money

In the meantime, follow the money if you desire to dive deeper into the rabbit holes. Who is funding what, and who is benefiting? But it goes beyond the money. For the ones in control, it is all about control and manipulation. They don't need to hoard more wealth; it is about literal population control. Money and creation power is being siphoned off the population to further drop us into fear, scarcity, and disempowerment. But again, it's less about money than control. This agenda was decades in the making, over a century at a bare minimum, some say since the Declaration of Independence, hidden behind the false hope of the American dream.

It was always just meant to be that: a dream. And most of us were never meant to achieve it. That's the sad reality. America was The Great Experiment. The American Dream was a fluffy distraction as, little by little, they contaminated our food and corrupted our medical system, creating more and more pharmaceuticals and pumping increasing amounts of chemicals into our bodies, polluting the water and adding fluoride to keep us asleep and shut down, all the while degrading our consciousness through the manipulation of media and pop culture while creating the illusion of choice in our false democracy.

Little by little, we got here, one national disaster after another, one global catastrophe after another. 2020 was a culmination of it all, and the level of extreme chaos has only continued. None of this was an accident. It was all premeditated. People have been in an uproar about false narratives created around Project 2025, not realizing they are a distraction from the true Agenda: 2030—an agenda for global control. You will own nothing and be happy.

Who funds the media, who funds the politicians, and who subsidizes the food supplies that are compromised?

Perhaps the Roman Empire never fell, it just morphed and migrated to different power centers to confer the illusion of progress and keep the masses complacent. *(And who were the rulers of the Roman Empire?)*

But with all these insights to consider, the one thing that should alarm us the most is that the Truth is being shut down. As we grapple with rediscovering the Truth of our world, it's harder than ever to discern truth from fiction. Censorship and false information are everywhere. Tech giants and corporate media are shutting down voices that counter the mainstream narrative. Differing viewpoints are how progress is made. Unity consciousness is organic, not forced or fake.

The news cycle moves so fast it's making our heads spin, one unprecedented event on the heels of another with no time to process what has happened. This is Disclosure, the time of Revelation, and most have not been prepared for it. The amount of corruption and Evil coming to light can be such a shock to the system that many will continue to turn a blind eye and numb until it's impossible to go on.

I encourage you to question everything. Follow the money. Question everything you have been led to believe and how the system operates. Question everything the media tells you. Question everything the politicians say. Question the agendas. Question who this policy might serve. Question whether any of it is truly serving you. Is this empowering you? Is it expanding your freedom or constricting your liberty?

The suppression of Truth is a coordinated attack on freedom and sovereignty. Sovereign beings born of love are who we are, and we are here to remember that this is our divine birthright: sovereignty. We're here to embody our most whole, most expansive expressions as divine sovereign beings.

These ideas have been trickling into my consciousness for a solid decade. Yes, it's confronting. Sometimes, it takes multiple times to hear something for the kernel of Truth to land deeply enough that you are ready to acknowledge it. Sometimes, the bandaid needs to be ripped off. Trust and remember that the Light has already won; this is the Dark's last attempt to grasp control. They're desperate and are not going down without a fight, but their time is over. Perhaps it's all happening to serve the collective awakening.

It's time for us to connect and come together to anchor in the Light of Truth and spread the Light of Illumination. Share the love as much as possible. Thank you for staying open and for showing up for yourself because the more you show up for yourself, the more you'll be able to show up for others.

It's not all darkness and despair; remember: the Light has won. This is no longer about the Blue Pill versus the Red Pill; this is the Black Pill versus the Gold pill. The antidote to the black pill is the Gold pill, and this book guides you on the golden path to the Emerald City that lies within, the treasure chest of your heart: your eternal Home.

Chapter Fourteen

THE TRUTH SHALL SET YOU FREE

From Surviving to Thriving

"The greatest homage we can pay to truth is to use it." ~ Ralph Waldo Emerson

The Truth often hurts, but it also sets us free. The Truth will only hurt an ego operating in distortion, ultimately serving our greater evolution and empowerment. During this powerful time, darkness is brought to Light, and truths are unveiled. Higher Truth is pouring in to liberate our consciousness.

Many refer to this time of chaos as the Great Awakening. Societal upheaval is a symptom of the paradigm shift we are in the midst of. This time was predicted—it was always meant to happen.

The shift is upon us. The Awakening is here. Humanity is about to enter a whole new era, a golden age of harmony, love, and Light.

However, as discussed in the previous chapter, the Truth underlying this most critical moment in human history is being suppressed precisely because the Truth will set you free.

And that is what those in control don't want: for humanity to be free.

If the Truth has been hidden, it means we've not been truly free. Even under the guise of freedom and democracy, humanity has been enslaved for millennia.

If you question such 'alternative' narratives, remember this: The Truth is stranger than fiction.

Anytime you doubt people who are spewing ideas that may be called a conspiracy theory by others, zoom out and consider that when we look at facts, the vast majority of 'conspiracies' have happened in reality. Rather than 'conspiracy theories,' we have the reality of conspiracies against the thriving of humanity. Pejorative terms such as 'conspiracy theorist' and 'anti-vaxxer' effectively shut down the possibility for further inquiry and discussion.

We're not actually free. The Truth has been hidden to keep us from being free and sovereign unto ourselves, and we've been sold the idea of progress and democracy to keep us complacent. We've been living under an illusion of freedom where the Truth is largely the opposite of what we've been led to believe. In essence, we've been stuck in an inverted matrix where everything is the opposite of Truth. To face and heal a shadow government, we must face and heal our own shadows.

Life is all about growth and expansion. If we are alive, we are meant to grow. We are meant to expand emotionally, mentally, psychologically, and spiritually. We are meant to evolve at a soul level. That is what we come to Earth to do. We incarnated here to learn our lessons, grow into the greatest version of ourselves, and take one step closer to achieving our fullest potential in this embodied human form.

As humans having an embodied physical experience, it's challenging to ascend into our highest capacities and potential of ensouled higher self consciousness. Earth is a very dense experience of polarity and duality. Lower energies based on polarity and physical limitation keep us separated from Truth, love, each other, and our power. But we are here to learn to transcend the separation and integrate the wisdom. Everything that happens to us is a lesson that brings an opportunity to grow. Heartbreak, loss, health crises. These experiences present opportunities for us to reconnect with Truth and love. Every lifetime we incarnate here, we have another chance to learn and grow, and we repeat the lessons until we get them.

Yet, we have been living in an inverted matrix with an anti-life agenda that is working against humanity's evolution. The odds have been stacked against our soul's ability to grow and transcend the matrix of duality and illusion.

Take the word Live. If you flip it around and spell it backward, it spells Evil; lived becomes the devil. And if you look at the world around us, what are they trying to stop us from doing?

Those in control are trying to stop us from living the fullest expression of our lives and being free. Life on Earth is about remembering our essence as free, sovereign beings. That is who we are: powerful divine beings meant to expand and ascend in frequency and consciousness.

In the paradigm that is crumbling, everything has been set up to serve the opposite agenda, which is the anti-life agenda, AKA evil. The agenda is against a thriving humanity. As a cancer survivor, I'm not about simply surviving. I decided very early on that I wouldn't just get through it and survive. I wanted to thrive. How we choose to identify has an impact. I decided not to be a cancer survivor, stuck in the struggle of survival mode, but a cancer thriver—someone who transformed the pain into power. So, I looked at every possible angle. I chose to do the deeper healing that was required to step into the energy of truly thriving because even though on the surface I looked reasonably healthy, I obviously wasn't thriving before I was diagnosed; otherwise, I wouldn't have gotten cancer in the first place.

At face value, I looked like I was living a decent life. Deep down, there was a niggle that knew I wasn't in alignment, but I couldn't even put a finger on why, what, specifically, I was supposed to change, or how to do it. While I eventually allowed an inkling of an idea to emerge, it took me quite a long time to figure out what I was meant to be doing because it ran counter to the expected and accepted narrative of success.

Because I was not living in accordance with my soul's purpose nor taking proactive steps to change things because I was perpetually exhausted, my energy was completely constricted. I also had a history of trauma, creating multiple layers of stuck energy that contributed to the perfect storm that is cancer. My energy field was small, and I was not in my power. I was living in stress and survival mode because my life was not in alignment. My diagnosis hit me like a slap in the face, but in a 'Hey, it's time to wake up and live!' kind of way.

I realized it was an opportunity, that I was getting a second chance. It was an opportunity to see what was not in alignment—what in my life was not working for me—so that I could wake up, fully live, and begin to truly thrive.

My story is not unique. Society is set up in opposition to our soul's compulsion to expand and our body's capacity to thrive. I was disconnected from my Truth, and when I zoomed out, I realized most of the population was. People are waking up now. And that is precisely what the Great Awakening is: the mass rise in consciousness of humanity—the waking up of the masses. To be sure, we are up against a perfect storm with environmental factors contributing to our illnesses—from Monsanto to EMFs to chemtrails and polluted water, it's chemical warfare.

But what's the difference between someone who gets cancer and someone who doesn't? I believe that the root cause lies in unresolved trauma and inner conflict, a lack of alignment in one's life, and a disconnection from self and a higher power.

Most people have been disconnected from their Truth because we've been disconnected from our power and from nature. Severing us from who we truly are as powerful sovereign divine beings connected directly to Source is the original Fall. Divinity is real. Nature does heal. We've been fed a lie that we need pills and chemicals to be healthy. But we are born of nature, not separate from it, and the ultimate Source of life is the Sun. The inverted matrix is inorganic; it's time to return to our natural organic state.

I connected with a naturopath during my diagnostic process who shared that, according to her perspective, Lymphoma is connected to buried emotional trauma. Immediately that resonated as Truth. As I intuitively unraveled the complexities of epigenetics and learned that the long line of cancer on my dad's side of the family—seven immediate family members who all passed from cancer, treatment, and treatment-related complications—was *not* genetically related, it became all the more evident that cancer was connected primarily to suppressed trauma and emotion and additional epigenetic factors. Importantly, I shifted the sense of hope, that surviving cancer was indeed possible. Three family members have since been diagnosed with all different forms of cancer. At first I thought I had failed. However, they have, in fact, all survived their diagnoses, when all before me had not.

From Constriction and Contraction to Evolution and Expansion

The news portrays one tragedy after another. Disaster, doom, death—it's not just the news, but the vast majority of entertainment is filled with apocalyptic visions and graphic violence. All of it keeps us in a state of chronic stress. Tragedy and distraction inundate us by the minute. Unless we are careful and deliberate about where we place our focus and attention, it is incredibly easy to get sucked into the vortex of fear, drama, and trauma.

All of it is geared toward energy constriction and contraction rather than expansion. That simple phenomenon is preventing us from achieving our potential. Fear keeps us in narrow tunnel vision and prevents us from thinking critically and seeing possibilities beyond the narrative. The education system is also designed that way, stuck inside concrete walls that suppress creativity and critical thinking. Asking questions is how we learn; now, it is virtually taboo to question the prevailing narrative.

The vast majority of the system is designed to keep us thinking within certain parameters because it needs good little soldiers to fill the rank-and-file corporate bureaucracy. Of course, we need doctors and accountants to help us navigate the complexity of the broken tax code, but the system itself does not serve our core needs.

If achieving our highest potential was indeed the goal, emotional intelligence, mindset, and self-regulation would be key subjects. History would look entirely different, and philosophy and critical thinking would expand to include ancient wisdom. Science would expand to include the quantum. The Cartesian dichotomy separating mind and body would be discarded entirely. Identity psychology and ego integration would be the core of self-development classes. Practical 101s on how to be an independent, self-sufficient, contributing member of society would be incorporated into the standard curriculum, including financial management and communication skills. Learning how to grow food and be self-sufficient would be prioritized.

Truth can't be suppressed forever. That's why we're in this global situation now. Universal Truth cannot be denied. The forces that feed off fear are trying to keep Truth hidden in the shadows through manipulation and control precipitated by chaos and fear to prevent this awakening process. However, the facade is beginning to break down, and people are starting to see through the illusion. The matrix is cracking and slowly beginning to shatter. We see widening division in society precisely because so many are still stuck in the illusion of the matrix and are scared to let go of the illusion of certainty. They're afraid to step outside the uncomfortable tiny box of the known in which they've been living.

Yet, like a snowball that eventually becomes an avalanche, people are starting to see the hypocrisy and how nothing adds up. Collectively, we are beginning to understand that we've been living in an illusion that has not worked for us. The 100th monkey effect suggests that through quantum entanglement, new behaviors and ideas can spread from one group to another, even if separated by physical barriers. Once a critical mass is reached, the evolution and expansion of consciousness is inevitable. While the original quantum entanglement explanation of the monkeys' behavior has been questioned, the findings point to the power of paradigm shifts,[139] which we are undoubtedly in the midst of. With the internet and meme culture, physical barriers have been broken down, and people can access these new ideas more than ever. Again, this is precisely why so much disinformation and confusion is being pumped out to distract and confuse the Truth. However, the evolution of human consciousness is inevitable. The question is, who will proceed on the path of Ascension over the coming years?

We are here to reclaim our sovereignty and liberate humanity's hearts and minds. We must continue doing the work, waking up to the truths of our origins, divine nature, and the illusions that have kept us from accessing it all.

These narratives have been pushed on us from multiple areas. Science has an agenda. Like it or not, many scientific narratives are part of this greater agenda. On the whole, science has been hijacked, manipulated, and used to keep us separated from divinity. Science and $cience are entirely different entities. We were taught that the power of science is its objectivity, but considering the impact of funding and publishing, we cannot deny the inherent bias.

As I neared completion of my Master's degree, I debated pursuing a PhD. Being the nerd that I am, I loved writing the papers for my degree, and when I handed in my dissertation proposal, my advisor told me I had a PhD project on my hands. Stubbornly, I moved forward and did receive top marks, with 'for further research' as a conclusion based on the initial experiments. But my intuition felt a strong *No* to further study in the ivory towers. There's a saying in academia: Publish or die. If you don't get funding for the subjects you want to research, finishing that PhD will be challenging. Good luck getting published.

Without the proper funding or papers published in suitable journals, say goodbye to a professorship. Say goodbye to tenure. To succeed in academia or research, you must primarily operate within the currently supported paradigm unless you have independent funding and can conduct research autonomously. Even then, you'll have to be published in an accepted journal to be taken remotely seriously.

The ivory towers of academia are essentially just as compromised as the sterile corridors of medicine and the prison-like schools of our education (indoctrination) system.

Then, we have the scientific process itself. 'It's Science' has become a pithy retort to shut down anyone questioning the accepted narrative. But the very premise of science is based on questioning and replication. Let's dig into the science and see if it follows the proper scientific process and holds up in independent trials. If there are no safety protocols, placebo, or control group to compare the experimental group against, that's not real science.

Long-term studies are essential in determining new drugs' safety and side effects. A six-day safety study, or even a few months, is grossly insufficient. Without proper safety trials or replicable procedures, it's not true science.

Even the term 'side effects' is misleading. Let's just be straight: side effects are effects. Call me crazy, but I don't personally think that it's pro-life to be saying take this drug that might prevent that symptom, but it may also kill you. Alleviate something minor with the risk of something significant. Cancer, paralysis, death. We see these listed as potential side effects for nearly every pharmaceutical advertised as if that is normal. It's not.

If one death from a virus is not acceptable, one death from the supposed preventative most certainly is not either. But because someone profits from the intervention, deaths and side effects are swept under the rug, and those who speak out are silenced. Worse, those who experience side effects are often ignored and gaslit.

Rates of autism are dramatically increasing, and there are direct correlations with vaccines, yet authorities and those who trust them are pretending there's nothing there. They attribute it to better detection, which may explain recent year-on-year increases, however when you consider that in 1980 the incidence was about 4 per 10,000 children[140] and now in 2024 it is 1 in 36 children,[141] that argument falls flat.

As somebody with a heavy science and research-based background, I have a hard time with the 'trust the science' narrative because the entire premise of science is to question, test, and re-test. Without bias, manipulation, or a deeper agenda, we'd more robustly investigate the safety and efficacy of vaccines and new drugs pushed into the marketplace. Medications for obesity with dire side effects are being pushed while ignoring the root causes of the epidemic: our corrupted food system, polluted world, impossible cultural norms of beauty, and underlying trauma connected to bodily shame that causes many to subconsciously build a layer of physical protection as a barrier to unwanted attention.

The Paradigm Shift

Furthermore, the current paradigm under which our scientific community operates still ignores significant developments in quantum physics. Thomas Kuhn's *The Structure of Scientific Revolutions* challenged the prevailing view of scientific progress as 'development by accumulation,' proposing instead a model with periods of revolutionary science that catalyze a Paradigm Shift, much like the Copernican Revolution. His controversial ideas introduced a more realistic humanism into the core of science, suggesting that less rational humanistic elements influence scientific progress. Likewise, less rational ego-based attachment may hinder progress.

The fact of the matter is the manner in which we still conduct science is inherently limited because one variable compared against another variable is not the way the world works. We live in a highly complex universe. Both the observer effect and confirmation bias have been found to influence outcomes. The observer effect describes the phenomena seen in quantum science that the observer's expectation can influence the study's outcome. This is the Law of Assumption in action: what we believe to be true about ourselves and the world—our expectation—shapes and creates that reality.

Objective reality is not objective at all. I believe in the power of science. However, we have to learn to detach from our previous teachings and recognize that science is limited by human understanding and perception. Science is a human construct, only as good as those conducting it. Science provides a framework for understanding and harnessing the inner workings of our universe. However, we must remember that it, too, is meant to continuously evolve. We must acknowledge the limitations due to biased interpretation and even manipulation of results, agendas behind who is funding and publishing safety studies, and the inherent limitations of studying a quantum world with Newtonian methods.

Politicians, media, big corporations, and even celebrities have been pushing a narrative, and we must ask why. They hope that after enough pushing, we will be exhausted enough to give in and comply rather than stop, pause, and think for ourselves. They bank on herd mentality to prevent us from activating our critical thinking capacity. Blind acceptance of the narrative is the aim. 'Repeat a lie often enough, and it becomes Truth' is a law of propaganda sometimes referred to as the illusion of Truth by psychologists, often attributed to Nazi Joseph Goebbels.

It is time for us to stand in our power, do the research, and connect and converse with people also engaging in critical thinking. Staying open and tuning in to our intuition is vital. Squashing the voices of the opposition and leaving no room for discussion should be highly suspect. How do we develop and progress as a society if we cannot have a calm, respectful conversation about our different ideas, opinions, and perspectives? How do we create innovative systems and structures and facilitate more growth? It's a widely accepted fact that the sharing of ideas in coffee houses helped to spark the industrial revolution. Progress and innovation come from sharing ideas, shifting perspectives, and broadening our views on life and how the world works.

So, if we have just one prevailing narrative, how will we progress, grow, and evolve as a society?

Remember that science itself is a human construct, and it is evolving as we evolve. Most people forget that science now differs from science fifty years ago, a far cry from one hundred years ago. We must acknowledge that science is constantly evolving, and it is meant to. Technology is continually evolving as we evolve, and science will continue to evolve as our consciousness expands.

Our understanding of reality—what we think is true now—could be blown out of the water in a mere decade. Our knowledge of the world is already shifting dramatically—this is the Great Awakening, after all. We now have a vastly different understanding of reality than in pre-Copernican times. Looking back even further to the ancients, it is clear they had a great deal of wisdom in astronomy and complex geometry. I believe that our ancient ancestors, in many ways, were far more advanced than accepted narratives give them credit for. We believe we're the most technologically and intellectually advanced human civilization, but I question this. With so much lost and suppressed knowledge, it's hard to know for a fact, but we must also understand that history, or 'his-story,' is written by the victors. The victors have self-serving agendas, and patriarchal bias always paints the enemy in a poor light.

Patriarchy, religion, and the repression of women and the feminine have all served to keep us out of balance and from the ultimate Truth. Mind control and programming run deep. This goes beyond the media, politicians, advertising, and entertainment.

It comes from religion and generations of suppression and trauma. Keeping people in fear of a vengeful God is not spiritual Truth. God is love. Patriarchal religion inverts everything true. If we live in fear, we are more likely to become dependent upon a savior, which is another way to control us. Part of waking up to our true power is addressing the Truth of our world and the systems and structures of oppression. Lifting the veil reveals the Truth, and Truth shall set us free.

Now is the time to realize that we are shifting into a paradigm of living in our sovereign power, but we must choose this path. The choice is the initiation. The Great Awakening is leading us to the path of Ascension. Humanity has been going through a collective dark night of the soul, and no matter how much we want to blame the dark forces, it's all happening for our highest good.

Global crisis leads to our collective breakthrough. United we stand, and humans unite to support other humans, as we have seen time and again in the face of crisis and tragedy.

As we begin to remember that the power lies within us, we will realize that we are far more effective at building a more beautiful future through grassroots efforts to mobilize collectively. The Silver Lining of the horrific tragedy of Hurricane Helene was precisely this: souls united toward a common goal, mobilizing more quickly than the government to rescue and support their fellow citizens. This is the way of the Aquarian Age. Together, we can illuminate the shadows and face the collective darkness to realize the deception, rise in our power, and build a New Earth based on Truth, Light, and Love.

The Work

Consider your own beliefs. Are they conducive to growth, creating abundance, and living in love? Or are they limiting your perception of reality and what is possible? Think about where your beliefs come from and what kind of programming you've been exposed to since birth. With curiosity and no judgment, examine your limiting beliefs and where they came from. What's not serving you?

Tune into your intuition and your heart wisdom to know the Truth with a capital T. Once we are connected to Source, once we are connected to our hearts and our intuition, everything comes back into alignment. We become one with our inner power and a conduit for the divine, limitless and powerful beyond measure. This is the real work we are being called to do.

It's a choice—it's always a choice. But if you want to experience a life of freedom, expansion, and growth, if you want to reclaim your power and stand in your Truth, then make the choice.

Choose to tune in. Choose yourself over the agenda. Take what they've been telling you and flip it. Think the opposite; do the opposite because the Truth has been flipped upside down in our inverted matrix. Everything that they've told you, the opposite is closer to the Truth.

What is the Great Awakening?

Awakening opens your eyes—all three of them—to the Truth. It is an expansion of consciousness, a reclamation of Truth, a journey of remembrance of who you are, your nature, the universe, and how it works. Awakening is a journey of unlearning and relearning the Truth of our society and the systems and how they operate.

Awakening, fundamentally, is remembering your true nature and the fact that you are a limitless, powerful, divine being born from Source.

Collectively, we are experiencing a mass awakening. With social media spreading information faster than ever, censorship is on the rise, and Truth is being suppressed. But they're only delaying the inevitable, and each deceptive move they make triggers more to see the forest from the trees.

Universal Truth cannot be denied. The shadows are coming to the Light because the Truth cannot remain hidden in the darkness as Earth receives high frequency light codes of illumination, and the more of us who awaken and raise our vibration above that of fear and control, the higher the collective frequency will rise.

Awakening is simply becoming conscious and breaking free from the prison matrix and remembering the sacred nature of our reality. It is standing in your power and sovereignty. It is simple yet profound. Simple in theory yet simultaneously complex in process, as there are layers upon layers of deconditioning, layers of our being that all need to be cleared. Simple does not mean easy.

But the process is worth the effort. When we operate from an integrated wholeness where mind, body, and soul are aligned with the highest good for all of us, everything naturally flows and expands. Realign with your Truth, mind, body, and soul integrated in a state of harmonic wholeness, and everything will fall into place.

Trust and faith are essential. Find peace within so the external cannot rattle or shake your internal foundation; your inner compass will guide you through these tumultuous times. It's time to heal back into the wholeness that is the Truth of our being.

As scary as it may be to step up and speak out in your authentic Truth, especially if people in your life might not understand, you must decide what is more important. I always return to what feels right and true. And that comes from within, my Truth with a capital T that cannot be denied. My own Gene Keys are Truth and Illumination, after all, so I cannot suppress what I am here to express. The more you show up for yourself, the more you can show up for those around you and help uplift humanity to rise above the fear agendas of power and control agendas.

True power is a power that flows from within, and it's a power that binds and unites. Tune into your heart's wisdom to uncover the Truth, which indeed shall set you free.

Chapter Fifteen

PATRIARCHY AND THE PARADIGM OF SEPARATION

It Ends With Us

"Patriarchy is like the elephant in the room that we don't talk about, but how could it not affect the planet radically when it's the superstructure of human society." ~ Ani DiFranco

Patriarchy and the paradigm of power over, separation, and control have dominated humanity for millennia. Archeological and historical evidence suggests that around 5,000 years ago, human society shifted from matrilineal, female-centric modalities into a patriarchal, masculine-dominated way of life.

The discussion that ensues about the woes of patriarchy is not about replacing men and reverting once again to a fully female-centric society. Men, too, have been victims of the tyranny of patriarchy, their hearts cut off and compassion extinguished. The battle of the sexes has created an epidemic of dissatisfied and disenfranchised men who bare the brunt of the blame, when largely they themselves are not the ones at fault. Unwitting victims and perpetrators of generational trauma, we must all take responsibility for the role we play in perpetuating this disharmony. What is required is a balancing of the scales to come into true harmony and union. Society needs men in their pure, divine power, just as we need women in their expressed divine essence.

We need everyone to show up as their whole selves, valued and empowered, working harmoniously. Like yin and yang, integrated and in ever-flowing harmony, the call is to come into union and harmony both within and without. We all contain feminine and masculine energies within us, and pitting men versus women only perpetuates the paradigm of separation. Replacing men with women, and vice versa, is still to operate in the paradigm of polarity and separation.

Feminism has failed because it fell into the fallen paradigm of pitting women against men, further exacerbating the issue. It has women stepping into the shoes of men in their corrupted masculine energy, still thoroughly imbalanced in their essence, suppressing their natural femininity and emasculating many men in the process. It is not moving us forward. Women stepping up into leadership by embracing their feminine power while also letting the men know that it's okay for them to show up in their powerful divine masculine will help shift our society into an era of harmony.

Distorted feminine energy is part of the collective shadow. Part of the awakening process is seeing that this paradigm of separation hasn't worked for us and that to enter the new paradigm, we must embrace the divine feminine in her fully empowered feminine essence. So, we'll examine where things have gotten a little off track and why things have gotten skewed, resulting in this wild world we live in now.

For both parts, it's a process of integrating the dual energies of masculine and feminine within. We all contain masculine and feminine energies, and ascending our vibration is about coming into harmony and union. Healing ourselves first and coming into wholeness, harmony, and love within will heal the world—as within, so without.

The rise of the divine feminine energy is about women rising into their power, but not above men. We must allow the energy of the divine feminine to rise both within and without so that we come into equilibrium, peace, and harmony. Feminine energy resides within all humans and is felt as our emotional, intuitive, heart-centered aspects. By embracing the wisdom in our hearts and wombs—physical and energetic, men and women—we allow the capacity for integration and inner union into wholeness. Divine union within catalyzes sacred union in the physical and the rebirth of true love onto Earth.

The expression of the patriarchy is more than overt domination and control of men over women; it's about the masculine principle superseding the female principle, bringing us out of balance energetically on every level of society. Women who have stepped into a masculine energy and fully operate within the structures of the patriarchy are still essentially perpetuating a distorted system that does not work. This energetic imbalance is why the feminist movement has failed women. To succeed, women have been forced to mold themselves into this patriarchal model. Women wearing business suits in executive offices and on political podiums in itself does not solve the fundamental issues of the patriarchy.

Putting on a pantsuit and stepping into men's shoes removes femininity from the equation, and the removal of feminine energy from society at large is the fundamental issue at hand. Of course women should have the option of moving up the ladder of success and breaking through the glass ceiling as they desire. Of course women should have equal rights, pay, and respect in the workplace. Women embodied in their feminine power having leadership roles in society is key to healing collective turmoil.

However, by and large, collectively, we—men *and* women alike—are still operating through a patriarchal model, a masculine way of being that's about pushing, driving, striving, and achieving. Doing, doing, doing. This societal directive does not serve women in particular because when women disconnect from the natural cycles and rhythms that are innate to us, often done through artificial means such as hormonal birth control and being on the corporate clock, it suppresses our ability to show up at our best and be in our full power. Boss babes eventually burn out.

Authenticity is the most powerful vibration of all. The SPANE scale of emotions measured its vibrational frequency to be 4000 times more powerful than love itself. We must move through love to get to the heart of our authentic Truth and then embody and radiate this unique fractal of frequency into the world.

For those who wonder why still in this day and age, after all these years of breaking barriers, so few women hold leadership positions, this is my theory: it is because women wearing pantsuits in the boardroom are still not operating from a genuine space of true, authentic, integrated power. This is why, collectively, women hit a glass ceiling: we are not operating in our authentic power. It's nigh on impossible for us to show up fully in our power in the current mode of operation because it is not in energetic alignment with our core authentic soul truth, nor is it in alignment with the natural rhythms and cycles of the feminine. Our hormones do not lie—we have different phases of the month that, when left to their natural devices, dictate different energy levels. This fluctuation also applies to our daily rhythms; our hormones operate in waves. Caffeine, birth control, and blue light disrupt our hormones, removing us from the wisdom held within and the authentic Truth that contains the gold of our soul.

Men, too, contain feminine energy; we are all a balance of both. The imbalance in society is also due to men suppressing the feminine within. Mind over heart. Doing versus being. Thinking versus feeling. Men suppressing their emotions because 'boys don't cry' is part of the problem. Awakened women want a strong masculine in their powerful protector provider energy. However, only when a man opens his heart can he fully show up in that energy. This emotional safety enables her to flourish and blossom into an ever greater level of power and devotion, which in turn motivates him to show up with strength and leadership.

This same process occurs within us as we walk the path of mastery into embodied wholeness. Sacred inner union calls for both the masculine and feminine energetics to be unlocked and harmonized. A healed inner masculine allows a woman to feel safe and stable as she steps into her power. Similarly, a healed inner feminine enables men to feel safe to soften into emotional vulnerability. I do distinguish biological sex from masculine and feminine energetics, and in partnership, a woman can embody more of the masculine traits while a man can embody the feminine energy.

Biological differences do, however, impact how we show up and operate.[142] These differences should be honored, not swept under the rug, and not made out to be shameful or something we should try to overcome. Honoring women's nurturing instincts and the role of motherhood should be our collective priority. Women should have the right to choose what is best for their lives without being shamed and to honor their deepest instincts and desires.

That should include the celebration of motherhood, as well as a shift in the way we define jobs and careers to enable women to step into their influential leadership as creators, healers, and way-showers while also honoring their natural cycles and rhythms and the gift that it is to carry and bring forth the miracle of life.

The energy of the Mother is so desperately needed in a world that's lost its humanity. It is time to re-mother humanity and return the eternal wisdom of the Mother to her rightful place. The Divine Feminine energy itself needs to be honored if women are to have true power and influence in our world. In a world that celebrates superficiality, authenticity is a potent key code of transformation, and a woman who steps into her authenticity by embracing the power of the feminine within becomes an unstoppable force.

We have naturally evolved with different biological capacities for a reason. Grandiose mistakes like that are not made in evolution. It just doesn't work that way. Whether you believe in evolution or in the divine creation of humanity, we wouldn't have been created with such distinct biological roles if we were meant to be exactly the same. We're not. We're meant to complement each other biologically and energetically.

This distinction goes far beyond basic biology. We must embrace the energetic differences between the masculine and the feminine, both within and without. To heal, we must recognize that competition over cooperation is not serving us and that the patriarchy is a paradigm of separation and disconnection—disconnection of mind and body, disconnection from the land, disconnection from natural rhythms and ways of being, disconnection from our souls, disconnection from our selves, disconnection from source and spirit, disconnection from each other, and disconnection from the sacred feminine.

Fundamentally, this disconnection must be illuminated, as it is the source of all societal issues we now face.

Humanity evolved historically in communities, tribes, and small social groups. Modern society, especially urban communities, is detached from that original way of being. I'm not saying we should go back to cave days and hand-to-mouth living, but community is vital to thriving, as is communing with the land.

The call now is to be conscious about creating that kind of community for ourselves because we can co-create something even more beautiful as we come together. The call is to live in sacred devotion to cultivating life and communion with the land. It's crucial to recognize what has not been working and shift into ways of being and operating that can propel us forward—together. The more we share and support each other, the more we can all rise and create something more beautiful that works for all.

The Cult of the Individual vs Self-Actualization

There is a distinct difference between taking personal responsibility for yourself—being the CEO of your own life—and the cult of the individual.[143] Filling your cup first is zero percent selfish, and it's not about placing your individual wellbeing *over* other people's needs at any cost. Rather, it's about being fully nourished to pour from an overflowing cup of love. If you are not filled up yourself, you are not in a position to serve at your highest capacity because you have less to give energetically.

When I was recovering from cancer, and in the months leading up to diagnosis, I had limited capacity to give to others because I barely had enough energy to get myself through the day. I had to muster any ounce of energy I could to show up for my students, relying on caffeine and chocolate to make it through my sessions. It was not sustainable. I hit burnout. Underlying this was undiagnosed Stage three Adrenal Fatigue. Not to mention—cancer. Without any sense of hyperbole, my life force was nearly extinguished.

If you're running on overdrive and are about to hit an empty tank yourself, how much can you show up for the people in your life? How much life do you even have left to live?

Emotionally speaking, when stressed out, strung out, and overextended, you're much more likely to overreact if something triggers you. If somebody says something and it lands the wrong way, it doesn't necessarily mean that they meant it in the way you're interpreting through your lens of stress. When your emotional self-regulation capacities are weakened, your ability to reflect and express equanimity and compassion rather than reacting and lashing out at them in return is completely diminished. Then, the situation escalates.

Interpersonal relationships are directly impacted when we are overextended and haven't filled our cup by taking care of our needs first. The way society is built now, so many of us are running on overdrive. Divorce is on the rise. People run away at the first sign of discord rather than sitting down and discussing what caused them pain. We're empty tanks. We've reached a place of utter disconnection.

Not to mention the physical fallout that results when we are not taking care of ourselves: illness and chronic disease are on the rise, as are mental imbalances. These are all consequences of a paradigm that has kept us out of balance and disconnected from half of ourselves.

Self-care, self-love, and filling our cups are not a luxury but a necessity for healing the world; society hasn't been structured to enable that. It's a matter of examining what has not been working for us and thinking about how we can rebuild something that does support the thriving of all of society.

The cult of the individual is about ego, power, greed, and control. Personal responsibility and filling your cup first are not. Serving our needs first enables us to step up and serve compassionately and more completely.

Humans evolved in community,[144] yet we've been separated from each other, from ourselves, our internal source, our connection to a greater power, and our connection to nature. Modern society has been disconnected from all that truly matters.

Returning to our center point and tuning in is key to reevaluating our values and what truly matters. Community is about not just sharing but balancing responsibilities, honoring individual gifts, dividing roles, and complementing each other's talents and proclivities. Honoring and valuing our complementary natures is how we genuinely honor both the masculine and the feminine. It's not about everybody doing the same thing.

While women are capable of showing up and doing many jobs equally, some better, than men, some may prefer to focus on childrearing and managing the household. These roles have become devalued yet are essential for the healthy development of children and society. Meanwhile, there are many essential roles filled predominately by men. Thank you, men, for showing up and enabling society to function.

Harmony in society relies on everybody having a role and having that role acknowledged and respected through honoring the different gifts and capabilities that we all have, including women and the feminine within all of us. We must step back and figure out how to integrate that more completely and beautifully. How can we structure society to nurture and honor the multifaceted gifts women contribute while celebrating and nurturing the different seasons and phases of life? Likewise, how can we structure society to enable men to step fully into their potential while feeling valued, honored, and respected?

Religion and the Patriarchy

Religion must inevitably be addressed when discussing the patriarchy because it extends beyond the economy, politics, and business. It touches interpersonal and intimate relationships as well as our primary relationship—that with a higher power—and one of the primary drivers of the patriarchy's perpetuation has been religion itself. Patriarchal dominance has been precipitated, pushed, and perpetuated by male-dominated, male-led religion. This has less to do with particular religious beliefs—although beliefs of Western religions are undeniably rooted in patriarchal ideology—but rather the social institution of religion itself. Not all religious institutions are equally distorted, but the epicenter of modern Christianity, which boasts 2.4 billion followers[145]—the Vatican itself—is entirely skewed and patriarchal in the way it operates. It's far more concerned with controlling the masses than facilitating any connection with the divine.

The Bible itself has been highly edited. Removal of the gospels that spoke into principles of the divine feminine and direct communion with God fundamentally distorted the essence of the original esoteric teachings. Less than ten percent of Jesus' life is covered in the Bible, and over 500 gospels were sifted through by Roman orthodoxy to select the 27 books of the New Testament.[146] Thirteen of the selected 27 are attributed to Paul,[147] a man who did not know Jesus himself, while the selection process was debated for over three centuries by people with political and personal agendas. Furthermore, gospel editing was spearheaded primarily by those with political and personal agendas who hired 'correctors' to edit the texts. Our understanding of the Bible is quite deliberately completely skewed because our version is a highly edited fragment of the original.

We're living half-lives because we've been taught half-truths. The Nag Hammadi is a collection of gospels discovered in 1945 that were buried in the desert of Egypt around the time Roman persecution began so that they weren't burned and eradicated.[148] In these unedited, uncorrupted texts, we find discussion of the Sophia principle, the universal aspect of divine wisdom and feminine consciousness; the feminine aspect of the Divine. Gnostics held that Sophia was the Holy Spirit aspect, the Bride of Christ. The Holy Spirit was the Divine Feminine, and she was effectively erased.

Hidden teachings from the Nag Hammadi and Dead Sea Scrolls prescribe no separation between humanity and the divine. The rift exists solely due to our ignorance and internal disconnection. To paraphrase the Gospel of Thomas from the Nag Hammadi:[149] *"He Who understands all, but lacks Self-Knowledge lacks everything."*

Gnosis, or a direct knowing and inner connection with God, was a cornerstone teaching of Mystery Schools—the very schools Yeshua trained in himself. The Gospel of Mary declares: *"Be vigilant, and allow no one to mislead you by saying: "'Here it is!' or 'There it is!' For it is within you that the Son of Man dwells."*[150] Yeshua and his counterpart, Mary Magdalene, taught that the Kingdom of Heaven is revealed through self-discovery, and access to the kingdom lies within.

The Gospels of Thomas and Mary both tell us that we all have the power to commune with the Divine, to speak with God directly, and to receive answers for ourselves. Cultivating this connection is up to us and requires practice, like meditation or exercise. We are not the helpless sinners that the religious institutions have damned us to be. Nor are we required to belong to a church or pay tithes to prove our devotion to the divine.

'Love your neighbor as yourself.' This teaching is about self-love first. The true path to God is through the heart of pure compassion, which fosters harmony within and without, allowing the wisdom of the feminine to guide us.

Pope Gregory the 9th defiled the name and role of Mary Magdalene and women at large when he labeled her a prostitute in 591 AD.[151] Finally, restitution came 1500 years later when Pope Francis declared in 2016 through Vatican decree[152] that July 22 would be Mary Magdalene's feast day, making her a saint on par with the apostles. What is still not yet widely known or accepted is that Mary Magdalene was just as powerful as Jesus Christ himself, his counterpart in marriage and ministry. In Truth, he needed her to attain his full potential. She is an ascended master, as is Mother Mary, and the one Jesus entrusted with his message of resurrection. The sacred power of the divine feminine was deliberately edited out of religious teachings to suppress feminine power further and prevent women from embodying and expressing their power as healers and leaders, spiritual or otherwise.

Not only were influential female leaders removed from the literature, but their reputations were also defamed. Centuries later, witch hunts removed millions of healers from society. That's straight-up patriarchal persecution. Roman soldiers sought out any woman in the community who was in her power, a healer, and connected to nature and source. In Truth, it wasn't just women who were persecuted, but also men who recognized the power of the feminine archetype and honored and utilized nature in her purest form.[153]

These individuals were well-respected for their abilities, gifts, and knowledge. The witch hunt wasn't about women using magical powers for evil. They were persecuted, slandered, and ostracized for the expertise and the wisdom they carried from being connected to ancient and eternal Truth, divinely led to help, guide, and serve people. The eternal power and wisdom of the feminine were repressed. Essentially, the witch hunts were a genocide of the feminine principle and a massive ancestral, generational, and collective trauma that still needs to be healed in society. Until we fully address these deep collective wounds, we will continue to be mired in division and energetic enslavement. We cannot heal what lies buried in the shadows.

After the sanctioned female genocide of the witch hunts, female suppression continued through legal suppression. Women weren't allowed to own property, they weren't allowed to vote, they weren't allowed to pursue higher education, they weren't allowed to pursue careers in technical fields, and to this day, women still do not receive equal pay. Depending on the culture and country, women continue to be suppressed overtly and discreetly in myriad ways.

The process of women stepping into our power is ongoing, but slowly, surely, headway is being made as many of us begin to remember the codes and gifts contained within, remembering our lives as priestesses, healers, mages, and sages. It's time to fully embrace an age where the feminine and the masculine are equally honored.

The days of women being relegated to the sidelines as they have for millennia are running short. Society is in a state of disharmony and emotional suppression that has caused a great deal of pain for both men and women alike. Specific issues, such as sexuality and sensuality, have mainly been taboo, matters very much related to the feminine and her suppression. Recently, any woman in her feminine power has been named and shamed for one reason or another. What discussion there is around sexuality in the collective is largely distorted, continuing to perpetuate suppression and distortion of the sacred feminine.

Kundalini is the divine feminine life force energy coiled at the base of our spines, the energy that is the spark of all life that pulsates through all living creation. Once activated, it moves up through each of the energy centers to culminate in transcendence, a state of pure bliss and oneness. Shakti is the divine feminine energy of creation that activates the Kundalini awakening, and once our chakras are clear of blockages and trauma, the energy can move freely through our chakras to facilitate and activate our highest potential of pure creation power. Sex and the sensual aspect of the feminine became taboo for a reason—because it is pure life force power.

This pure, potent energy of sacred sexual alchemy has been purposely distorted and desecrated, corrupted and polluted, suppressed and rejected through systematic hijacking and manipulation. Religion removed the Sacred feminine and damned her through original sin, pornography and prostitution pillaged her innocence and desecrated her purity, while authoritarian patriarchal regimes suppressed her magic and pilfered her freedom. Culture has over-sexualized this divine gift while distorting beauty standards and perpetuating body shame, while the medical establishment and pharmaceutical industries have controlled her body. Many mainstream spiritual teachings such as Tantra and Kundalini yoga have only served to bolster distortion by watering down the teachings.

Esoteric practices have been systematically suppressed through institutionalized shame, the lowest frequency on the scale of emotions.[154] It is no wonder we have been so disconnected from Source and suffering from epidemic chronic depression and disease—we have been disconnected from the power and magic of our bodies, the Earth, and the True source of Divinity for millennia.

Reclamation is upon us. As always, it starts within.

Dismantling the patriarchy is an inside job. The first step is to acknowledge where we have been shaming the feminine within—men and women alike—and where we may shame women in our lives. First, we must recognize that these biases and judgments exist due to cultural conditioning. We must acknowledge the suppressed emotions and uncover grief, fear, trauma, anger, and pain.

Furthermore, we must address these wounds by going deeper and acknowledging that this has been happening for centuries, embracing the Truth of our worthiness, healing it within, releasing the shame, resentment, anger, grief, and pain related to persecution and suffering, and integrating the wounds of the shadows into wisdom and alchemizing them into strength and inner power. Finally, we can say, "This ends with me."

Embracing all aspects of ourselves, notably those suppressed feminine aspects, which include our emotions and the need to rest in certain parts of our cycle, allows us to integrate the parts of us we've been cut off from. Reconnecting with the natural cycles and rhythms and honoring our energetic needs for rest at certain times gives us permission to heal and rebirth those parts of us that have been suppressed. As a culture, we've been trained to give without end and place our energy outside ourselves.

Healing the feminine requires allowing ourselves to turn inward and live in accordance with nature's rhythms, to embrace a cyclical rather than a linear way of being.

Reconciling this imbalance and healing both the feminine and masculine wounds is how we begin to raise the life force to spiral into a whole new way of Being based on light, love, and the Truth of the sacred, birthing a New Earth and co-creating Magic with the Divine.

CHAPTER SIXTEEN
THE BIG SHIFT: RISE OF THE DIVINE FEMININE
THE RESURRECTION OF A RADIANT FUTURE

"The feminine spirit is the matriarch of creation; she contains the mysteries of life." ~ Tanya Markul

The Dalai Lama famously said, 'The World will be saved by Western Women.' Indeed, Western Women are in a powerful position as they have been granted the opportunity to balance the scales by reclaiming both their power and their rightful position in global influence. Indeed, the shift in consciousness underway is not to tip the scales in the opposite direction but to bring them back into balance to right the trajectory of our collective evolution. The rise of divine feminine energy is a core aspect of this shift, accompanied by the crumbling of patriarchal suppression and societal structures controlled and dominated by masculine principles. As the old falls away, we're shifting into a new paradigm of harmony and union.

The rise of the divine feminine is vastly different from the feminist movement. While the movement played a pivotal role in reclamation and recognition of female power and potential, women have been denying their femininity to make their mark in this skewed system. The feminist movement was co-opted in subtle ways that do not align with the true feminine energy of a woman (or anybody) in her authentic feminine power.

Feminine energy exists within everybody. Again, everybody, both men and women, contains masculine and feminine energies. This discussion isn't about the physical expression of male and female but about the masculine and feminine principles of energy. It is a massive distinction: biology versus energy. People embody these energies in different ways and to varying degrees. However, integrating these energies within is a significant aspect of our inner work as we awaken, ascend, and continue to evolve on the spiritual path.

For those who don't identify with being spiritual or on the spiritual path, those who may identify more with the realms of psychology, personal growth, self-development, and positive thinking as many of these teachings run parallel to each other, this ties to the notions of integration, wholeness, and self-actualization.

Healing Back to Wholeness

This phrase dropped in after a high heart activation I received in 2019. 'Healing Back to Wholeness' refers to the journey of returning to—healing back to—our original state of divine union within. Wholeness is a state of feeling fully at Home in your body, fully You. It's the journey of soul integration, and a significant component of what is being integrated is the dual yet complementary energies of the masculine and the feminine, reuniting them back into harmony and balance.

To reiterate, the rise of the divine feminine isn't to overtake or surpass the masculine; rather, it's to bring the two back into a unified and complementary whole—an integrated, harmonious, beautiful balance so that they can nurture each other and be fully expressed. Union can happen within a partnership, but it must also occur within.

In Truth, for a partnership to manifest its fullest and most harmonious expression, it's incumbent upon each of the individuals within the partnership to return to this integrated sense of wholeness within themselves first. Many relationship mentors discuss the need to heal the wounds within to attract the ideal partner and manifest a beautiful relationship, and to a degree, this is very true, or else we will continue to attract karmic partners that play out the same patterns until we learn the lesson. However, much healing and evolution can occur within a healthy partnership itself. Conscious relationships where both partners are committed to growth can provide the most profound and liberating healing opportunities, as much of our wounding and past pain is relational. With that said, most of the work still must be done within, and some divine unions require a significant amount of the work to be done individually for union to be possible. Partners help mirror wounds that still need healing and integration, and often, we manifest particular individuals into our lives to do just that.

Whether in a relationship or alone, inner integration must be done within each individual, and both paths lead to a beautiful place of harmony and wholeness.

The feminine principle is cyclical, engendering a sense of connection to nature and her innate rhythms in the flow of life. Like water, feminine energy flows, ebbing and rising with the tides of emotions and powerful waves of intuition and inspiration. The masculine principle, on the other hand, is linear. Like a beam of light illuminating the path forward, the masculine drives us to pursue our goals, directing our vision and action to create all that is meant to manifest through us.

As with the cycles and rhythms of nature, we have four seasons every year, and every year, it's the same four seasons. The wheel of the year spirals continuously in tune with feminine energies. But each year, the trees grow taller, and the flowers bloom bigger and brighter. Over time, we grow and change, an extension of the masculine principle of expansion. When the feminine and the masculine merge in perfect harmony, the most brilliant and expansive possible expression emerges.

It's the same with us. When we're fully in sync with nature, with the rhythms around us, and with the rhythms within while growing forward to manifest our vision through the power of creation, then we're fully in sync with the essence of life itself, with the force of the universe backing us.

This harmony is the essence of true power—being in flow with the divine You-universe within and without. Connection to the All is our true source of power. We are one with everything in the 'uni-verse,' the one song-weaving threads of harmony through the web of creation.

The rise of the feminine calls us to embrace the dark. Healing and integrating the shadows into the light facilitates our becoming and rebirth into the most whole and complete version of ourselves, with a depth of wisdom and the brilliance of a vast wholeness of being.

The most beautiful creations of life, including life itself, emerge from the dark, the womb space, the void. Like a seed planted deep within the ground, all creation springs from the dark void.

Once we gain perspective and reframe the darkness in our lives, we can begin to see its beauty because it contains the possibility and potency for growth, transformation, and creation. The dark night of the soul that so many experience is precisely this process of planting and nurturing the seed still buried deep within the darkness. It is where the seed for a more beautiful future is planted before it can emerge and blossom. The seed must germinate in the dark. Before it can fully emerge and blossom, the seed must first come into being in the womb of the Earth, just as we begin life as a tiny cell forged through the unification of the masculine seed and feminine egg in the womb of our mothers.

Everything begins in the void of creation. Life begins in the darkness of the womb of creation, where the feminine holds the potential and the masculine generates the spark.

We need both, and we must remember that without the mother, without the feminine principle, there would be no life. Creation potential is lost without the mother and cannot be replaced by artificial means.

In this time of turmoil, artificial intelligence, and transhumanism, where we have lost our connection with nature and reverence for the feminine, we are being called to remember this fundamental Truth of our existence. The Trans agenda seeks to further displace and replace both the feminine and divine humanity in society. Roughly 90% of AI specialists are male;[155] our virtual, automated, and inorganic futures are being built based on inherent bias. We cannot allow this to transpire.

Transhumanism erases the soul with a parallel attempt to erase the womb, the link between transhumanism and transgender. There is a vast difference between celebrating individual expression—which I honor and respect for autonomous adults—and pushing an agenda on minors. My four-year-old niece entered pre-school wanting to be a unicorn when she grows up. Just days later, she changed her mind and now wants to be Tinkerbell. True story. Adults can make drastic life-altering decisions. Children's brains are not yet formed, nor have their hormones kicked in. We won't fully open the can of worms that is Atrazine[156] and the impact of microplastics on endocrine function here,[157] but the disruption of our biology and the epidemic of suppressed testosterone[158] cannot be ignored either.

Honoring and embracing the cycles of darkness that give birth to the light will guide us back home to the organic Truth we hold within. We are collectively being called on a quest to go within and reclaim what is true for ourselves. Tuning into our heart's wisdom and tapping into our intuition will help us stay anchored in our higher self and deepest Truth.

Connecting with nature and grounding on the Earth herself helps us to reconnect with the feminine source and our natural essence. The sun represents the masculine, while the Earth represents the feminine. Without the light of the sun, life would not exist. But it is the mother who holds life itself. Earth and moon represent the physical bodies of manifestation reflecting and feeding off the sun's light, the masculine that generates the spark of life. The moon, deeply connected to Earth and women's cycles, represents the essence of the dark feminine and her natural rhythms.

However, the moon represents the control center of the lunar matrix, which has subverted the organic Mother's essence by perpetuating subconscious illusions through the masses. Through mind control and sexual trauma, many women have been disconnected from their natural divinity and serve to perpetuate the inverted matrix that is anti-life and anti-soul. Sexual perversion and trauma are the primary methods used to control humanity. By controlling our centers of creation and life force energy, they siphon our essence and power. This subject is dark and very deep, but the call is to transcend the lunar matrix and reclaim our divinity and our sovereignty by clearing out trauma and dismantling systems of mind control.

Embracing the shadows and whatever darkness lies within is the process of integration that will help us move forward from a space of wholeness and empowerment to create a new earth based on principles of harmony, love, and joy. A world of peace and abundance that works for us all. It must start within.

To integrate our internal masculine and feminine energies, we can energetically anchor into the crystalline core of the Earth, connect to the sun, and merge the energies within. These purified solar masculine and solar feminine energies marry together in the heart space to birth the holy child through the unified holy trinity field within.

Integrating into wholeness, reclaiming our power, and tapping into our intuition enables our beauty, magic, and power to emerge. This is the path of true mastery. We are all healers and creators, and we all—men and women—contain the power of the feminine within. It is up to us to access and unleash this potent potential for creation.

While we carry forth unique features, qualities, and characteristics within each lifetime, we all contain the potential for everything. In any given lifetime on Earth, these qualities manifest in particular variations so that we can learn specific lessons and experience the vastness of the human condition in its complete spectrum, both light and dark. We contain the seeds and energies of all within and are far more capable than we have been led to believe.

The Suppression of the Feminine

The patriarchy and the three patriarchal Abrahamic religions have adopted a doctrine of power over. Inherent to hierarchical structures are imbalances in power. Christianity—which has shaped global politics and power structures since its adoption in 380 AD as the official religion of Rome—has been using fear as a control and oppression mechanism to keep people out of their power, as have land-ruling 'elites,' many of whom claim their legitimacy was given through the blessing of God, giving them the divine right to rule over a population coerced by carrots and sticks to be obedient and compliant.

The illusion of choice and freedom granted by democracy has led to a blissfully ignorant and pliable population. With science, technology, and the perceived elimination of barriers through equal access to education along with the veneer of a free-market capitalist economy to bolster this facade, many have created some semblance of the American dream. Liberty and justice, however, are proving to be illusions sold to the masses to keep them obeisant.

As discussed in a previous chapter, when we're in an energy of fear, obedience, and compliance, we cannot take responsibility for our lives because we are not in our power. We place power and agency outside ourselves, seeking a savior to swoop in and fix things for us. Christianity has Jesus, while America and the West have their politicians, celebrities, and strong-armed, agenda-filled 'philanthropists.'

When you take responsibility for your thoughts, your actions, and all that you experience, you operate from empowerment within rather than reacting and responding to things that happen to you from without.

Victim mentality is so insidious and pervasive that we often are completely unaware that we are operating in this energy. One of the deepest layers of victim programming is that our genes determine everything—essentially, we are a victim of our genes, helpless when it comes to disease. While genes do inform virtually every aspect of our makeup, they do not, as we have been led to believe, dictate our destiny.

Our cells live in an open flow where they receive information from the outside environment, influencing gene expression from within. Information flows in and out. Our environment does, in fact, influence how genes are expressed, such as whether they are turned on or off. As this is not a chapter dedicated to the subject, I will simply underscore this profound shift in understanding the fundamental nature of our existence: that our cells' interactions with our environment determine our biological 'destiny.'

Furthermore, it shows us that consciousness creates reality. This profound shift in perspective once again places the power within. Once we recognize that we can profoundly influence the outcome of our lives by making choices aligned with our highest good and taking responsibility for the surroundings we immerse ourselves in, we fundamentally shift how we show up in the world: as powerful creators rather than helpless victims.

Beyond biology, many of us have been programmed with limiting beliefs, such as the notion that life is working against us and will never work out for us. Narratives that we've been hearing our whole lives, filtered through different mediums such as our parents, school, movies, television programs, pop culture, religion, society, and our immediate surroundings and community, often serve to keep us down and small.

The Truth is, it's mainly by design, though the vast majority who perpetuate these disempowering narratives are entirely unaware they are caught up in the web themselves. The patriarchy needed to demonize women because women who were in their power were—are—sovereign beings. Healers and midwives. Priestesses. Leaders and wisdom keepers of their communities. Stewards of nature and carriers of ancient generational wisdom through the lineage.

This shift began long before Christianity. Evidence of this paradigm shift places the suppression of goddess culture at around 5,000 years ago when women were revered. Christianity cannot take full blame as it was an expression of the rise of the patriarchal paradigm. However, it most certainly has perpetuated and even escalated the suppression and persecution of women in the last couple of millennia.

The task now is to remember the Truth and recognize the female birthright as powerful creator beings and healers—for women to remember that we are magical manifestors, that we are Queens, priestesses, and goddesses in earthly human form, and for men to honor them as such by working to embody the Priest King energy. We must all honor the power of the feminine within and the women in our life.

Women used to be revered for their feminine essence and oracular capabilities. Priestesses, in particular, used to be the conduits who conferred sovereign power to ruling Kings through the act of sacred divine sex.

How beautiful and revolutionary to consider that women are the direct connection to Source, and it's through our womb portal that we confer the power to the men. Considering how at odds this is with our society's current views of women, it's genuinely quite astonishing to reflect through these different layers and perspectives just how much we've been removed from our power, how much that power has been removed from us in many ways through the desecration of our womb and denigration of our feminine essence.

Set the World Ablaze

The dark night of the soul that humanity has been stuck in for millennia as the light of Truth has nearly been extinguished is now ending. We've been lost in the dark, but the light of Truth has now been set ablaze. It's up to us all to remove residual soot and smoke that is still blocking us from seeing the light and allow the pure fires of alchemy to transmute the grit into gold. The veil is lifting, and our capacity to see clearly is returning.

Now is the time to reclaim our power and unleash the fullest expressions of ourselves, to unleash our voice, and to be the unstoppable creators we were born to be. It is time to embrace our divine birthright as sovereign beings, create the beautiful realities we envision, and do it all from a heart-centered space because creation born through connection to the heart center is for the good of all.

Women in their true power are natural healers because they work through the heart and womb in the vibration of love, service, and creation. Feminine intuition is the power we have been separated from: our heart-wisdom, the frequency of love, the Truth of love.

And it's not just women; it's humans operating in the space of wholeness and connected to the feminine aspect of the divine, working with the pure intention of love and service rather than ego, greed, and power.

Abundance is beautiful, and our perception of money, wealth, and prosperity must also be healed. But just like everything else co-opted in service of power and control rather than love and the good of all, money and our perception of it have become distorted. Money is a tool. Currency is meant to flow. Abundance flows when we feel the flow of love and gratitude within, and it is our divine right to receive prosperity and the resources to build a beautiful future.

Poverty consciousness is a mind control virus placed on humanity and the feminine in particular to insert guilt, shame, and unworthiness as it pertains to abundance, wealth, prosperity, and money. 'Money is evil' is a program of the inverted paradigm to keep us separate from our divine worthiness and our divine inheritance that is incredibly resourced and abundant. Manipulation and suppression of the feminine have occurred mainly through money and sex. Money and resources in the hands of heart-centered creators will change the world for the better. We have visions of a more beautiful world and know how to create it.

Honoring the Feminine

The feminine principle recognizes the body as divine. The body is a sacred vessel, which I call the body temple. By exalting Mother Mary's virginity, the church essentially removed her humanity by excising her sexuality, thus creating an unattainable symbol of exalted holiness. None can match her; therefore, we are all lower, bound by the sinful nature of our passions and sexuality.

Mary Magdalene was depicted as a prostitute. She was far from that. She was Yeshua's partner in every sense of the word, an ascended master on his level of spiritual attainment. Women have been offered the dichotomies of the unattainable virgin or desecrated whore with little room in the middle for a path of redemption.

As we combine all these pieces to reveal the grand tapestry of the power of sacred femininity, it's reality-shattering to see the Truth revealed, like a diamond materializing where there was once coal. It's humbling to realize how powerful we are and that we contain so much beautiful potential within.

Surrender is key. The divine feminine asks us to let go of our ego-driven agendas and need for control, to simply surrender and allow divine inspiration to flow, directing us on the course of our soul's truth north.

At first, surrendering feels like the opposite of power, so we resist. We associate 'surrender' with giving up and allowing defeat, but it isn't weak at all. Surrender is a powerful, courageous choice. It indicates the utmost trust in the universe and trust in ourselves—trust that all will work out for our highest good, whether we can see that possibility or not, especially when we cannot.

Surrender to the universe, surrender to the circumstance, surrender even to the masculine energy in the context of a relationship. Surrendering herself to a man might seem counterintuitive to a woman in her power; how could a woman in her power surrender? But a woman in her power can fully let go and trust, surrender herself to the process, to the being she is with, to the whole universe, and ultimately to God. When she feels safe, deep down, she *knows* that all is as it's meant to be and that all will unfold for her highest good because she is held in the arms of God.

When it comes to the power of manifesting, surrendering to the process is the female energy of receiving and becoming a magnet for all that we desire and require. Not grasping, pushing, forcing, or doing, doing, doing. That's the masculine mode of manifesting through outward-focused action.

Surrendering and allowing all to flow is a female principle of magnetism and creation. We put the intention out there firmly, take aligned and intuitively guided action, but then step back and allow the universe to deliver in the most aligned divine timing and in the most aligned divine way. We let go of the how and Trust.

This is utterly counter to the way that many people have been moving through life. In the old paradigm we're shifting out of, the way of making things happen through force has dominated. Manifesting through willpower can work, but eventually, something will fall out on the other side. Energetic self-sabotage or the dropping of the proverbial other shoe will ensue as this kind of manifestation was born of misalignment. Rebalancing and shifting into the feminine allows all to unfold in the right divine timing.

It is from a place of surrender that all flows. The patriarchy had to keep women out of their power to control the population and their ability to create their reality.

The Virgin Queens and Goddesses

Predating Christianity, the goddesses that people worshiped, like Isis, Ishtar, and Diana, were also called Virgins. The word Virgin had a very different meaning then: a woman who was free and sovereign unto herself. Goddesses like Ishtar, Diana, Astarte, and Isis were also called Virgins, not because they were pure and inexperienced but rather because they were strong and independent. Celebrations of fertility were replaced by veneration of the Virgin Mother.

Note: Many of these goddesses were co-opted, corrupted, and even cloned by the dark forces, so the avatars many connect with may have contained reversals and distortions. These distortions and false clones have recently been dismantled as of just prior to publishing, however it will take time for the residue to fully be cleared. I encourage you to exercise the utmost caution and discernment if you endeavor to connect with these energies until you have cleared your own field of ego distortions. However, we can still examine the pure origins of their archetypal energies and representations.

This conception of the word Virgin is entirely different from our modern-day definition. A Virgin was free, independent, autonomous, and untied. As a Virgo born under the sign of the Virgin Goddess, my path has called me to reconnect with the deeper truths of the divine feminine. Elizabeth I, the Virgin Queen herself, was born September 7 under the sign of Virgo, the Virgin Goddess, as was Mother Mary, the Virgin, who was born September 8. What a different nuance this provides to our conception of their power and the role they each played in human history. Mother Mary was an extremely advanced soul in her own right, an initiate prepared for her destined path of immaculate conception from birth through her sacred lineage, and some say the level of spiritual mastery required for immaculate conception as an embodiment of the Sophia marks her as the most advanced soul ever to incarnate on the planet, more powerful even than her son.

Remember, we live in an inverted matrix where so much Truth has been flipped completely upside down. One of the greatest weapons wielded against humanity, both men and women alike, is sexual perversion and distortion. Pitting men against women in the battle of the sexes has entrapped us in the prison of duality. Without control over our own sexuality and integrated embodiment of our lower energy centers, we become much more easily manipulated through energetic hooks, cords, and siphoning. Now is the time to reclaim the Virgin energy held within to embody the sovereign goddess queen and inner king, the high priest and priestess, the witch, the magi, the healer, and the Holy Mother Father's creative essence at our core.

Magic is real, and everybody is a magician. Light magic is internal alchemy; dark magic is external manipulation. Both dark magic and light magic exist, but until recently, these practices have largely been co-opted and demonized to keep all of humanity—men and women alike—out of their power and to perpetuate the state of separation.

This separation occurs within as much as without: the separation of the divine feminine and the divine masculine within and the imbalance that results from exalting the masculine over the feminine rather than empowering us to become integrated whole beings. If we are separated from the source and Truth contained within, we are not in our power.

Returning to that space of wholeness returns us to our center of power. Again, this journey guides us to be in the flow, surrender to the process, and move with the cycles of nature. Honoring our intuition, trusting our judgment, respecting the need to rest and to take a step back as our body and soul call, and letting go of preconceived ideas of forcing, pushing, and achieving and the do-do-do, go, go, go mentality catalyzes our evolution

Release the striving, go with the flow, and surrender. The call of the divine feminine as She rises within is to move in this cyclical manner, reclaim our birthright, and remember who we are at our core: powerful divine creator beings here to heal and liberate the hearts of humanity.

I will close this chapter with a powerful quotation from a book that I read at the time of the original recording: *"We know that by reclaiming our birthright, we will reclaim our power as human beings and be able to stand tall again in the face of those psychopathic mad men who want to steal it from us in their crazed bid to exploit and ultimately cull the human race." ~ Unknown*[159]

Mike drop executed with the Sword of Truth.

Powerful and poignant words that speak to the heart of this massive shift in humanity. It is time to reclaim our birthright indeed. This shift is necessary because it is heartbreakingly evident that the systems in place are failing humanity. They need to break down. We must rebuild a world where resources are not hoarded, mismanaged, polluted, or corrupted. We have an obligation to future generations to reclaim our power and break free from the grips of what, in truth, are psychopathic tendencies of the ruling 'elite.' But in highest Truth, they have no power. Without the heart and soul of humanity, they have nothing. It is time for us to take back what is ours.

It is time to rise and create a New Earth enabled by the rise of the divine feminine, based on the feminine and the masculine returning to integrated wholeness, unity, and harmony. A world that prioritizes harmony, love, beauty, and abundance for all above all else; scarcity is a lie, there is plenty for all. These are the principles we should be living by. These principles will unite and elevate humanity into a new Golden Era of Love and Light.

The Truth is as beautiful as it sounds. We've been living in a world of black and white and shades of gray when, really, our world is one of vibrant technicolor and shimmering radiant iridescence beyond our wildest imagination—colors so vivid they go beyond our current spectrum of limited perception. So throw away all that you've been led to believe about our limited capacity and dream into reality all that your heart desires.

Because your heart's truest desires hold the keys to the kingdom of Heaven itself.

Chapter Seventeen
SOULAR POWER
The Source of Light and Life

"When the mystics descend into the depths of their own being, they find 'in their heart' the image of the sun, they find their own life-force which they call the 'sun' for a legitimate, physical reason, because our source of energy and life actually is the sun. Our physiological life, regarded as an energy process, is entirely solar." ~ Carl Jung

Finally, it is time to address the primary source of it all: the Sun. The source of all light and all life.

What has been swept under the rug in the past several decades is the sun's healing power and activating potential. Without the sun to activate photosynthesis and heat the planet, there would be no life. We know the sun triggers Vitamin D production within the body, one of the powerhouses for our immunity. Beyond this, the sun penetrates Earth and her inhabitants with light codes and frequencies.

So, we must also ask why, in the midst of a global health crisis, we were told to stay inside and hide from the source of light and life itself. We'll review the sun's tangible health benefits and then address the relationship between the sun and Ascension.

Sunshine State of Mind

The sun is the primary vehicle for the light codes penetrating our planet and triggering the rise in frequency. But from the most basic perspective, the sun literally is light, and the more we soak it up, the lighter we feel.

Consider the common daydream when stressed out at work: most imagine a relaxing vacation on the beach, playing in the sun, or hiking up a mountain on a gorgeous sunny day. Most people gravitate toward nature in some form when they're feeling stressed out.

We innately know that the sun is healing, something we have known from time immemorial. In fact, according to a 20-year Swedish study, non-smokers who don't get enough sunlight have a similar life expectancy to smokers in the group with highest sun exposure. Not only did avoiding sunlight shave over two years from their life expectancy, but it also increased their risk for cardiovascular disease.[160]

Yet, with the constant push for sunblock and heightened focus on the risk of too much sun exposure, we've lost touch with the fact that the sun is beneficial for our wellbeing and the catalyst for the chemical reaction we need to create vitamin D, which is crucial for our health. Vitamin D is essential for immunity, and it is vital for bone health as it helps our bodies absorb calcium and phosphorus.

Beyond these baseline benefits, sunshine has also been proven to boost our mood, tangibly generating a sunshine state of mind. I feel so rejuvenated when I go to the beach, free and at ease, happy-go-lucky like a mermaid fairy. Laying on the grass or going for a walk instantly lifts my spirits. It has been proven that sunshine can help mitigate depression and potentially anxiety as well.

Regular sun exposure is, in fact, according to research, linked to benefits on mood-boosting hormone production:

- increased serotonin levels – the happy hormone that is really a neurotransmitter crucial in regulating mood, appetite, and sleep, associated with improved mood and overall mental well-being[161]

- regulation of melatonin production, which regulates sleep-wake cycles and our circadian rhythm[162]

- lower cortisol – the stress hormone – which helps manage stress, maintain healthy immune function, and support overall wellbeing[163]

- increased endorphins, the natural pain-relieving and mood-enhancing hormones that lead to an overall sense of wellbeing and even mild euphoria.[164]

Sunshine is a mood booster, scientifically proven to be so. Seasonal affective disorder (SAD) is a diagnosable condition that recognizes people's moods become more depressed as the light fades into darkness by the end of autumn.[165] It literally abbreviates *sad (just like the Standard American Diet!)*. There is a direct correlation between people who live in northern climates and those who experience less light in the winter and the incidence of SAD.

Without adequate sun exposure, there is a direct association with lower moods and a measured correlation with depression. This is all because people are not getting enough sunlight. Sun lamps were created for those who suffer from depression in dark winter climates. In the winter months in our modern society, daylight hours are typically spent at work, and sometimes, it can be too cold to be outside.

Regarding the health benefits of vitamin D, studies have found that the vast majority of, if not all, cancer patients are low in vitamin D when diagnosed.[166] That was the case for me. While going through my diagnostic process, I also met with holistic practitioners; one of them immediately checked my vitamin D levels, which were very low. So, I was put on a high-dose supplement at once. I took that throughout my diagnostic process and added sunbathing in direct sunlight without sunblock for twenty minutes per day, successfully elevating my vitamin D levels so dramatically that my oncologist asked me to stop taking vitamin D because my levels were so high—and this was early on in treatment.

Finally, it is hypothesized that sunlight exposure may trigger the release of nitric oxide in the skin, which is linked to a host of health benefits. Dr. Richard Weller, a dermatologist and researcher at the University of Edinburgh has conducted extensive research into the effects of nitric oxide, including lowered blood pressure, improved immune function, and enhanced wound healing.[167]

I implemented a lot of protocols and practices on the side to help support my body through treatment. I cleansed my body, ate predominantly plant-based foods, took magic energy elixirs, and saw energy healers. All in all, I handled treatment—600 hours of chemotherapy—so smoothly that the doctors asked me how I was doing so well by the final round. I also responded quickly to treatment. So, I have to believe that everything I did to support my system did help.

With the myriad modalities supporting me, it's impossible to pick apart exactly what did what, but I know everything I did helped, including the vitamin D protocol. According to one study on vitamin D levels in breast cancer, they found that people who were below 24 nanograms per milliliter were nearly three times more likely to have stage three cancer than those with higher levels of vitamin D.[168]

There's a distinction between being low and clinically deficient, but the lower your levels are, the worse the progression of cancer seems to be. Without a doubt, the correlation with vitamin D deficiency exists. Interestingly, they have found the exact same correlations with the Coronavirus—low vitamin D leads to higher susceptibility[169] while supplementing results in quicker recovery.

These findings speak volumes about the importance of both dietary supplementation and that we were born to live in nature. When we entered the world as a species, we lived closely aligned with nature. We evolved in community and in communion with the land and her creatures. Our bodies were designed to be out in the sun, not slaving away in cubicles amidst a concrete jungle. Of course, we must take certain precautions so our skin doesn't become scorched by the midday summer sun, but even those with fair skin can build up a tolerance.

With Irish and Scottish heritage plus ancestry from Norway, Sweden, and Germany, I have trained my fair skin to not require sunblock by going out earlier in the day and later in the day for an hour at a time or so. It depends on the sun's strength and the exact time of day. Pushing 10:30 or 11:00 am, my skin starts to say enough, and I try not to go out before 3:00 pm or even 4:00 pm, depending on the time of year. During midday, I would be cautious beyond ten to twenty minutes. Otherwise, I choose organic sunblock without toxic chemicals—many known carcinogens—that are absorbed directly into the skin with regular sunscreen.

Contrary to popular belief, the sun's ultraviolet or UV light is extremely healing for us. It has been demonized in our society. We are told to slather our skin with sunblock, cover up with clothes, or stay inside because it will give us skin cancer. Yes, skin cancer does happen, but that is not the complete picture. Too much sun can burn the skin if you're not careful about when and how. But skin cancer was barely discussed before the 1950s and rates have risen 2000% since, while we have spent increasing time indoors. In fact, vitamin D deficiency has also skyrocketed 490% in the same time period.

But it seems sunburn is directly correlated to internal toxicity, particularly due to seed oil consumption and—paradoxically—sunblock usage. Higher consumption of seed oil leads to a higher risk of melanoma.[170] Our consumption of polyunsaturated fatty acids (PUFAs) has unwittingly climbed dramatically as it gets hidden inside products, and seed oil acts as a catalyst for lipid peroxidation, which causes damage to skin cells and our DNA, thus driving rates of cancer up. UV rays alone cannot drive damage, so it's the SAD double whammy as the Standard American Diet causes cancer while backwards medical advice drives us indoors, perpetuating SAD in a significant portion of the population.

My increased sun exposure during my diagnostic process coincided with a total body detox. My pale skin developed a golden glow. If we are mindful about going out when the sun is less intense, we will derive massive benefits. Beyond melanin levels, what causes some to burn more in the first place is internal toxicity of the body. The less toxic your body is, the less prone your skin becomes to burns.

Sunlight doesn't just get absorbed by our skin, however. The eyes absorb sunlight through the rods and cones, and sunlight helps regulate the body's circadian cycle by producing melatonin through the eyes through a process called photoreception.[171] Melanin protects the skin from harmful effects of ultraviolet (UV) radiation, and when activated our cells produce more melanin, creating the tanning effect. Sunglasses can block much of this response—and the sun's ascension activation potential—even with sufficient skin exposure without sunblock by potentially tricking the body into believing it's getting less sun than it really is, which may result in sunburn.

We are not meant to look directly at the sun midday. But sunglasses are a different story: by constantly wearing large dark shades according to fashion trends, we block light from entering our eyes. Walking around without constantly wearing sunglasses will help us absorb more of the sun's frequencies. Just as the sun feels warm to us, the sun is streaming in vibrational energies beyond our physical perception. These light frequencies are absorbed more readily and thoroughly when we don't wear sunglasses or sunblock, and these are the frequencies of ascension that facilitate the expansion of consciousness and awakening of our gifts and our power.

I've also been training my light blue eyes to need sunglasses less and less. I used to own numerous pairs of dark-lensed glasses, all of which I lost (many of which were quite nice, oops!). Interestingly, the only pair I have left is a light cream with light gray-brown lenses, which I purchased over 16 years ago in Tokyo! The last pair of designer dark lenses disappeared on my birthday on a European beach. I put them down for a minute to take a photo, and poof, they were gone. And yet, I've managed to hang on to this one pair for over a decade and a half. It was almost as if the universe had been forcing me to remove the shields to allow more light in all along.

Taking this a step further, we get into the subject of sun gazing. This practice has been potent for those who practice regularly. My practice is irregular as I haven't had consistent sunrise or sunset views, but it is worth researching and giving it a whirl, as long as you take precautions only to do it in the windows when it is safe to.

Start with five to ten minutes* at sunrise and give to ten minutes just before sunset because that's when the light is gentlest and UV rays not harmful to our eyes. Midday sun can damage your eyes, so please be cautious and follow appropriate guidance. If done appropriately, sun gazing can amplify the absorption of healing frequencies and help activate our DNA. *Some sungazers do say that due to the sun's shift in frequency to a bright white, sun gazing has become more challenging, so start with just a minute or two just after dawn and as the sun is setting, but if this practice feels too intense for your eyes, even when done in the appropriate windows of time, stick with simply reducing sunglass usage.

It is important to note that the medical community has not conducted formal research on the practice of sun gazing and does not endorse it, reiterating that looking directly at the sun can be damaging to your eyes. While they acknowledge the benefits of sun exposure and the benefits of meditative practices that involve focusing on an object, they advise against the specific practice of sun gazing.[172] They key factor is timing: if attempted, it is only recommended in the first few minutes post-sunrise and last few minutes, as stated above.

Returning to the days before big pharma and the burgeoning medical industry, they sent people to the seaside to heal when sick. Novels from the 1800s and early 1900s would describe the upper class being sent to the seaside or to the Mediterranean to recover when they were struck with illness. It all sounds very quaint and lovely, but this was actually what they did. Upon further research, I found that back in the thirties, they were studying the impact of the sun on over 165 different diseases. Sunlight proved to be abundantly effective in mitigating diseases including tuberculosis and hypertension, diarrhea, personality disorders, and almost every single form of cancer with no further official treatment. Curious how that information was buried, isn't it?

I believe, down to the core of my being, that the sun's powerful energy can heal us. However, the extent of its benefits goes far beyond being skin-deep. The sun does not just improve our immunity but heals our bodies physically.

Light is illuminating Truth and awakening us to the depth of our spiritual potential. As the solar cycle and ascension codes have amplified, we've received increased light codes and energy over the last several years. During this time, intense energies from the sun have been streaming into the planet in an escalating capacity, preparing us for the shift. The intense energies from the sun are light codes streaming in to activate our dormant DNA, helping us to release the densities and catalyze our ascension.

The sun's frequency is ascending, shifting from streaming golden light to luminescent white diamond codes onto our planet. Looking up at the sun or through photos, it is evident that it looks different—much brighter—than it used to.

These heightened frequencies facilitate our work to release traumas and do emotional healing—to quite literally release the baggage that has been weighing us down for lifetimes. Depending on where you are in your healing journey may influence how intensely you experience what's happening energetically. It's a double-edged sword—those conscious of this process tend to have heightened sensitivity and awareness so that we may feel the ascension symptoms more, in one sense. Many of us also transmute for the collective. Yet with ongoing work, even with the increasing frequency from both time and energetic perspectives, the fewer symptoms we may experience and the lighter we feel as we continue on the journey and receive increasing quantities of diamond light codes.

Those who don't feel them are typically just numb and unaware of what is occurring when they experience symptoms and inexplicable illness after illness. Headaches, fatigue, sinus infections, fevers, heaviness, lethargy, digestive issues, mood swings, and so on result from our cells detoxing and our bodies purging all the old, dense, toxic energies. It's forcing us to release the baggage—both physical and energetic.

The journey is unique to us all. We get what our soul needs from it, and our journeys are not linear but cyclical. We may come back around on the spiral where the same issues arise, but we get to rise higher after that subsequent period of healing and integration. There have been multiple times I felt better than ever, and then boom, I was slammed with energies again and brought to my knees, deeper into the shadowy depths than ever before. On the other side, however, I keep rising ever higher, lighter and freer yet more embodied in my wholeness.

DNA Upgrades

Most of us learned in 9th-grade biology that we only use about 2% of our DNA. You may also remember they call the rest a highly scientific term: junk DNA. According to our textbooks, 98% of our DNA is *junk*.

I don't buy it. Many doctors and scientists agree—that 98% of unaccounted-for DNA is not junk. Biology and evolution do not make such massive mistakes. When functioning optimally, the human body is one of the most complex yet efficient technologies in existence, if not the most. The human body is downright miraculous when you consider the precision of the millions of functions that occur to keep us alive without conscious thought. As complex beings, we do not have that extra DNA by accident. This junk theory doesn't make sense: if evolution is as beautiful as it is, we wouldn't have that much random junk sitting around within our DNA or genetic sequence.

So, if not junk, what is all this extra DNA? It is dormant, unactivated DNA. Because it's not activated, we're not using it, meaning we have incredible latent potential that already exists within. We simply need to find the keys to unlock and activate these gifts. As of right now, we are aware that the human body codes for about 23,000 genes. Through this process of Ascension, we are evolving into a different form of being by activating this dormant DNA. We are evolving into Homo Luminous, Human 2.0.

Solar Consciousness and the 144,000

Solar contains the root 'Sol,' which is Spanish for sun. In French it is 'soleil' and in Latin it is 'solis.' Sol sounds very much like *soul*, the light of our innermost being. We are literal beings of light ascending from carbon-based DNA to crystalline or silica-based DNA. We are transitioning into a more crystalline state, which means embodied light. Crystalline consciousness is the state of awareness encompassing the diamond light consciousness into which we are being activated. In a far more literal sense than most may grasp, we will be embodied beings of light.

This transformation doesn't happen overnight, but this is the progression of humanity's evolution. We are stepping into a fuller expression of who we are: light. We are in the process of this collective activation and the Ascension of humanity into a new version of being, a new paradigm, a new era—a new Golden Age.

The sun codes help us do this through light frequencies and vibrations. Remember, everything is energy in the quantum reality in which we exist. Currently, we express 23,000 genes; some say we are evolving into a state where roughly 144,000 genes are activated—this constitutes a massive upgrade.

People within the spiritual community consider the numbers 144 and 144,000 significant, and it is a well-known component of Biblical prophecy, with several verses in Revelations elucidating who the 144,000 are. I do not interpret this number to mean a specific group of 144,000 individuals or 144,000 'pods' of lightworkers that many also refer to as the Chosen Ones. Nor are the Chosen Ones those who follow a specific man-made religion. Instead, it is a latent potential that lies within, a frequency of being that can be activated in souls who choose to walk the path with purity of heart and devotion to anchoring the Truth of Love onto the planet and walking the way of Christ Consciousness as an embodiment of love.

Energetically, 144,000 refers to the activation of our seven primary chakras, with every petal of each chakra open. When you add the petals of the first six chakras, you get 144, and the 1000 petals of the crown chakra act as a multiplier to get 144,000. As we unblock our energy centers and allow our life force energy to rise up the spine, we activate and open each petal, embodying this 144,000 frequency. So, the 144,000 is a frequency of potential fully activated and embodied within the ascending individual.

Additionally, our current limited biology expresses roughly 23,000 genes, with only a fraction expressed at once in the average human. Some in the spiritual community say that our biology itself is also upgrading from 23,000 genes to 144,000. Interestingly, researchers discovered that the number of novel single nucleotide variants (SNVs) stabilizes at about 144,000 new variants per genome. There's that number again, showing up in our biology.

Human potential is vastly expanding if such a massive upgrade and activation of our DNA is also occurring—upgrading from 23,000 to 144,000. Imagine what might be possible for us when our entire spectrum of DNA is activated and those genes come online. Again, this will not happen overnight, but imagine the exciting prospects for self-healing capacities and superhuman capabilities.

Just think of those magical miracle healings that will all be able to access and perform for self and others—all the time. 'You will do greater works than me.' I'm paraphrasing Jesus here, but the Bible verse from John 14:12 says, 'Truly I tell you, the one who believes in me will also do the works that I do. *And he will do even greater works than these*, because

I am going to the Father.' To break the meaning of this down, those who follow the path of Christ by activating Christ consciousness within [the one who believes in me] will activate and access the same power he held [will also do the works that I do] by becoming an open vessel for God source energy [because I am going to the Father].

Astonishingly, he also suggests that if we follow the path he walked, we will be able to access more miraculous superpowers and supernatural capabilities than he had time to display during his time here on Earth [and he will do even greater works than these]. Christ, as the son/ sun, seeded the blueprint for solar/soular consciousness to activate our organic ascension template to fully embody high dimensional capacities in physical form, which is a miraculous achievement. These are advanced esoteric spiritual concepts. However, this is the direction humanity is heading for those on the organic ascension path.

Superpowers will be coming online along with healing abilities. Clairvoyance, clairaudience, claircognizance, clairsentience, mediumship, and telepathy will become common. Many individuals already have these capacities activated, and many find these gifts are now coming online or strengthening. Teleportation, bilocation, and so-called miracles like walking on water will eventually become possible, and we will activate our light bodies and transition from carbon to crystalline.

Our capacity is far greater than you or I can even imagine right now, but what is clear is that we are activating higher levels of DNA. The sun also activates the pineal gland, which helps us stay connected to source energy. This tiny gland is vital to our spiritual growth—it is our third eye, our inner knowing, our point of clear perception. It is also God's seal of protection against the dark forces trying to control and entrap the soul of humanity. Meditation and sun gazing help activate the pineal gland, facilitating the activation of our spiritual gifts.

The sun is streaming in very high-level frequencies: many in the 'New Age' talk about ascending into 5D (I believed this was the case myself for a while), but again, the sun is streaming in frequencies up to 12D. These are incredibly high-level frequencies and a massive jump in frequency and consciousness that we are embarking on, so naturally, we are being shaken to our core. Again, the different dimensions are not different places but rather different states of consciousness where our perception of time changes and our world experience expands into peace, love, joy, and bliss as our modus operandi.

Humanity has a beautiful opportunity to soak in all this healing and activating light because the sun is beaming in many powerful frequencies. From a soul perspective, it is a powerful time to be incarnated on Earth, upgrading and expanding our consciousness, and elevating our frequency. What a miracle it is to be alive in this supernatural human body.

Light Illuminates Truth

Why do you think the pandemic powers had us go inside? Why do you think they keep telling us to put on chemical-laden sunscreen? Why do you think sunglasses are made to be such a sexy accessory? Don't get me wrong, as I've shared, my eyes and skin used to be sensitive, and I love the look of my oversized sunglasses, but we don't have to wear them all the time. Just take them off once in a while.

We are here to anchor in the crystalline light that carries codes of divinity. Anchor the light by staying grounded in yourself, connected to Earth and your body. Take electrolytes, and put your feet directly on the ground. If you're in a cold climate, sun gazing will be extremely helpful because you can still practice sun gazing at dusk and dawn regardless of temperatures. Winter light can also be less harsh, so it could be an excellent time to begin, depending on where you are in the world and when you may happen upon these words.

Take off your sunglasses to begin allowing more light in. In winter, bundle up and go outside for a walk in the snow. Enjoy nature as much as possible, regardless of climate or time of year. Make fresh air and sunshine a priority. As we have seen with SAD, it is imperative to get sunshine.

Certain northern regions, such as Canada, Scotland, and the Scandinavian countries, experience extremes with light. I have been to Scotland in both extremes. I was there in June, around the longest day of the year, and it was light all day long. Meanwhile, I was there one winter for New Year's just after the Winter Solstice, the longest night of the year, and it was light for just a few hours. Copenhagen in December was the same, while the sun barely set in the Oslo summer.

Receiving natural sunlight in the darkness of winter can be a precious blessing in northern climates. Anything we can do helps. Sun gazing could be extremely helpful for people who live in those extremes. Sun lamps certainly help, but the real deal carries the codes.

After cancer treatment, I struggled more than usual in winter. I had always lived in northern climates, likely contributing to my low vitamin D levels. Finally, on an intuitive whim, in the early spring of 2018, I decided to move down to Miami. Deep down, I knew it would be healing for me.

After years of escaping the dreariness of winter for blessed but brief glimmers of the Florida sunshine, I knew I needed more beach and sun. My soul was clearly pulling me south, and I immediately felt at home. I used all the silly hashtags on my Instagram, like #lifeisbetteratthebeach, #sunshinestateofmind, and #vitaminsea. But as we have seen, sunshine is genuinely powerfully healing, and we've been increasingly detached and disconnected from that knowledge. Life by the sea was the medicine my soul needed.

I feel very blessed that I could make that transition with ease, but I also know that I manifested it, and I was called down to Miami, followed by Tulum, for my healing, to pick up soul codes and anchor in the light in different parts of the globe, and to initiate the next phase of my awakening journey which took me on pilgrimage to sacred sites around the world. Many of us are called to particular places in the world for higher soul purposes that are often beyond our conscious awareness. My whole life has been guided in this way, and only more recently have I become attuned to these understandings of the soul calling.

To recap this dense chapter, the core message is to relax and, quite literally, soak up the sun. This shift is about moving from doing into being. It's about honoring our cycles and rhythms. It's about being gentle with ourselves and observing our need to rest and relax. It's about soaking up the sun and allowing ourselves to simply Be.

As we ascend into light beings, we are called to fully receive the light codes and higher vibrational frequencies to embody the light and shine ever more brightly. We are here to create Heaven on Earth; that is our job, above all else.

Chapter Eighteen
Creating Heaven on Earth
The Rainbow Pillar of Light

"Heaven on Earth is a choice you must make, not a place you must find." ~ Wayne Dyer

We are in the midst of an unprecedented time in history, at the brink of the dawn of a new golden age, one in which we have the capacity to finally create Heaven on Earth, a veritable Garden of Eden without the fall.

The matrix of illusion is breaking, and the light of Truth is shining through the cracks. From one of the darkest times in human history, a Golden Dawn is rising as Gaia's song is awakening our crystal hearts and calling us to live in alignment with cosmic law.

New Earth: Heaven on Earth

'New Earth' is a term bandied about by many in the spiritual community, but the term itself can be traced back to—once again—the Bible. Found in the book of Revelation (21:1), Isaiah (65:17 & 66:22), and 2 Peter (3:13), it is used to elucidate the ultimate state of a redeemed humanity.

It seems author C.S. Lewis also intimated the possibility of a Heaven on Earth in his works. In *The Problem of Pain*, he cited Romans 8:18, which says, *'The sufferings of this present time are not worthy to be compared with the glory which shall be revealed in us.'* [KJV] Lewis says, *'A book on suffering which says nothing of Heaven, is leaving out almost the whole of one side of the account. Scripture and tradition habitually put the joys of Heaven into the scale against the sufferings of Earth, and no solution of the problem of pain which does not do so can be called a Christian one.'* What he suggests is religion provides little tangible solution to the pain and suffering of our world, much less a means to access or create Heaven.

We are building a future post-resurrection Heaven, which the Bible itself refers to as New Earth. Resurrection is likewise an internal process. We are resurrecting our light bodies by activating our dormant DNA and clearing the distortion that has suppressed our energy bodies. We are resurrecting the life force within, enabling the redemption of our bodies to become vessels of the divine. Christ's resurrection body is the prototype for ours. As a way-shower, he seeded the blueprint for Christ Consciousness onto the planet so that we could walk in his footsteps to resurrect Heaven within to create Heaven without here on Earth. As within, so without.

There is no tangible difference between Heaven on Earth and the New Earth as they both refer to a reality of love and expanded consciousness. Both are contingent upon ascension into a higher vibrational frequency, individually and collectively, of the Earth herself.

Creating a New Earth occurs by anchoring the frequencies of Heaven onto Earth through our Body Temples as the pillars of light we are here to embody: Light, Love, Truth, Joy, Harmony, Wholeness, Bliss, and Abundance. As above, so below, we anchor the codes of paradise through our pillar of light, the rainbow body, the rainbow bridge guiding us home to a world of love.

Tibetan teachings discuss the rainbow body: *'Today you have the chance to walk the rainbow bridge. The bridge of ascension. The bridge of awakening. The bridge between the dimensions.'* The rainbow body is a state of transformation and transcendence where after death a person's body dissolves into pure light attained through years of devoted spiritual practice. It is complete liberation from suffering, union with the divine, and the attainment of the highest level of enlightened consciousness. When prana—universal life force energy—and kundalini combine and intertwine, a powerful multidimensional experience where the physical and spiritual worlds merge blossoms within our being.

Activating the rainbow body can occur through devoted spiritual practice and clearing out the energy centers—our chakras, which are associated with the seven colors of the rainbow. Purification of the body occurs by working with the different elements within: earth, fire, water, air, and ether. Full activation of the rainbow body is a highly advanced practice and most will not come close to attaining the full rainbow body. However it represents the potential available to us as we follow the golden path to the Emerald City, residing at the heart of our rainbow body.

Is there a connection between the resurrection of Jesus Christ and the phenomenon of the Rainbow body? There is scholarly debate surrounding this, however texts detailing his missing years suggest he studied with the masters of the East in India and Tibet, in the mystery schools of Egypt, and with Druid masters in Western Europe. Years of dedicated spiritual study enabled him to anchor the blueprint of Christ Consciousness into the planet and reveal the path of Christ.

In Christ-like thinking, we must know Christ: not the Jesus from the Bible, whom some even theorize is an egregore (a non-physical entity that arises from collective thought and emotion), not Yeshua, the man who embodied the Christ light and anchored the blueprint onto the planet, but the frequency of Christ consciousness that he embodied.

Ascension is, to put it simply, the internal process of spiraling upward, emotionally, energetically, vibrationally, through our thoughts, mindset, and feelings. These frequency states become more elevated and expansive. It is crucial to reiterate that ascension is a process that happens within our body temple, the vehicle or vessel for our soul. Ascension is not about leaving the physical body or this physical plane. Embodied Ascension, Incension, or Descension are terms people use to help elucidate the process humanity is being called to undergo—coming deeper into the body, into the heart, and uncovering our connection with God Source within.

You are likely familiar with the notion of Ascension from the Bible: Jesus' (Yeshua's) Ascension. He did ascend into his light body. But we must release the trauma-bond connotation created by the preceding crucifixion. Without getting caught up in the religious context or connotation, it's time to align our understanding of Ascension with broader spiritual science.

Religion and spirituality are different. While religion relies on dogma and doctrine created in the paradigm of fear-based separation, spirituality is a broader sense of connection with something greater than ourselves, and through inner gnosis coming to know our innate divinity that pervades all creation – God beyond religion.

It Begins Within

Ascension begins with awareness of our thoughts, emotions, feelings, being and essence, and the Truth of the world around us and how it operates. It is an awareness of our connection to ourselves, each other, Mother Nature, Source, and the Cosmos. Awakening is waking up to the Truth of who we are and our place in the Universe.

Awakening is a precursor to—or symptom of—the process of Ascension into a higher vibrational state of love, joy, ease, freedom, bliss, and abundance. Releasing the lower-density emotions and frequencies allows us to experience the world through this beautiful state of expansion, feeling lighter and freer, able to fully express our authentic joy and just Be.

Arriving at this state of Being takes deep inner work and is something we must choose for ourselves. Again, it's a choice. But the reward is the pot of gold at the end of the rainbow, the treasure chest, the holy grail. The 'Chosen Ones' are the ones who recognize the mission they came here to serve and who choose to allow the divinity within them to blossom. God's Chosen Ones are here to be the way-showers and create Heaven on Earth.

Heaven on Earth is a state where all beings operates at a higher vibrational frequency, and love, freedom, harmony, and bliss are the norm. We anchor this frequency by becoming the Rainbow Pillar of Light—our body temples purified and energy centers open and flowing to allow divine love to pour through the chalices of our hearts.

Harmony, above all, is key. Harmony, of course, emanates from the self: as within, so without. There's no critical self-talk, beating yourself up, self-punishment, self-judgment, blame, or shame. And when you're in harmony with yourself by accepting all aspects of yourself, you are in complete alignment with the totality of your being, mind, body, and soul. When our cells are in a state of harmony and coherence, our physical body experiences vibrant well-being, our energy field expands, and we radiate a powerful frequency of love that is healing to all those around us.

Creating Heaven on Earth begins with generating these vibrational alignments within—a state of Heaven within. Imagine living in harmony on all levels of your being and with others around you, animals, nature, and the Earth. Everything flows with ease and peace, and people don't fight for resources because everyone operates from an eternal state of abundance. Cooperation is the rule, and everything flows from the divine—that feminine principle of ease and flow guiding us to follow nature's rhythms and cycles, pay attention, tune in, and allow the heart to lead.

Tuning in with our feminine nature, trusting our intuition, coming into alignment with all aspects of ourselves, and being and creating in harmony on all levels—this is what carries us into the new era, this new golden age of light and love based on the notion of living in higher states of Being.

Ultimately, it's all about returning to love, the heart center, and heart wisdom because heart wisdom is the highest wisdom that exists.

Ascension is a journey of descending deep into the heart and liberating it from the shackles of fear and pain. It is a process of looking within and doing the inner work. It is a journey of connecting within, without, above, and below, with all the elements, realms, aspects, and dimensions. Fundamentally, we all return to this idea, this internal wisdom, and this sense of awareness that everything is connected. We are all one; nothing is separate.

The illusion we've been living in is one of separation. We are here to reclaim the Truth of love and unity through integrating the polarities. We are here to release the densities that keep us down so we can ascend into higher vibrational frequencies.

We've discussed many tools to help us ground down and anchor in these higher-frequency states. These include meditation, earthing, and purifying our physical vessels through detoxing, breathwork, inner child healing, frequency healing, and diving into shadow work.

Release, integrate, ascend. Release, integrate, ascend. Up the spiral we go.

Again, it's always a choice. Nobody will make you do this, but if living in peace, joy, and abundance and accessing Heaven on Earth holds any appeal, doing the inner work by facing the distortions head-on, surrendering to the proverbial dark night of the soul so you can release all that you are not—the ego identities that limit your soul's expansion—is essential. It involves looking at the darker aspects of self that we've suppressed and repressed to bring them into the light to transmute, integrate, and release them.

It's not an easy process, but it's a very rewarding one because, ultimately, the pot of gold we're all seeking lies within. Once we release all of the densities and the layers of trauma, negativity, and toxicity that often aren't even ours, the limiting beliefs and ancestral traumas that we've inherited, once we release them and integrate the wisdom, we can access levels of joy, love, freedom, and abundance we never would have thought possible.

Forgiveness is vital to the process: forgiveness of yourself, your parents, ancestors, and those who hurt and betrayed you. Forgiveness is not about making them right. It's about releasing yourself from the trap of anger and resentment because this burden weighs down so many. Feelings of unworthiness and not good enough are some of the heaviest burdens we universally carry. Guilt and shame are two of the lowest frequencies, as well as feelings of hopelessness and despair, which mire us in disempowerment. Resentment, anger, and judgment keep us out of our true power.

Once we start to work through that muck, we begin to release the heaviness. We start to feel lighter and lighter as we release the density of the trauma and pain, which often manifests as physical weight loss as well. This release happened to me, as my weight suddenly stabilized with ease when I reached a certain point in my journey. Body became easy when I allowed myself to release struggle and experience ease, anchoring the belief that 'Body is Easy.' Even as the journey has continued to spiral me deeper into myself, my physical vessel maintains with absolute ease because this belief that the body is easy has fully anchored into my cells.

While the process might be fraught with emotional turmoil and tears, it's a beautiful journey of release and integration. You look lighter and brighter and begin to radiate with the essence of eternal youth. I call it the energetic glow-up. It's a beautiful process of unraveling and blossoming to remember that you are worthy of a wonderful life.

It's challenging work, but we are all incarnated here to do it. We were chosen to be here at this time to anchor in the frequencies of Christ consciousness and create Heaven on Earth. We are here to be the pillar of light connecting above and below, the higher realms of the divine, Father Sun with Mother Earth. Because you are here, living on Earth in these prophesied 'end of times,' you are a powerful being.

It is an ongoing process, but it has definitively begun. Many estimate that our window to choose the path of ascension and the path of the light remains open through 2032, through which point our world will be mired in chaos and turmoil. While I believe these timelines are constantly shifting based on our collective frequency, now is a critical window for our souls to make a choice. Why delay the inevitable?

On December 21st, 2020, we experienced a significant influx of light energies from the Sun on the day of the Great Conjunction between Jupiter and Saturn, which coincided with the Winter Solstice. This conjunction initially inspired me to share the original Light in the Darkness live series—to help spread the message of the light. Ever since, light codes have only amplified and increased and the awakening has rippled out through the collective consciousness. We can anchor the light within ourselves and embed it into physical planet Earth for the collective. Together, we can co-create Heaven on Earth. United we stand, and through unity consciousness, we build a more beautiful future.

Anchor in those beautiful ideas of what Heaven on Earth looks like to you. Consider your vision of what a pristine, beautiful Garden of Eden would look like to you. Crystal clear waters, pure air, vibrant flowers, majestic trees, flowing rivers, and diamond waterfalls, abundant life of all forms. Societies built on a foundation of harmony, peace, and true freedom and justice for all, where love, Truth, and trust are the foundation for all relationships, systems, and structures. Beauty all around, natural abundance, whatever that looks like to you, call it in, pull it down, anchor that vision into the chalice of your heart and into the Earth's crystalline diamond grid.

We're all being called to step up and do this work. We're all being called to become our biggest, brightest, most brilliant selves and to do what it takes to make that vision a reality.

Ascension is a path that we choose. It's a path of returning love. It's a path of returning to the heart center. It calls us to establish an intimate connection with higher consciousness, with the divine. It guides us into total alignment, mind, body, and soul.

It is a journey of coming into alignment in every layer of our existence, in every capacity, in every dimension, in every manner possible. We eventually arrive at a state of pure divine alignment. And from that alignment comes that sense of ease. And from that space of freedom and flow comes the ability to manifest instantly and with joy. Easy, blissful instant manifestation energy is what we are entering here in Heaven on Earth.

Five-D is the vibrational frequency most commonly associated with the dimension of Heaven on Earth. It delineates the frequency of consciousness of a dimension where we live from a pure heart-centered space. It's simply about returning to your heart center and living in this space of love.

Living with an open heart: simple enough in concept, yet not necessarily easy for us mind-based trauma-burdened humans to achieve.

However, some also say that timelines have shifted (they have constantly been shifting as we go through this ascension process because we are continually changing our realities—this is the nature of the quantum realm in which we live) and that we are passing 5D and ascending right into 12D, or an even higher level of consciousness and embodied frequency.

Remember, our minds are still operating in limitation, so these notions go beyond what we can mentally grasp. It requires a great deal of surrender and trust. The only thing we need to concern ourselves with is to keep choosing love in each moment. Even when we're in the midst of a tidal wave of shadows and heavy emotions, we process and honor the feelings, and then the sea calms, and we return to love. Hold love and compassion for yourself as best you can when passing through those dark moments.

The Rose of Your Heart

I always envision the heart center blossoming like a beautiful flower emerging from the soil into its fullest, most magical expression of beauty, life, and abundance. For me, it's a Rose. Many perceive it to be a lotus, as the chakras are often depicted as such.

Imagine your heart center blossoming open and seeing a beautiful light shining from within—a diamond shining brilliantly through its infinite iridescent facets. The chalice of your heart opens, aligned and attuned with the highest frequencies for the good of your soul and the good of all. From that space, manifestation becomes easy and even instant, and you're in the diving flow of abundance, receiving the nectar of the divine because your heart's desires are ultimately in service to All.

Whatever you call in or envision to create from that space of deep heart alignment is for the highest good of all. The universe has your back when you surrender to the divine and allow your deepest desires to pour forth so manifestation flows with ease and grace.

Awakening and ascension is a journey of remembering the Truth of who you are. Then, continue to do the work, meditate, sit with yourself, and figure out your blocks. What are your limiting beliefs? What are you holding onto and carrying that is no longer serving you? Then, drop and release it. It's not a snap of the fingers, and it's done kind of process, and can be hard as heck. But it does get easier.

The easier it gets, the easier it gets. The better it gets, the better it gets.

Ongoing journaling as a point of reflection on what triggers you, what lights you up, what feels off, and what feels good helps us reflect and find clarity on all of the above. Getting really honest with yourself and, crucially, getting curious about your path and what is possible facilitates transformation.

Ask yourself from a space of non-judgmental curiosity: Why is that trigger coming up for you? What is that really about? What is the root of it? And is that true? Does it have to be true? Then, replace these notions with ideas that support your growth, rewiring your thoughts to align with the frequency of your higher Truth, your higher self, possibility, and beauty. When you are in tune with that, then everything will flow. Everything will manifest when you live in this heart-centered space of love, beauty, bliss, joy, and service for the highest good. With your heart blossomed wide open, you know that you are one with all. That is the space from which we create Heaven on Earth.

Choose your higher timeline now and keep doing the work, one step at a time, and you will be able to take those steps over the rainbow bridge and find the pot of gold that exists. It exists for all of us who choose it—all who decide to show up and do the work.

Lightworkers have been assisting the planet's grid, clearing density and anchoring in the light. The old grid has been compressed and refined into pure crystalline diamond light that refracts its rainbow brilliance through the grid of Gaia. We are not alone in this process; many have stepped up to shine their light and guide us in the right direction. Keep going, keep choosing, and don't give up on yourself because it is not an easy process, but it is so rewarding.

Life will eventually bring us to this decision point, whether we are ready or not. I was forced into it with a cancer diagnosis. I didn't fully see the bigger picture regarding my specific path and role, but something inside kept pulling me and saying, *You're not done yet. Keep going, keep going. You still have more work to do.* In the past several years, it has all come together, full circle, up the spiral. And I know the journey ahead holds much more magic as I continue. Up the spiral we go as we spiral closer and closer to our center point, creating the pillar of light within.

This process is not linear but journeys us all on an upward spiral. We typically have to come back to the same lessons over and over, but each time, we've gained a little bit more wisdom and a little bit more insight, bringing us higher up the spiral.

No matter what, freedom is possible and available to us all. No matter where you have been or what depths of darkness you may currently be experiencing, liberation is possible. Open your heart to possibility, higher aspects of yourself, and the idea that you are a divine, beautiful being. We are all connected and attuned to these higher frequencies of expansion; we only have to open and allow them to flow through to reveal the pot of gold waiting within.

Reality is Expanding

Understand that there is so much more to our existence than we have been led to believe. We are connected to great universal intelligence. We are all one, and we are all divine sparks of creative consciousness. We're not necessarily all God, but all sparks of God Source

Divine Creator Intelligence. That's the Truth with a capital T, as I see it—a beautiful, empowering, liberating truth.

In simple terms, the process of illumination is one of reclaiming your power and stepping into your fullest potential. It is a process of returning to the Truth of who you are and living that fullest, brightest expression of yourself.

Tune into your heart, go within, and sit with your inner Truth. Your heart knows what is best for you. If you quiet the mind and tune in—which is not easy because we've been conditioned out of that connection—the more you Trust. The more we tune in and listen to the niggles, and the more we follow them, the more we build inner trust.

Start with the small things, and then slowly, bit by bit, your life will become more and more aligned. Life will expand in ways you never even thought possible. Eventually, it becomes beautiful and fun, even magical and filled with everyday miracles. It isn't always easy, but it is a fun and liberating journey of self-discovery as you remember the Truth of who you are.

I encourage you to sit and meditate this week and envision your most brilliant vision of Heaven on Earth and then to anchor this vision down into your current reality as a legitimate possibility, not as a place that's separate from where we are here, but as a place that we are living in now. Anchor this beautiful vision of infinite possibility into the Earth through your clear channel of divine beauty, bliss, and light, through your heart, all the way down through the middle of the Earth into her core so that we are drawing up her Heart codes and anchoring divine light codes that will help to release us from the shackles of darkness and fear into the heart of our home: Planet Earth.

Remember that this is all about Being the light—becoming our most illuminated, brilliant selves. To become the beautiful light beings we are, connect with the sun, receive the golden and white diamond rainbow light codes, and anchor in these powerful frequencies of light, pulling them down from above through your vessel as a pure conduit of divine light. Anchor the light into the center of the Earth and envision the most beautiful expression of Heaven and Earth that you can imagine blossoming from within.

Additional Resources:

You can find my Free Higher Self New Earth Frequency Meditation on my website and inside my community.

Chapter Nineteen
We Are Not Alone
The Diamond Web of Connection

"In the deepest sense the search for extraterrestrial intelligence is a search for ourselves." ~ Carl Sagan

"In very different ways, the possibility that the universe is teeming with life, and the opposite possibility that we are totally alone, are equally exciting. Either way, the urge to know more about the universe seems to me irresistible, and I cannot imagine that anybody of truly poetic sensibility could disagree." ~ Richard Dawkins

As tumultuous, confusing, and isolating as these times are, we must remember that we are not alone. So many have felt isolated and alone physically, psychologically, and emotionally. Forced into isolation by Covid mandates, many experience ongoing repercussions of being lonely and disconnected. Social distancing is social isolation, and it has had lasting impacts on our mental health and emotional wellbeing, as well as on many people's social circles.

The human species evolved in community. From birth onward, we need human connection to survive. A few decades ago, Romania inadvertently created a disturbing social experiment with devastating consequences. Thousands of institutionalized abandoned orphans were deprived of human contact, and for those that did receive adequate nutrition (many did not) simply lacking a caregiver had the potential to wreak a lifetime of havoc on mental and physical health, with attenuating social and emotional consequences.[173]

At the most fundamental level, we need connection and community. That is not just how we operate socially, emotionally, and psychologically but also how we thrive.

Naturally, everyone has different degrees of need and desire for social interaction. Some of us are introverts, others are extroverts, and others are extroverted introverts, like myself. While some people prefer to be alone more often than others, fundamentally, we are wired for connection. From infancy, we are wired to connect with our caregivers to learn and grow.[174] Mirror neurons in our brains help us learn by watching another perform a task and firing when somebody *else* does something: our neurons mirror the actions of others.[175] The Hebbian theory that explains associative learning is often summarized by the phrase, 'Neurons that fire together, wire together.'[176] This phenomenon is the basis for neuroplasticity and learning, which occurs powerfully when a task is modeled and we then repeat it. It could even be argued that this phenomenon shaped human civilization and cultural evolution.

Neuroscience has proven that we are indisputably neurologically wired to learn through interaction. Yet recently, authorities attempted to separate us from one another entirely. Isolation engenders a lack of trust, further shutting us down and closing us off to connection. The consequences of closing schools and daycare and keeping fragile young children in isolation during their formative years is already becoming apparent.[177] Repercussions on mental health and learning have been swept under the rug by the decision-makers; as a society it is time we face the music and take concerted action to mitigate long-term outcomes for vulnerable populations.

On the flip side, the physical isolation encouraged many to turn inward, which for those with adequate awareness and tools was a blessing. Many found community online. For some, the pandemic became an opportunity to shift and transform. For others, the fear and isolation took over, shut them down, and had long-lasting effects on their overall wellbeing. The divergence in response to the pandemic was evident to many: it created a poignant choice of fear versus love. No matter what one's choice was before, there is always an opportunity to choose again.

Find Your Tribe

This time of ongoing upheaval has caused many people to recognize what is no longer in alignment with them, including people and relationships. If you feel like you don't relate to particular people in your life anymore, find community with others on a similar path, cultivating a vibration like yours. Your community is out there. Your tribe is out there.

One of the beauties of social media is the ability to connect with others thousands of miles away. While everything is constantly shifting, and in some ways, it is getting harder and harder to connect, the people you align with exist. Isolation is a common part of the journey of spiritual awakening and dark night of the soul, a phase that both calls us inward and acts as a form of spiritual protection from distractions that might cause us to stray from the path.

Professional support is also advisable, whether that's a therapist, coach, mentor, or guide. People are there for you in some capacity, and we all need support at some point on the journey. Higher divine guidance also reminds us that we are never alone. We all need connection and community. At a certain point, we need to both stay open to new connections and make the effort to put ourselves out there and connect.

In looking at the social factors related to illness and recovery, research has found through studying cancer patients and their level of connection and support related to loneliness and isolation, those with more social support had improved survival rates, while the inverse was also true.[178] Those with less support, who were more isolated and alone and didn't feel like they could connect or talk to people about what they were going through, had a much more grim outcome. Loneliness and isolation are significant factors in depression.[179] People tend to self-isolate when they are struggling. This pattern is something to examine for ourselves: when we feel low, do we tend to isolate ourselves or reach out for support? I know I have historically been an isolator.

As an introvert, empath, HSP (highly sensitive person), projector in human design, and stereotypical Virgo hermit with a Taurus moon, I need alone time to hermit in my cave. When I'm not out traveling or exploring, I am a homebody and need to disconnect. It's a delicate balance between needing alone time to regenerate, isolating because you're feeling low, and allowing yourself the time to recuperate your energy in times of stress.

We must be mindful of whether we are isolating or cocooning too much. A common trauma response of not having your needs fully met as a child is hyper-independence, over self-reliance, and not feeling safe asking for help.[180]

If you know somebody who may be struggling, check in on them and see how they're doing. They may need that—to have somebody reach out to them. Many people are not in a space where they feel comfortable reaching out and asking for support. Simply ask how they're doing, offer your ear, listen with compassion, and hold the space. The number one thing people crave is to be heard and feel understood. Listening with compassion and holding the space without trying to fix anything can be powerfully healing.

The Hive of Connection

Community and connection are critical, and the web of connection goes beyond what we might imagine. When we come together to raise our frequencies, it helps to raise the collective vibration. This is why mass meditations are powerful. When a group comes together to meditate and raises their frequency all at once, it can tangibly impact the frequency of the planet. Mass global meditations were held in the 1980s, after which they studied the energetic frequency of the planet and measured crime rates.

Astonishingly (or perhaps 'but of course' now with these understandings of vibrational frequency and quantum connection), they significantly reduced crime rates and generated prolonged measures of peace. One such mass meditation reduced the world's crime rate for an extended period. It was statistically significant, and subsequent studies have found similar results extending to war and terrorism.[181]

Vibration is very real and potent. The more we come together and raise our energy and frequency, lift each other, support each other, and consciously create these higher vibrational states, the more significant the strides we will make toward healing the collective shadows and raising the collective consciousness as it ripples out through the quantum.

Collectively, we are stronger together. United we stand, divided we fall.

If we collectively focus on a future of harmony and abundance, if we collectively focus on a timeline that averts total devastation and destruction, the potential of that timeline occurring is much greater.

There is much more to our world than meets the eye. Interdimensional beings—angels, elementals, ancestors, multidimensional aspects of self and other, and what some might call aliens—are all around us, supporting and guiding humanity beyond our conscious perception. They tend to stay in the background until we ask them to show up because we live on a planet of free will, and they cannot interfere with our process and will only make themselves known once we are ready. They may show up in subtle ways, such as through physical signs, as I mention below, or through energetic means, such as ringing ears. Stay open and trust.

Connection with your higher consciousness, guides, and angels can provide powerful solace, support, healing, and guidance. We all have higher guidance there to support us. They are always there, but we must call on them and request support. In fact, they are *waiting* for us to ask for support.

Our interdimensional guides and protectors—our angels, ancestors, ascended masters, and our own higher selves—very much want humanity to ascend and succeed in this collective Ascension process. They are trying to connect more, making their presence known through signs and synchronicities. But in a world of free will, they cannot benevolently interfere without our request, approval, or openness.

Ask, and you shall receive. *(And be sure to call in protection and for only beings of the highest light and love to be able to come forward.)*

Trust the signs. Follow the feel good, and the feathers.

When you see synchronicities such as repeated numbers—especially 444, which I often see—that is a sign that you are being guided, protected, and supported and can call on that support. Today, I found a white feather, the 14th feather this week (!), and a huge painted gold feather in a shop. I don't believe in coincidences at this point in my journey, and the synchronicities and guidance eventually become impossible to ignore.

Of course, you don't need to see numbers or signs to feel connected to your guides or higher self. You can simply connect. Ask. Get quiet, raise your vibration through meditation, and ask for protection. Release any fears and put a golden pillar of light around you for protection to prevent any unwanted or deceptive energies from trying to enter the space. Call in clearing and protection from Holy Mother Father God and the angels assigned to you by God,[182] then open your channel for receiving. Open your crown chakra and your heart to receive.

Call on your angels and guides for support and guidance, and they will show up for you. Getting comfortable and trusting the process and what comes through will take some practice for most. Like exercising your muscles, it takes practice and consistency to strengthen your connection. Tune in, get quiet, and connect. Breathe. Be still. Surrender. Trust. The guidance is there. They are always there and waiting for you to call on them.

We are aspects of them. They are aspects of us. We are all connected.

You Are The Savior You Have Been Seeking

Unity consciousness is the destination of this grand journey. Living in this paradigm of separation and hierarchy, we have placed experts, authorities, teachers, healers, and gurus on pedestals and perceived them to be more capable and powerful. That is inherently disempowering and puts us in a state of victimhood. Many in such positions have abused their power. This is the lesson of the time: to take our power back and source it from within.

When we look outside of ourselves seeking a savior, we are put in a lower vibrational state, keeping us in disempowerment. We must recognize that we are all one, all connected to the same universal God Source consciousness because we are all divine. We are all sparks of the divine, having the full spectrum of embodied experience through us, and this experience of separation is a journey to return us to the unity of love.

Religious association with God as a male figure in the sky so many of us are familiar with has polarized and disconnected so many of us from Source because we don't feel connected to that narrow and distorted understanding of a higher power.

Release any preconceived notions that you may have of God or interdimensional beings, who some might call angels or aliens. Much of our collective perception of such beings is distorted. Stay open to who your guides might be. Stay open to the possibility that, at your core, your soul is equal to them. Don't place them on a pedestal because if you make them higher than you, that will potentially block the connection or create room for distorted entities to pose as angels or ascended masters, offering kernels of truth through layers of distortion and lower frequency.

Discernment is of the utmost importance as we open our hearts and minds to other realms. There are energies that seek to interfere and even hijack our connection. This is why clearing our field and calling in protection is essential as we begin to open up. The more we clear our energetic field of distorted perceptions and wounds, the more we hone our capacity to read energy and discern what is truly of the light. False light clones cannot come in and pose as an ascended master, angel, or interdimensional being when we have clarity of perception and protection in place. These distorted energies are falling away, but their residue still remains.

Yeshua never wanted to be seen as a savior. He came to be a way-shower, teaching us how to become like him. Religion distorted the original esoteric teachings to control the masses through the displacement of power, seeking a savior, and redemption through external validation.

Go within, raise your frequency and vibration, and recognize the divinity within. It is safest to connect through the pure frequency of Holy Mother Father God and hone your discernment before connecting with other beings.

Higher dimensional beings like the Andromedans, Plediains, Sirians, Lyrans, and Arcturians, for example, have been making their presence known to more and more people on the planet. These higher-dimensional beings may show up as light or geometric patterns and frequencies. Many of us are starseeds with origins and past lives on these planets. Our souls are connected to multiple places in multiple dimensions. Think of them as soul family here to support you in different ways.

Angels, fairies, goddesses, and other mythical beings are also here to connect and guide us. Before connecting, always ask for protection from Mother Father God and the angels assigned to you by God, and only allow in energies of the highest light and love. Whoever comes through for you, allow it, as long as they are of the light. You can ask, and when you are tuned in, you will know—again, honing your intuition is key. Connect with your Higher Self first and strengthen that connection. Don't try to force it. Don't get discouraged if you don't feel a direct connection. Keep doing the inner work and meditation. If you want to hone this connection, you can receive formal guidance on connecting to the Akashic records, as I have done.[183]

Again, they might not make themselves seen visually, much less in human form. You may receive messages and knowings, or they may first make themselves known to you through your environment. I receive many signs, synchronicities, sensations, and knowings myself. Sound frequencies, lights, and sacred geometry patterns may also come into your field. They will communicate differently depending on your soul gifts and how activated and attuned you are.

Stay open to the multitude of ways they may show up. You can ask specific questions, but I also like to ask open questions such as 'What is in my highest good to know right now? What message do you have for me? What do I need to know today?' Often, they have a specific message that needs to come through that we wouldn't even think of asking.

Asking only specific questions may limit the information available, even though much more is available if you allow it. Everything is available; we just have to stay open to receiving it. That said, sometimes it is not in our best interest to know certain information yet, as it is a lesson we have to play out for our soul's growth. The key, though, is to get good at asking questions—knowing the right ones to ask.

We Are One

The fundamental aspect to integrate and anchor within is the wisdom and knowledge that we are all one, all connected through infinite source intelligence. We all originate from source, and when you truly recognize that, you see God and yourself in everyone.

I am you, and you are me. We are one.

This fundamental perspective shift can help end the wars, anger, hate, and fear. Embodying this understanding that we are all one will end the source of all ills: the fear of the other rooted in separation.

Harming anyone else is to inflict harm upon ourselves. Loving thy neighbor as thyself is the Soulution.

This wisdom helps us come home to the heart. It's grounding, connecting, and empowering to remember that the true you is, after all, the center of the Universe, just like everyone else. We are each the center of the You-niverse as the threads of creation weave through us, creating a brilliant tapestry of life. We are all one, and we are all beautiful, powerful, worthy creator beings who create the world around us. It's time to remember this and build a more beautiful world. Together, magic and miracles can happen.

Unity consciousness is the return to love.

Chapter Twenty

Living the Prophecies: Co-Creating Heaven on Earth

Astrology, Prophecy, and the Birth of Christ Consciousness

"God has not given us prophecy to scare us but to prepare us."
~ Joel C. Rosenberg

The light at the end of the tunnel is here. We are seeding and birthing a new reality. It is time to unite the pieces. The Ascension is now. As dicey as things in the world may get, cultivate a strong energy field and keep your vibration in the frequency of authenticity. Like an Eagle soaring through the sky higher than the rest as a master of alchemy, rise above it all and stay above the fray while remaining anchored in the journey. It will take each and every one of us to come together and build a new reality. You are the Prophecy, here to the return the Planet to Love.

The Times of Prophecy: Legends of a Golden Age

As we embrace the End Times as a New Dawn for humanity, Native prophecies are emerging into the collective consciousness. These prophecies speak directly to the themes discussed throughout this odyssey that journeyed us through the heart of darkness to emerge into the light. The Mayan prophecy and Revelations spoke of the End Times not as an armageddon—a New Age misconception—but as the end of an old cycle and the start of a new. Rather than destruction, the prophecy can be interpreted as a time of rapid evolution.[184]

Many other Native prophecies speak of these times, pointing to the importance of both our choices and our actions. The Hopi Prophecy decrees:[185]

> *"When the earth is dying there shall arise a new tribe of all colours and all creeds. This tribe shall be called The Warriors of the Rainbow and it will put its faith in actions not words."*

This reflects similar prophecies of the Rainbow Warriors told by the Cree, Navajo, Hopi, Salish, Zuni, Cherokee, and Sioux, often referred to as the Whirling Rainbow Prophecy:[186]

> *"There will come a time when the earth is sick and the animals and plants begin to die. Then the Indians will regain their spirit and gather people of all nations, colors and beliefs to join together in the fight to save the Earth: The Rainbow Warriors."*

> *"There will come a day when people of all races, colors, and creeds will put aside their differences. They will come together in love, joining hands in unification, to heal the Earth and all her children. They will move over the Earth like a great Whirling Rainbow, bringing peace, understanding and healing everywhere they go. Many creatures thought to be extinct or mythical will resurface at this time; the great trees that perished will return almost overnight. All living things will flourish, drawing sustenance from the breast of our Mother, the Earth."*

> "The great spiritual Teachers who walked the Earth and taught the basics of the truths of the Whirling Rainbow Prophecy will return and walk amongst us once more, sharing their power and understanding with all. We will learn how to see and hear in a sacred manner. Men and women will be equals in the way Creator intended them to be; all children will be safe anywhere they want to go. Elders will be respected and valued for their contributions to life. Their wisdom will be sought out. The whole Human race will be called The People and there will be no more war, sickness or hunger forever."

Lakota legend speaks of a beautiful woman who appeared bearing gifts of a sacred pipe and bundle to the people.[187] She told them she would return as a white buffalo calf at a time of a trouble world to restore harmony and spirituality. The birth of a white buffalo calf is seen as a sacred sign of prayers heard, while acting as both a warning and a blessing. During the spring of 2024, I learned of reports of three white buffalo calves birthed across the American West, which, amplified by the holy trinity, I believe portends spiritual rebirth and the promise of a blank slate for humanity.

The seven fires prophecy of the Anishanaabe speaks of the phases of learning for those on Turtle Island—a Native term for the North American continent—that represent key spiritual teachings and was given prior to the arrival of the Europeans. The prophecy states that when the world has been befouled and the waters turned bitter by disrespect, humans must choose between two paths: materialism and spirituality. If humanity chooses spirituality, we will survive. If we continue down the path of materialism, it signals the end. In *The Mishomis Book: The Voice of the Ojibway* by Edward Benton-Banai, 1988, the prophecy says:

> "The Seventh Prophet that came to the people long ago was said to be different from the other prophets. This prophet was described as 'young and had a strange light in his eyes' and said:

> "In the time of the Seventh Fire New People will emerge. They will retrace their steps to find what was left by the trail. Their steps will take them to the Elders who they will ask to guide them on their journey. But many

of the Elders will have fallen asleep. They will awaken to this new time with nothing to offer. Some of the Elders will be silent because no one will ask anything of them. The New People will have to be careful in how they approach the Elders. The task of the New People will not be easy.

"If the New People will remain strong in their quest the Water Drum of the Midewiwin Lodge will again sound its voice. There will be a rebirth of the Anishinabe Nation and a rekindling of old flames. The Sacred Fire will again be lit.

"It is this time that the light skinned race will be given a choice between two roads. If they choose the right road, then the Seventh Fire will light the Eighth and final Fire, an eternal fire of peace, love brotherhood and sisterhood. If the light skinned race makes the wrong choice of the roads, then the destruction which they brought with them in coming to this country will come back at them and cause much suffering and death to all the Earth's people."

William Commanda, carrier and custodian of the Wampum Belt and the Seven Fires Prophecy, and founder of the Circle of All Nations, declared in August 2022: *"The Time has come to light up the Eighth Fire."*

The Eagle and the Condor is another ancient prophecy that speaks of the splitting of humanity into two paths: that of the Eagle—the path of the mind, the masculine, and industry, and that of the Condor—the path of the heart, the feminine, and intuition.[188] This prophecy states that beginning in the 1490s would be a 500-year cycle during which the Eagle people would rise to overpower and nearly overcome the Condor people. This precisely aligns with historical records of Christopher Columbus landing in the Americas in 1492 and the ensuing colonialism and industrial revolution that followed, pillaging the land and decimating so many.

However, the potential for the two to rise in union and harmony to awaken humanity would arise with the transition into the next 500-year period, which aligns with the 1990s, just a couple decades shy of the Mayan calendar's end. This is not just about the people of different nations, but the balancing of the masculine and the feminine, the mind and the heart, science and ancient earth-based wisdom.

We must remember that prophecy only speaks of potential. For this potential to be realized, the harmony and balance must arise within so it can emanate without. Representing the unification of the path of self-actualization with the teaching Love thy neighbor as thyself, the way of mastery and the way of love merge to create a middle way, the ultimate path of harmony.

Golden threads of promise weave through legends and prophecies that span the globe across the ages, speaking of rainbows that symbolize God's grace and an age of coming peace and harmony. Seven, a sacred number, is reflected in many traditions as well.

The Bible mentions rainbows in both Genesis and Revelations:

> *"12 And God said, "This is the sign of the covenant I am making between me and you and every living creature with you, a covenant for all generations to come: 13 I have set my rainbow in the clouds, and it will be the sign of the covenant between me and the earth. 14 Whenever I bring clouds over the earth and the rainbow appears in the clouds, 15 I will remember my covenant between me and you and all living creatures of every kind. Never again will the waters become a flood to destroy all life. 16 Whenever the rainbow appears in the clouds, I will see it and remember the everlasting covenant between God and all living creatures of every kind on the earth."*
> *Genesis 9:12-16*

> *"The one sitting on the throne was as brilliant as gemstones—like jasper and carnelian. And the glow of an emerald circled his throne like a rainbow."*
> *Revelations 4:3*

Biblical prophecy also speaks of the seven signs of the Second Coming of Christ: earthquakes, disease, famines, great storms, lightnings, and thunder. These seven prophecies must be fulfilled before Christ returns.

But what is the Second Coming of Christ? It is the birth of Christ consciousness within all of us. We are meant to walk the path, anchoring the blueprint Yeshua seeded into our vessels so that we can do greater things than he. These crises can be seen as collective wake-up calls for us to enact the prophecies as bearers of the Christ light within.

Legends of a Golden Age span the globe, from *Chryson Genos* in Greek mythology to *Gullaldr* in Norse mythology and the Satya Yuga of Hindu myth when humanity is righteous and devoid of wickedness.

Many believe we are living at the end of the Kali Yuga, the fourth, shortest, and worst of the World Ages. The End of times does not mean the end of the world, rather, the end of the Dark Ages, an era, and the end of Time itself. Apocalypse means to reveal, and what is being revealed is the Truth of our Spiritual Nature and the quantum reality in which we reside.

Closely matching the Precession of the Equinoxes, a full Yuga cycle lasts approximately 26,000 years.[189] The precession of the equinoxes refers to the gradual rotation of the pattern of stars that impacts the position of key markers in our night sky, with one revolution lasting 25,920 years. In accordance with this greater cycle, the Kali Yuga marks the relatively shorter transition between the descending Yuga, which lasts roughly 12,000 years, and the ascending Yuga, which lasts another 12,000 years. The planet takes 72 years to move one degree through the zodiac, and 25,920 to complete one full 360 degree circle. The Kali Yuga itself is said to last roughly 1296 years, the darkest time of the cycle when we are farthest from the super sun we revolve around, with the lowest point of possibility.

As we move closer to the Super Sun, realization of our electric potential will arise naturally. According to certain calculations, we have already left the Kali Yuga long behind and are on the ascending side of the cycle, and by the year 2082 we will fully enter the Treta Yuga, the light half of the Ascending cycle of Virtue that lasts 12,000 years. This theory based on the Mahabharat places the start of the Kali Yuga at around roughly 3102 BC, which closely aligns with the rise of patriarchal dominance and suppression, leading to millennia of a dark age of disharmony, destruction, and devastation.

However you choose to interpret and weave these prophecies and legends into your own worldview, it is evident that humanity is undergoing an extraordinary shift in consciousness that is calling us to rise in love and harmony.

Over the past several years, I myself have had numerous dreams with a prophetic or revelatory quality, several involving water. Waters rising only to suddenly give way to a bright new reality with a rainbow arcing over sparkling waters; another depicting what could only be described as the 'firmament' breaking, allowing a deluge of water to flood down, instantaneously flipping the world only to reveal a peaceful and pristine realm; a goddess holding a lightning bolt; darker aspects about our matrix reality being revealed; a sense of waiting in the underworld, pearls of wisdom embodied, unafraid of the power within, prepared to emerge; a sense of pure golden peace, merged with the essence of divine love itself. My meditations bring me into a realm of pure ethereal beauty, where joy and love lead the way.

Ultimately, these prophetic teachings speak to the victory of good over evil as the age of darkness comes to an end. Through facing the fear and the demons in the underworld of our subconscious by illuminating Truth with the supernatural force of God consciousness, we are blessed with the precious gems of wisdom to give birth to a brilliantly abundant Sacred New Earth.

Alignment and Co-Creation

We are not meant to create Heaven on Earth alone, but rather as vessels of God Source consciousness, co-creating with the divine. Co-creating from embodied energetic alignment magnetizes instant manifestation into your reality. Shifting your energy is the fastest way to create a sustained new reality.

By nature, we are creative beings. When we manifest in alignment with our soul, we are actually co-creating with the divine. The truth is that we are always manifesting and creating our reality. It is incumbent upon us to become aware of our creative power so that when we create, we do so when aligned with our higher self, the universe, truth, and love.

When we create from a heart-centered space, we move from a place of service. Opening your heart enables you to act from heart wisdom. Living with an open heart is the way to co-create Heaven on Earth. The heart is the seat of the soul, and when operating from the frequency of soul alignment, you can instantly manifest and attract all that you desire into your reality because you are aligned with what is in the highest good for all.

Co-creating from the heart rests on service and gratitude, which attract more resources and opportunities, generating further momentum and expansion. What you give out comes back to you multiplied. When aligned with our most profound truth and innermost knowing, everything we envision and desire quickly manifests for us because the Universe wants us to succeed. Or, it simply responds to our frequency and matches what we send out with more of that because we live in an infinitely abundant, ever-expanding universe.

God, Source, Creative Intelligence, the Universe, whatever term you prefer, wants us to expand. Because expansion is the natural order of the cosmos, to stay small and constricted is to oppose the flow of the Universe, which compels us to step into our fullest expression and live beautiful, epic, abundant lives. We can serve even more powerfully when we are wholly in our power and living in joy and bliss. That frequency is where the magic happens. We are entering an era where instant manifestation will be even more prevalent because time accelerates as we enter a higher vibrational reality, so everything moves faster, and manifestation becomes instantaneous.

In higher vibrational frequency consciousness, we do not have the same barriers of time and space. We must focus on raising our vibrational frequency to cultivate this ability to manifest instantly and with ease. That means living in joy and releasing fear. The journey of facing our shadows and raising our frequency is not instant, so don't put pressure on yourself because that will only backfire. The collective shift will continue over the coming years, and no, it won't be all magic, rainbows, or butterflies. However, once we begin the work, we will notice the shifts, and sometimes, they can happen in quantum leaps and bounds.

A great deal still needs to be released from the collective, so we must do what we can individually. I know my work is ongoing. Will it ever truly be done? Maybe not until we return fully to Source! It is a process. Release any sense of pressure or expectation for yourself to get through it quickly. The energies are aligning for us to do this work far more rapidly than we could before, to start processing and releasing much more quickly.

It's a fascinating time for the entire Universe right now. What are humans going to do? Are they going to succeed? The vast majority want us to.

Remember, too, that light is born in the dark. So please be gentle with yourself when the darkness rises up because it's within all of us. We live in this polarity for a reason—to transmute the shadows and integrate the dark. Darkness is nothing to feel ashamed about or beat yourself up over when the old stuff comes up. Face it, embrace it, and release it.

It's an upward spiral, so we keep returning to our lessons to peel back all the layers and fully integrate the wisdom in the shadows. Like peeling back the layers of an onion, we shed the layers one by one until we finally arrive at the core, the golden treasure of truth buried deep within the chest. Our diamond heart is then revealed and polished, ready to shine bright in its infinitely faceted brilliance.

Our crystalline hearts become both a chalice for and a beacon of divinity. How can you serve more? Allow the divine to flow through you.

Adapting to the New

Humans have a natural gift of adaptation. Through necessity, we can rapidly adapt to new environments. However, adapting our consciousness in the absence of extenuating circumstances proves to be more challenging. Awakening to our personal truth is (ideally) the first step. Then, we awaken to the reality of what is happening in the world, the battle of the dark and the light, and the illusions cast by the inverted matrix of enslavement through fear-based mind-control. Those in power are trying to conceal the truth in every manner possible, through our apps, through the media, and through toxic chemicals that blanket our minds and hearts with the burden of toxicity.

We must be conscious about where we spend our time and energy and where we receive our information. Adapting our consciousness to have heightened discernment in a world of artificial intelligence, disinformation, and deep fakes is crucial. While we can access these new elevated states of consciousness, the 3D world has been shifting rapidly into one based on control, with attempts to loosh our attention and siphon our energy.

Fortunately, the 2024 election results—which came through just in the nick of time prior to publishing for an 11th hour update—signaled a major timeline shift for humanity. As hard as it still may be for some to believe, the lesser of two evils presided, and this was a win not just for the United States but for the freedom and future of global humanity. It signaled the fall of the first beast system, yet collectively we must remain vigilant to not fall into the trap of giving our power away to a savior through the second. We the People chose a path forward that did not perpetuate the establishment, which was in truth rooted in an insidious Satanic agenda. Again, however, as we move forward and proactively dismantle the system that operated through force, we must remain vigilant so as not to allow a more deceptive Luciferian agenda to infiltrate and subtly entice us to give the sovereignty of our souls away, as could happen with AI. When the second system falls, the new Golden Age will formally be ushered in.

The old paradigm systems and structures will crumble because they do not align with the frequency of truth. By design, they haven't been serving us for many years. So we must adapt the way that we live our lives and the way that we show up in the world because we are the ones who must build the New Earth. We no longer have time to be passive observers or commentators. It is time to act, to step up, and lead.

The good news is that humans are brilliant at adapting. We can adapt to almost any environment and survive challenging circumstances. The human species has survived and overcome many disasters throughout history. We are designed to evolve and adapt. Our brains adapt quickly because we can rewire them quickly (relatively speaking, with concerted focus). We are currently in the process of rewiring our entire biology so that we can adapt and create remarkable technologies and systems we can't even fathom yet.

Speaking our truth and making ourselves heard is part of the healing process for so many. Speaking our truth into the world helps to heal the collective suppression. Finding my voice and having the courage to put myself out there has been a journey, so I understand the inner work required to reclaim your power and express yourself. After an entire childhood of being painfully shy and a long, arduous journey of healing the anxiety over being seen and the fear of rejection, I am doing it. The programming runs so deep for so many. It takes courage and a lot of shedding before we can get to this space of actually doing the thing, but confidence builds through action, one step at a time.

Speaking our truth comes in all shapes and forms, and often, it simply means expressing our truth to our loved ones. Many of us stray from the expected path because it doesn't feel right, realizing that living your life by other people's standards is more painful and soul-crushing than you can bear. Yet, it requires great courage to go against what our family, friends, and community expect of us. As vulnerable as it feels, it is always worth choosing your soul.

For those who always felt like the black sheep, maybe you're actually a sparkly iridescent winged unicorn here to inspire and guide others to break out of the mold. Writing, sharing, and speaking up, expressing ourselves through any medium, even art or music, allows us to shine our light—our truth. Use whatever form of expression you've been gifted with and become the leader you came here to be. Lead with light, lead with love.

We've all been gifted with brilliance that has been buried. Focus on what lights you up and brings you joy. What skills do I want to sharpen? What gifts do I want to share? What feels right for you?

Crossing the Rainbow Bridge

Entering the realm of magic requires that we shed the heavier, denser energies that are not a vibrational match for the Kingdom. We are being called to release what blocks us from taking that next step to cross over the rainbow bridge into the beautiful abundance that awaits on the other side.

Heaven on Earth exists on a different vibrational frequency. To enter the Kingdom of Heaven, we must release the dense, heavy, fear-based vibrations: anger, resentment, guilt, shame, helplessness, victimhood, depression, anxiety, stress, worries, and fear itself. We can't carry fear across the rainbow bridge. Thank goodness for that!

Operating from a space of neutrality, we are triggered less and less. Once we've released the core wound, there's nothing to react to. Finally, we enter a profound peace, fully compassionate with ourselves and others. The peace that passeth all understanding.

Heaven on Earth is harmony, bridging differing perspectives into a harmonious union. Rather than discord, we find union and commonality. Harmony is a different way of operating and being from what we've experienced in this realm of separation.

Heaven on Earth is available to those who are ready and all who choose to walk the path of light. I've witnessed glimpses and glimmers, calling in rainbows and experiencing instant manifestation. Community where all are conscious, compassionate, and whole, living their unique, radiant expression of love. Crystal clear waters, fresh air, and pristine surroundings. Abundance and plenty for all.

What is it that you envision in your heaven-on-earth reality? Tune in with yourself and receive that clear vision from within. What is your truth? What is the reality that you desire? Tune into your heart's wisdom and allow the clarity to emerge. Freedom. Harmony. Love. Peace. Unity. Abundance. Harmony in all layers of our being, with others, with nature, with higher consciousness, and with the Universe's one song of creation. Your heart knows everything, and it will happen when it's aligned.

Together, the call is to raise our frequency and maintain this state. The more we all do this, the better off we will be in the long run, and the more quickly it will happen for the collective. So, let's raise the planet's vibration, anchor the higher realms by bringing light into the planet, and co-create Heaven on Earth.

What can you do to bring a little joy into your day? What can you do to ground yourself?

Dance. Sing. Laugh. Meditate. Get out in nature. Soak up a little sun. Dance in the rain. Take a bath. Do yoga. Move your body. Sweat. Take a nap. Climb a mountain. Read a book. Watch a comedy. Cuddle with your loved ones. Cuddle with your puppy. Call a friend. Cleanse your crystals. Gaze at the stars. Do nothing. Simply Be.

Prioritize self-care, whatever that looks like for you.

Prioritize whatever you can do to support, nurture, and nourish yourself. Energetic alignment is the foundation for magic and miracles.

The opposite of trauma isn't being healed; it is play, laughter, joy, love, connection, freedom of expression, and a sense of profound wholeness, a remembrance of your innate worthiness and holiness.

Liberate yourself from the shackles of illusion that keep you trapped in lack and suffering, and be the beacon of light and love to spark the remembrance in all those around you, until all of humanity is a living reflection of divine love.

Chapter Twenty-One

YOU ARE THE MIRACLE

Mastering the Way of Love

"There is only one path to Heaven. On Earth, we call it Love."
~ Henry David Thoreau

We have arrived at the culmination of our voyage, yet this is truly the point of inception. This journey has taken us through a labyrinth of remembrance of who we are, the power we hold within, and the truth that we are all fractals of the light of source consciousness.

You are the light; the light you shine comes from the embodiment of your soul. When you embody the light of the crystalline diamond within, anything is possible.

I received a message as I was running through final edits of this book: *Prepare for Miracles*. The task is to not just be ready to receive miracles, but to have the capacity to hold the Miracle frequency, as the living breathing walking talking miracle that you are. You are the miracle, here to anchor this remembrance onto the planet and spark the resurrection of this consciousness in others.

Having nurtured these ideas and expanded your energy and consciousness, the task now is to embody the frequency of infinite possibilities to usher you through the portal of emergence. This is the path of mastery that guides you along the way of love.

Energetic alignments with celestial bodies, seasonal shifts, solar flares, and natural cycles support us in this journey of remembrance and expansion. Portals of energy assist us along the process. But they all serve to help us remember that You are the portal. Your heart is the portal to expanded consciousness, available to you always.

Everything happens for a reason and is aligned with our highest expansion. It is here to support us in expanding our consciousness and energy. This is what we are here for: evolution and expansion.

We're entering a collective era of sovereignty, ease, and flow. The energies are supporting us; let it be easy. It's time to release limitation and expand our idea of what is possible for ourselves and the world and allow ourselves to anchor that vision.

Really, this is all about you: honing your sense of connection with the whole, grounding it into your body, and anchoring it into the planet so that the collective consciousness can expand.

Journal into reality the beauty you envision. Anchor that vision down through your divine vessel. What do you want to create? What kind of beauty, what kind of joy? What do you see and envision for the New Earth, Heaven on Earth? What kind of world, what kind of communities, what sort of systems do you want to create?

Expansion is a powerful energy that propels us to grow by stepping into our power. The Jupiter and Saturn Great conjunction occurred on December 21, 2020, the day I recorded this original video; these Great conjunctions occur every 20 years. The Winter Solstice is the shortest day of the year, amplifying polarity and highlighting the call to shine our light in the darkness, to *Be* the light. Jupiter carries the energy of abundance and expansion, bringing powerful energy to expand the light. From then on, the days got longer, and the light of our sun has only gotten brighter.

Saturn anchors Jupiter's expansive energy, making it practical so that we can create the systems that we envision will work for us—to practically build a new economy, a new education system, a new political system, a new healthcare system—in a manner that works for us and serves us. This metaphorically represents the foundation we are being called to create within and without.

As within, so without, the lesson of this time is to remember the light of divinity within and to be the beacon of love anchoring the truth of light so humanity can rise into remembrance of the miraculous.

While the timeline began in 2012, a year that many experienced their initial Awakening—the same year I received the message 'The System, The Shift, The Awakening'—the

Jupiter and Saturn conjunction energetically ramped up the Awakening and ushered in the new paradigm, as have other major planetary shifts such as Pluto moving into Aquarius in January of 2024 according to Tropical astrology, signifying the Dawn of the Age of Aquarius. Pluto's shifts are generational, and we are completing a greater cycle that is part of the Precession of the Equinoxes. These grander cycles take years to realize fully, and we are very much in the early stages of the shift into the Light; however, from our human perspective, this shift is occurring rapidly. To completely transform our world in a mere decade or generation (give or take) is an astonishing consideration. We are seeding the blueprint for a new reality, and it may take generations or even a few centuries for the world we envision to be built. However we should not underestimate just how much can shift within a single generation

As 2024 comes to a close, we are experiencing major timeline shifts. Jupiter and Saturn square twice, on August 19 and December 24, with the three-part series completing on June 15, 2025. With the Pisces Lunar Eclipse that occurred on September 17, 2024, sweeping out the remnants of the Age of Pisces as Pluto experiences his last hurrah in Capricorn in our lifetime until he moves back into Aquarius for good on November 19, 2024, we are witnessing the Fall of the of Empires. Pisces—the last sign in the wheel of the zodiac—governs illusion and deception as well as our connection to the divine, and the eclipse lifted the veil, revealing the dark underbelly of entertainment, political systems, agribusiness, and corrupt media in grand fashion. The Age of Illusion is Over.

On September 7, 2024, a dark and stormy day, I looked out over the New York City skyline to see Upper Manhattan enshrouded in dark clouds and another dark cluster hovering directly above Lower Manhattan. I went still, and a deep sense washed over me: 'It's Over.' A few hours later, the clouds began to lift, and the skyline glittered in gold as the setting sun reflected off the glass buildings. Twenty minutes later, I looked out and saw a bright pink sky and gasped when I stepped out. There was a double rainbow arching over the valley and framing the skyline. I knew God had won, and the timeline they attempted to usher in on September 11, 2001, was finally over. The Age of Illusion, deception, and control is over. The Roman Empire—which never truly fell but only transformed—is Fallen.

The next day, I learned that the New York City police commissioner's home had been raided, along with several others of the Mayor's inner circle. Followed by a rigged debate, Diddy's arrest as a distraction for the UN WHO meeting on the Autumn Equinox, and the leaking of New York City's Covid czar's sex parties during lockdown, disclosure is coming in rapid fire. Hurricanes Helene and Milton shed a glaring spotlight on the failure of governmental systems and the media while billions more have been sent overseas for false wars. Celebrities and CEOs are falling from grace faster than you can say Kanye.

Now is our time to reclaim our world and resurrect the organic Truth of the Light. According to astronomical and astrological alignments, much evidence suggests that Yeshua's birth might have been on September 11, 3 BC. Of course, they would have chosen to invert the essence and meaning of such a potent number. Both 9 and 11 carry powerful spiritual energies unto themselves, and when brought together, they mean emergence, spiritual awakening, and enlightenment. Emergence became emergency, birth became death, and hope became fear and tragedy.

The grid of darkness is being dismantled, refined under pressure to become the brilliant diamond grid of consciousness, radiantly reflecting the iridescent rainbow prism of luminous beauty and possibility.

We are the second coming of Christ, birthing Christ Consciousness into the planet through our Body Temples as we resurrect the light within, anchored into the pristine diamond consciousness of Source.

Dark truths are coming to light, and old systems are crumbling. We are finally coming to remember that the devil himself was a lie, an illusion that messed with our minds to keep us trapped in the prison of fear.

And when we stop feeding the beast, all that remains is the Truth of Love.

This is a renewal of righteousness. Seeds have been planted, and inspiration and ideas for the future abound. Together, we will co-create a beautiful reality based on community, harmony, and cooperation.

Life itself is a pilgrimage, and if we treat it as such, with the same level of ceremonial devotion, each action we take becomes a sacred reflection of divinity to resurrect a world of love and unity.

Competition vs. Cooperation

In 2012, when I was in grad school, I wrote a paper for social evolutionary psychology about the evolution of competition and cooperation from the level of the cell to the level of society. If we look at the biology of the human and the biology of a cell of any being, we are designed to live in a state of cooperation. Every cell is its own sovereign entity that needs to have its own needs met, while every system within our biological entirety must also have its needs met. Every cell has its role within the body. And every organelle within the cell has its role. They each have their own governance.

They each have their own transportation system, energy production, and waste management, much like a human operating within society. Looking at the cells operating within the whole of an individual healthy human being, we are living in perfect harmony. Every cell that makes up our being—all 50 trillion—lives in harmony. From that place of harmony where each is fulfilling their role and getting their needs met, the body as a whole thrives.

The whole doesn't function properly as a unit unless each unit has its needs met. If the cells in one system break down, the whole body begins to break down.

When a cell malfunctions and begins to consume more than its usual share of resources and rapidly replicate, multiplying its dysfunction, it becomes cancer. Viruses kill hosts to reproduce themselves. Bacteria invade and infect healthy cells with their defective programs. Parasites feed off of healthy cells, eventually killing the host. A healthy body with a healthy immune system eliminates these threats and invaders to return to homeostasis. Fevers, colds, and stomach aches are our body's natural defenses to clear our systems of pathogens. To heal, it gets worse before it gets better. This purification is happening in our society—we are purging the cancerous and parasitic entities, the viruses that have infected our minds, and the bacteria that erode society.

Our body can return to homeostasis when we purge the threat and purify our system. We thus ensure the survival of each cell within our body. Any surplus goes into the community bank when each component meets its needs. Cells store nutrients, muscles store ATP, and a healthy body only consumes what it needs for optimal vitality. It naturally regulates appetite and sends signals that say, 'I need to move' or 'I need to rest.' From there, we can thrive.

If we build a society based on these same principles that biology has designed within our vessels, if we tune in and learn from organic systems and natural biology, then we have the potential to create something that works for the collective and to create something that resembles Heaven on Earth. To be clear, this is *not* the same as communism or socialism, political models that are inherently totalitarian, placing control of resources in the hands of the few. The new model is a system of sovereign self-governance genuinely created by the people, for the people, where self-responsibility naturally emerges from self-actualization and merges with generous service to the whole. Innovation and creation are nurtured as life force is kindled and nourished for the soul's flourishing.

Perhaps it could incorporate a blending of the most noble values and rights upheld by the United States Constitution and the Iroquois Confederacy League of Nations with a hearty dose of Round Table ideals. The Confederacy was united under a common goal to live in harmony, and is believed to be a model for the American Constitution.[190] It stands out against other systems for its unique blending of law and values, where law, society, and nature are equal partners that each play a vital role. King Arthur's legendary Round Table symbolized common purpose and equality so none seated could claim precedence over the others.

For such a utopia to work, we must genuinely embody unity consciousness. Communities have not yet worked for this very reason—our consciousness was not ready. What is needed is a return to stewardship of and communion with the land, while embracing the progress and innovation enabled by technology, tempered by reverence of the divine feminine and a spiritual consciousness. There will likely be a period of transitional governance as we create support systems for communities to develop and mature. While my own visions are holistic and expansive, I certainly do not pretend to have all the answers for the specifics on how it will all look, but that's quite the point—I, alone, am not supposed to have every solution. Together, we share ideas and unite our visions to drive the evolution of our societal systems and structures as we continue to evolve our consciousness.

Many lightworkers and conscious New Earth visionaries have already envisioned models of new communities centered around healing centers and temples, holistic education, biodynamic farming, and mindful living in communion with the land; ascension hubs in alignment with the energetic grid of the planet and healing sanctuaries for both people and animals to come together and cultivate our hearts and minds for a more beautiful future. There is a way forward that integrates the best of our modern technological advances with conscious ethics and morality.

Science without spirituality is worthless. Spirituality without science is impractical. Together, however, society can blossom and flourish like never before.

Breakdown to Breakthrough

Just as we can get excited about triggers as they present an opportunity to shed another layer and expand into the next upgrade available, we can, on some level, appreciate and embrace the collective chaos because it's a sign that, as a society and as a culture, we are evolving. For that evolution to occur, we must detox and dissolve all that is not aligned with our collective ability to thrive. We are ready to upgrade. We are ready to evolve. We are ready to step into a new paradigm, to a new way of being. We are ready to thrive.

Finally, it is time to create the new systems and structures supporting this vision: a new political economy, education system, healthcare system; a new way of living in harmony with the Earth, from energy production to food production, that supports our collective expansion and our collective ability to thrive. An era of prosperity is available to us: a golden age of beauty, light, love, and miracles. Individually, we are activating our dormant DNA and expanding our capabilities and what is possible when we come together.

Hidden gifts such as self-healing and so-called superpowers are coming online. We are ascending and evolving into beings of light that emanate the light from within. We are evolving into a new era of humanity, and it is high time for a revolution—one that occurs primarily within.

Fighting and discord are on the rise on every level of our culture, and this is precisely what is happening inside so many people's bodies right now. Even at the level of biology, we can see how deeply external separation, discord, and disconnection are impacting us. Autoimmune diseases are on the rise, a manifestation of the body attacking itself. Cancer, too, is a result of internal discord, a state of disharmony within the body.

As within, so without.

If we stop fighting and consciously decide to live in harmony, peace, bliss, joy, light, and love, disease will disappear. Our trauma burden will dissipate. Physical diseases will automatically heal themselves because we are not in the energy of separation. Conversely, if we choose to heal the internal discord, we will no longer emanate that vibration into the quantum field, having a ripple effect on consciousness that will eventually engender global peace.

The presumption of mind-body separation has dominated our perception of reality. However, numerous studies have shown that a positive mindset that generates thoughts and feelings of hope and faith impact physical health outcomes. In relation to disease, particularly chronic diseases like cancer, the more hopeful a patient is, the better their odds of survival. Evidence exists, and the placebo effect proves the power of belief, but the pieces haven't fully come together yet into collective understanding, much less how our systems operate.

The crumbling of the system is, in fact, to our ultimate benefit because it allows us to rebuild a society that will serve our highest expression and allow us to expand into our highest potential.

It's time to break open the box of limitation and scarcity, step out, and emerge into the light of infinite possibility. A crucial piece of this emergence is the ability to share information because the convergence of different ideas, understanding, and information allows the emergence of new systems that facilitate our collective expansion and evolution.

Consider a computer. Each individual part is its own entity, but when combined, the parts join to create a beautiful system, a computer that is more powerful than its individual parts.

We are on the brink of coming together collectively to take all the new technologies and scientific understandings that already exist but haven't been implemented. From that space of integration, we can create a better reality, a new educational system based on human potential rather than one that indoctrinates us into a system that churns us out like cogs in a machine.

Let's not forget that the darkness of the void is where all life and creation are born. This collective dark night of the soul is a beautiful, potent, powerful opportunity for us to co-create a new, more beautiful reality that will serve the collective by serving the individual in a capacity that facilitates our expansion and allows us to embody our potential.

Focus on possibility, and don't limit yourself. If you can dream it, it can happen. Will it happen overnight? It is unlikely, that is, until you can hold the miracle frequency. Energies of expansion facilitate the creation of our dreams. When we are aligned and in tune, body, soul, and spirit, we operate in service from the heart center. From there, the Universe conspires to allow our vision to blossom because it will serve the collective good. Co-creation and manifestation become seamless when we are in a space of serving. Allow it to be easy, allow yourself to embrace joy, possibility, bliss, love, and harmony, and anchor the vision with gratitude.

By shining bright, we let others know that it's okay to shine. Rise in love with yourself. Rise in love with life. Rise in love with the reality that you want to create. From that energetic frequency of love, we will create a beautiful, new Heaven on Earth. Love over fear, always.

Connect with Mother Earth. Connect with other people. Connect with yourself.

Now is the time for us to co-create this reality. The signs—the rainbows, the beauty, and the possibility of a veritable Garden of Eden—confirm that the time of prophecy is here.

Like a rose, we plant, fertilize, and cultivate the seed. We give it the time and space to take root, and when the time is ripe, it emerges into the light and blossoms into a beautiful manifestation of creative essence. We are the ones rising. We are the ones blossoming into the purest frequency of divine love.

Allow yourself to believe in possibility. Allow yourself to envision your dreams as manifested in the reality of our beautiful heaven on Earth. Connect above and below, receive the angelic light frequencies from the sun and celestial heavens above, and anchor that frequency into the planetary grid and into Gaia's Diamond Heart.

Everything we need is here to support us. We have all the systems, structures, and tools we need to create this beautiful reality. No matter what, don't give up. We are remembering that we are far more powerful than we have been led to believe. Stand in your power and speak your truth to create a new reality through the resonance of your authenticity. Speak into existence the beauty and love you wish to create.

You are everything you need. We are everything we've been seeking. The ultimate truth is that the light shines from within. We just have to remember it's there.

Release the layers to uncover the buried treasure that lies within. The treasure chest has been inside all along, waiting for you to uncover your pot of gold. Allow your brave heart to blossom and light up the world with your love and devotion. Prepare for Miracles by holding the miracle frequency and the capacity to receive divine blessings.

Love is the eternal answer, and it is You.

It's time to Reb*earth* a New Earth as a vessel of the Genesis of Heaven on Earth.

The Rainbow Warriors have returned and the resurrection of the Angelic Human Template is underway.

As Above, So Below, As Within, So Without.

You are the Key to Our Heaven on Earth Reality: Liberate your heart to liberate the Heart of Humanity.

And Let There Be Light.

EPILOGUE: WE THE PEOPLE

Writing Humanity's New Story

Many battles have been won, timelines cleared, and we are on the path of liberation. Yet there is still much work to do.

I type the first section of the following words for a literal 11th hour update prior to my 11/11 book birthing, as the world has changed with the US Election this week. The globe was watching and the results blindsided many with a sweeping win by the candidate who has been vilified by the media for years.

Many are celebrating while many are mourning, in total fear, pain, confusion, anger, and despair. Many are losing their tight grip on their perception of reality as the systems crumble. Mass disclosure is upon us, accompanied by mass psychosis. Cue the collective dark night of the soul.

Remember, though, there is nothing to fear; fear itself is the illusion. Politics was part of my own full awakening, as I realized the corporate media had been lying about so much and I began to dig deeper and see through the illusions of the system, which I outlined in Chapter 13.

This, however, is so much bigger than politics: it is revealing how people are waking up to the corruption of the establishment and the greater system in which they operate. That this will trigger another wave of awakening is a major victory in and of itself.

A major timeline shift occurred for humanity with the US election, signifying the clearing of a fallen system more sinister than what he represents. Believe it or not, this is the higher timeline for humanity. It is a signal that humanity is ready to reclaim their power and enter an era of self-governance.

Much of the outrage incited by the corporate media is based in lies and illusion. The accusations of people losing their rights are simply not based in reality; a true examination of the 47th President Elect's stance on reproductive rights and gay rights will quickly reveal that the media has outright lied on these issues. Medical negligence and malpractice is what contributed to the tragic cases of mothers dying in childbirth highlighted by the left; doctors must take responsibility for knowing the difference between miscarriage and abortion, which are distinct issues, as are the rights of gay marriage—which he has always been in favor of—versus legal transition for minors. Part of the mind control virus is the loss of nuance to absolute black and white thinking that causes people to cast judgement without curiosity or deeper inquiry.

As I've intimated throughout these pages, this is a necessary process of evolution and rebirth. In a world of free will, however, people must choose their path, and the highest timeline is to fully divest from the systems of hierarchy and control.

The old systems are crumbling, because they *must*. Pluto entering Aquarius on the 19th is part of this upheaval for the purpose of transformation, like the Phoenix rising from the ashes of the underworld, born again into a golden-winged form. The US is concurrently undergoing its Pluto return, which means Pluto has returned to the same position it was roughly 250 years ago, which was 1776. This indeed is a time of revolution, setting the stage for not just the next four or 20 years but for the next 250 and beyond. As we know, this is also part of a much grander cycle measured by millennia.

Whether you like the man or not, President Trump has proposed a bold plan to "return the power to the American people by cleaning out the Deep State, firing rogue bureaucrats and rogue politicians, and targeting government corruption." Regardless of political leanings, this intention to dismantle the Deep State should be celebrated. Many global shifts occurred within two days of his election, from Hamas calling for an end to war and Putin ready to end the Ukraine war, the NYC mayor ending vouchers for illegals, and China wanting to work peacefully with the US. (I will endeavor to keep an updated overview inside my group). With a strong coalition of former Democrats behind him, many feel this truly signifies a shift forward to mend or even rebuild a broken system.

Robert F. Kennedy Jr. has already proposed that on January 20, the Trump White House will advise all U.S. Water systems to remove fluoride from the public water. The form of fluoride used is an industrial waste associated with arthritis, bone fractures, bone cancer, IQ loss, neurodevelopmental disorders, and thyroid disease. Win for the people. He has also promised to end the FDA's 'war on public health' waged through suppression of modalities that advance human health and can't be patented by Pharma. Again, win for us all.

My greatest concern is his alliance with the king of Artificial Intelligence. We cannot allow ourselves to get wrapped up in either a savior complex nor the idea that an AI technocratic future is the answer. This is merely a stepping stone to divest ourselves from the dark web of control; the next step is to ensure our sovereignty from a technocratic state.

To quote RFK Jr's uncle from his state of the union address January 14, 1963: "This country cannot afford to be materially rich but spiritually poor." ~ John F. Kennedy

Nobody is our savior, and there is much work to do. This is not a solution but a stepping stone towards humanity's ultimate liberation. The task now is to hold the politicians accountable to promises made and eventually fully divest from the power structures and cultivate self-mastery as we transition into the age of We the People.

I know God (beyond religion) is in control.

Humanity is ready to write not just a new chapter, but a new book. It's time for the fairy tale to begin.

***

The path forward calls lightworkers, healers, and starseeds as vessels of the divine here to do sacred work to step up in their embodied leadership.

More than ever, it is incumbent upon every one of you reading these pages—to rise as a Light Leader.

Anchored in your truth, embodied in your higher purpose, fully expressed in your sacred wholeness.

You are here to be a radiant prism of light, reflecting the frequencies needed for those around you.

It is time to step into and Embrace your Sacred Power.

Your body holds the Wisdom; it contains the keys to your liberation, expression, and expansion.

As the collective stirs into its next wave of mass awakening, the task now is to liberate the hearts of humanity, and it begins with You.

Anchored in your Truth, Embodied in your Authenticity.

We are in this together.

You stepping forward powerfully will raise the tide and lift all the boats around you.

For all those who feel the call, it is time to uplift, inspire, and heal the heart of humanity.

If you are ready to liberate yourself from anxiety and self-doubt,

To feel free and fully expressed in your truth,

To be a powerful force of love,

To step forward confidently in your next phase of being, in your next level of Leadership,

I invite you to an immersive container where we anchor the sacred into the physical through wisdom transmissions, self-discovery tools, embodiment practices, shadow work, meditations, activations, and curated energy practices to access your infinite potential:

Illumina Wisdom School and Community

www.illuminawisdomschool.com

www.thisartcalledlife.com/illumina-wisdom-school

RESOURCES

Here is a list of Free Resources and Additional Tools for you to utilize on your journey, available on my website and inside my community:

- Higher Self New Earth Frequency Meditation and Activation
- Refresh Cleanse Guide with Recipes
- A List of Common Ascension Symptoms
- Shadow Work Journaling and Self-Inquiry Questions
- Energy Clearing Meditation
- Book and Resource List

Inside My Community Memberships and Courses:

- Breath of Life Breathwork Foundations Course
- Energetic Protection and Clearing Basics
- The Body Temple Blueprint
- Infinite Possibilities Mind Body Soul Reset
- Align & Shine
- Golden Keys to Abundance
- Expansion Path to Mastery

- Elemental Multidimensional Self

- A Vault of three dozen+ Meditations and Activation journeys

- 100+ video lessons on awakening, self-mastery, and ascension

- *Much more, and ever-growing and expanding..!*

www.thisartcalledlife.com/illumina-wisdom
www.illuminawisdomschool.com

ABOUT THE AUTHOR

Amanda Erin Kelly, MSc, is a first-time published Author and Founder of Illumina Wisdom School and Thisartcalledlife.com with a vision and mission to bridge science and spirituality. She graduated from Boston College with a BA in Psychology and Minor in French, then went on to pursue a Master's degree in Social and Cultural Psychology at the London School of Economics and Political Science.

A cancer diagnosis in 2016 catalyzed her journey of healing and awakening. Treatment was fast and furious and after 600 hours of chemotherapy her final scan in September 2016 showed no evidence of disease, she has been in remission since, thriving and feeling better than ever and she has made it her mission to share the knowledge and wisdom she has gained through myriad additional trainings and certifications in holistic wellness and spirituality.

On a lifelong quest of discovery, her soul has guided her around the globe, and she has lived in six countries, traveled to fifty, and visited over thirty states within the United States. As a Priestess of the Rose, her soul travels have activated soul codes of remembrance connected to ancient lands that have awakened a sense of devotion to guiding, teaching, inspiring, and sharing the wisdom of the cosmos and the ancient codes held within the Earth's grid, dancing, laughing, and enjoying the beauty and magic of the world along the path home to love.

Connect with Amanda:
www.amandaerinkelly.com
www.thisartcalledlife.com
www.illuminawisdomschool.com
www.illuminawisdom.com

ENDNOTES

1. Frank, R.H. (2011) *The Darwin Economy: Liberty, Competition, and the Common Good*. Princeton University Press.

2. Kuhn, T.S. (1962) *The Structure of Scientific Revolutions*. University of Chicago Press.

3. See Chapter 20 for more about these prophecies.

4. I share more about these dreams on my website and YouTube channel (as above).

5. See *The Biology of Belief* by Bruce H. Lipton, Ph.D. for a thorough examination of quantum biology and epigenetics.

6. HeartMart Institute https://www.heartmath.org/

7. For a comprehensive overview of plasma cosmology, refer to 'A New Science of Heaven' by Robert Temple.

8. Source: https://www.psfc.mit.edu/vision/what_is_plasma

9. The Illusion of Reality: The Scientific Proof that Everything is Energy and Reality Isn't Real

10. The Fourth Phase of Water by Gerald Pollack

11. For a comprehensive list of citations regarding the Photon Belt, view this page.

12. Association Between Sunlight Exposure and Mental Health: Evidence from a Special Population without Sunlight in Work. 2023, Jun 14. J. Wang, Z. Wei, N. Yao, C. Li, L. Sun. View Article.

13. The Effects of grounding (Earthing) on inflammation, the immune response, wound healing, and prevention and treatment of chronic inflammatory and autoimmune diseases. 2015, Mar 15. JL Oschman, G Chevalier, R Brown. Article.

14. NASA overview and animated visualization of the Schumann Resonance. View Here.

15. We must distinguish between erratic behavior resulting in admissions and accidents and internal medical incidences. Many also theorize that internal parasitic activity peaks at the Full Moon, which may contribute to erratic behavior. For an overview of anecdotal evidence: Full Moon Madness in the ER. View Article.

16. NASA.gov Jupiter Facts. View Here.

17. Ancient Sites Aligned with the Solstice and the Equinox. View Article.

18. Maharishi Effect Research Overview, Maharishi International University. View Page.

19. Based on the Tropical Zodiac

20. Based on the Tropical Zodiac. Not all astrologers ascribe to this zodiac, however I believe there is relative truth to all systems, and I believe the Tropical Zodiac is most relevant to our 3D matrix reality within which our ego operates. I intend to deepen this inquiry and discussion going forward.

21. While still considered theoretical by hard scientists, ley lines have been studied in depth for decades by those who note their mysterious yet highly specific alignments on the global landscape. Those attuned to energy can feel a palpable difference on ley lines, while many ancient sacred sites, temples, and cathedrals have been build on top of nodes of crossing and convergence. *Ley Lines: The Greatest Landscape Mystery* by Danny Sullivan provides a comprehensive guide to the subject.

22. For an intimate discussion of esoteric alchemy, see *The Magdalene Manuscript: The Alchemies of Horus and Sex Magic of Isis* by Tom Kenyon and Judi Sion.

23. Jesus's 'Lost Years' are discussed in the Lost Gospels, and the subject is treated in a documentary entitled *The Lost Years of Jesus*. A channeled text *Anna: Grandmother of Jesus* by Claire Heartsong also elucidates much of Yeshua's younger years that include his mystery school trainings.

24. World Mental Health Day is promoted by the World Federation for Mental Health.

25. Pendergrast, M. (1999) *Uncommon Grounds: This History of Coffee and How it Transformed Our World*. Basic Books.

26. Jupiter-Saturn Great Conjunction of 2020. NASA.

27. The Star of Bethlehem: Can science explain what it really was? Eric Betz. Article.

28. The Trouble with Ingredients in Sunscreens. EWG Research.

29. The Role of Vitamin C in Human Immunity and Its Treatment Potential Against COVID-19: A Review Article. A. Moore, D. Khanna. 2023.

30. Zinc and immune function: the biological basis of altered resistance to infection. A.H. Shankar, A.S. Prasad. 1998. Article.

31. Vitamin D and Cancer Meta Analysis. Article.

32. Half of All Americans are Magnesium Deficient. Article.

33. What is Breathwork. Article.

34. Impact of antibiotics on the human microbiome and consequences for host health. D. V. Patangia, C.A. Ryan, E. Dempsey, R. P. Ross, C. Stanton. 2022. Article.

35. Serotonin. Article by Cleveland Clinic.

36. The Gut-Brain Axis Influence of Microbiota on Mood and Mental Health. J. Appleton. 2018. Article.

37. The Enteric Nervous System and Its Emerging Role as a Therapeutic Target. M. A. Fleming II, L. Ehsan, S. R. Moore, D. E. Levin. 2020. Article.

38. What is Cognitive Dissonce Theory? S McLeod, PhD. 2023. Article.

39. Are Negative core Beliefs Ruining Your Life? R.E. Wilson Jr. 2021. Psychology Today.

40. The Body Keeps the Score by Bessel van der Kolk is a groundbreaking book on trauma and healing.

41. Between 2016-2020 alone, $24.5 billion was invested globally in cancer research. The Lancet Volumen 24, Issue 6, June 2023. Article

42. Positive and negative emotion are associated with generalized transcriptional activation in immune cells. D. Rahal, S. M. Tashijian, M. Karan, N. Eisenberger, A. Galvan, A. J. Fulgini, P.D. Hastings, S. W. Cole. 2023. Article.

43. The Dark Side of Emotion: The Addiction Perspective. G. F. Koob. 2016. Article.

44. Inflammation: The Common Pathway of Stress-Relation Diseases. YZ. Liu, YX. Wang, CL. Jiang. 2017. Article.

45. For a fascinating review of many such cases, I recommend Radical Remission by Kelly A. Turner

46. Effects of artificial light at night on human health: A literature review of observational and experimental studies applied to exposure assessment. YM. Cho, SH. Rya, B.R. Lee, K.H. Kim, E. Lee, J. Choi. 2015. Article.

47. The Shamanic View of 'Mental Illness': Birth of a Healer. Mad In America (2019) Article.

48. Dominance and prestige: Meta-analytic review of experimentally induced body position effects on behavioral, self-report, and physiological dependent variables. R. Korner, L. Roseler, A. Schutz, B. J. Bushman (2022). Article.

49. *Heal Your Wounds and Find Your True Self: Finally a Book that Explains Why it's So Hard Being Your True Self*. L. Bourbeau. (2002). Lotus Press.

50. Benefits of Gratitude: An Overview of Research and Findings. KD Miller, 2019. Article.

51. The Yerkes-Dodson Law. K Cherry, MSEd. 2023. Article.

52. Effects of Stress on the Body. H. Marks, L. King, PhD, 2024. Article.

53. For an in-depth treatment on the subject, see: Dispenza, J. *You Are the Placebo: Making Your Mind Matter.* (2014) Hay House.

54. The gut-brain axis: Interactions between enteric microbiota, central and enteric nervous systems. M. Carabotti, A. Scirocco, M.A. Maselli, C. Severi. 2015. Article.

55. The Significance of the Heart-Brain Connection. T. R. Verny, MD. Article.

56. Braden, G. *The Science of Self-Empowerment.* (2017) Hay House.

57. Heart-Brain Health: A Two-Way Street. E. Gehrman. 2023. Article.

58. Pain: Is is All in the Brain or the Heart? A.M. Alshami. 2019. Article.

59. Earthing: Health Implications of Reconnecting the Human Body to the Earth's Surface Elections. G. Chevalier, S. T. Sinatra, J.L. Oschman, K. Sokal, P. Sokal. 2012. Article.

60. Forest Bathing Studies OVerview. Forest Bathing Central.

61. Benefits of Sunlight: A Bright Spot for Human Health. M. N. Mead, 2008. Article.

62. Low Vitamin D Levels Are Associated with Long COVID Syndrome in COVID-19 Survivors. L. di Filippo, S. Frara, F. Nannipieri, A. Cotellessa, M. Locatelli, P.R. Querini, A. Giustina. 2023. Article.

63. Does Vitamin D Supplementation Reduce COVID-19 Severity? A Systematic Review. K. Shah, V.P. Varna, U. Sharma, D. Mavalankar. 2022. Article.

64. The Science Behind Meditation. E. Boynton, 2020. Article.

65. Hannuksela, M. L., & Ellahham, S. (2001). Benefits and risks of sauna bathing. The American Journal of Medicine, 110(2), 118-126.

66. Why Giving is Good for Your Health. 2022. Article.

67. Pfaff, D.W. *The Altruistic Brain: How We Are Naturally Good*. (2015) Oxford University Press.

68. Volunteerism and Mortality among the Community-dwelling Elderly. D. Oman, C. E. Thoreson, K. Mcmahon. 1999. Article.

69. Chronic Disease Prevalence in the US: Sociodemographic and Geographic Variations. G.A. Benavidez, PhD, W. E. Zahnd, PhD, P. Hung, PhD, J. M. Eberth, PhD. (2024) CDC. Article.

70. For a comprehensive overview of the relationship between trauma and the body and the DSM's failure to integrate research into its manuals, see *The Body Keeps the Score: Brain, Mind, and Body in the Healing of Trauma* by Bessel van der Kolk. 2014. Penguin Books.

71. Vasovagal Episode. R. Jeanmonod, D. Sahni, M. Silberman. 2023. Article.

72. For a comprehensive examination of our current systems' inadequate response to chronic disease and sidelining the connection to trauma, refer to *The Myth of Normal: Trauma, Illness & Healing in a Toxic Culture* by Gabor Maté with Daniel Maté. (2022) Avery.

73. Carl G. Jung's most famous and influential work is *Psychology of the Unconscious.* 1912. Published in 2023 by Dover Publications.

74. Dweck, C.S., *Mindset: The New Psychology of Success*. (2007) Ballantine Books.

75. Understanding Mental Illness Triggers. K. Ponte, JD, MBA, CPRP. 2022. National Alliance on Mental Illness. Article.

76. Montessori, M. *The Absorbent Mind: A Classic in Education and Child Development for Educators and Parents*. (1995) Holt Paperbacks.

77. 'America is About to Experience a Pluto Return'. M. Clark, 2022. The Independent.

78. Fact Sheet: Potentially Toxic Chemicals in Personal Care Products. NY Health Foundation, 2018. Article.

79. Environmental Exposures and Cancer: Using the Precautionary Principle. L. Cohen, A. Jefferies. 2019. Article.

80. Impacts of Fluoride Neurotoxicity and Mitochondrial Dysfunction on Cognition and Mental Health: A Literature Review. E. A. Adkins, K. J. Brunst. 2021. Article.

81. Association between fluoride exposure in drinking water and cognitive deficits in children: A pilot study. T. R. Godebo, M. Jeuland, R. Tekle-Haimanot, B. Alemayehu, A. Shankar, A. Wolfe, N. Phan. 2023. Article.

82. Chronic Inflammation. R. Pahwa, A. Goyal, I. Jialal. 2023. Article.

83. You can find additional free resources on my website and in depth resources inside my school.

84. Production-related contaminants (pesticides, antibiotics, and hormones) in organic and conventionally produced milk samples sold in the USA. J. A Welsh, H. Braun, N. Brown, C. Um, K. Ehret, J. Figueroa, D. B. Barr. 2019. Article.

85. Glyphosate Contamination in Food Products goes Far Beyond Oat Products. A. Temkin, PhD. 2019. Environmental Working Group.

86. CDC: Alcohol Use and Your Health. Article.

87. The gut microbiome: Relationships with disease and opportunities for therapy. J. Durack, S. V. Lynch. 2019. Article.

88. Always consult a professional before engaging in a detox or fast. You can find more resources in the back of this book and on my website.

89. Dr. Hulda Clark, *The Cure For All Diseases*. (1994) New Century Press.

90. You can find additional free resources and deeper guidance on my website.

91. About Genetically Modified Food. Center for Food Safety.

92. Roundup Lawsuit Update. M. Gaines, 2024. Forbes.

93. Exposure to glyphosate-based herbicides and risk for non-Hogkin lymphoma: A meta-analysis and supporting evidence. L. Zhang, I. Rana, R.M. Shaffer, E. Taioli, L. Sheppard. 2019. Science Direct.

94. Is the Use of Glyphosate in Modern Agriculture Resulting in Increased Neuropsychiatric Conditions Through Modulation of the Gut-brain-microbiome Axis? J.A. Barnett, M.L. Bandy, D.L. Gibson. 2022. Article.

95. Antibiotics and Mental Health: The good, the bad, and the ugly. K. Dinan, T. Dinan. 2022. Article.

96. New Covid Boosters Were Released Before Human Testing But Experts Say They're Still Safe. R. Sohn. 2022. Health.com

97. Fentanyl Fact Sheet, DEA.

98. A five-day course of ivermectin for the treatment of Covid-19 may reduce the duration of illness. S. Ahmed, M.M. Karim, A.G. Ross, A. Kabir, A.B. Aziz, W.A. Khan. 2021. Article.

99. Ivermectin, a potential anticancer drug derived from an antiparasitic drug. M. Tang, X. Hu, Y. Wang, X. Yao, W. Zhang, C. Yu, F. Cheng, J. Li, Q. Fang. 2021. Article.

100. FDA Rejected MDMA-assisted PTSD therapy. Other Psychedelics firms intend to avoid that fate. K. Kupferschmidt. 2024. Article.

101. Psychedelic-Assisted Therapy for PTSD. L. Morland, PsyD, J. Woolley, MD, PhD. PTSD.va.gov

102. What's Soil Health Got to Do with GMOS? Non-GMO Project.

103. Soil Depletion and Nutrition Loss. 2011. Scientific American.

104. Alzheimer's Disease is Type 3 Diabetes – Evidence Reviewed. S. M. de la Monte, J. R. Wands. 2008. Article.

105. Understanding the Link between Sugar and Cancer: An Examination of the Preclinical and Clinical Evidence. M. Epner, P. Yang, R. W. Wagner, L. Cohen. 2022. Article.

106. The US Spends $4 Billion a Year Subsidizing 'Stalinist-style' Domestic Sugar Production. V.H. Smith. 2018. Article. https://www.aei.org/articles/the-u-s-spends-4-billion-a-year-subsidizing-stalinist-style-domestic-sugar-production/

107. Meat and Dairy Subsidies Make America Sick. N. Barnard, MD. Physicians Committee for Responsible Medicine.

108. Antibiotic Use in Livestock and Residues in Food – A Public Health Threat: A Review. O.M. Chimpeteanu, E.N. Pogurschi, D.C. Popa, N. Dragomir, T. Dragotoiu, O.D. Mihai, C.D. Petcu. 2022. Article.

109. Sugar Industry and Coronary Heart Disease Research: A Historical Analysis of Internal Industry Docuyments. C.E. Kearns, DDS, MBA, L.A. Schmidt, Phd, MSW, MPH, S.A. Glantz, PhD. 2016. Jama.

110. Trends in Healthcare Spending. 2024. AMA.

111. Trust in physicians and hospitals plummeted since the Covid pandemic, Northeastern research says. C. M. Hibbert. 2024. Northeastern Global News.

112. Pharma Paid $1.06 Billion to Reviewers at Top Medical Journals. B. Baletti, Ph.D. 2024. The Defender.

113. The Flexner Report – 100 Years Later. T.P. Duffy. 2011. Article.

114. Diet-related disease are the No.1 cause of death in the US – yet many doctors receive little to no nutrition education in med school. N. Johnson. 2024. Article.

115. Based on the recommended CDC vaccine schedule.

116. ADHD Diagnostic Trends: Increased Recognition or Overdiagnosis? E. Abdelnour, M.O. Jansen, J.A. Gold. 2022. Article.

117. Zuckerberg says Biden administration pressured Meta to Censor Covid-19 content. G. Rajan, N. Bose. 2024. Article.

118. Who Owns the Federal Reserve. St. Louis Fed.

119. "A close review of 31 U.S.C. disclosed that the Internal Revenue Service, a Private Corporation, is not shown as a division, bureau, or any part of the U.S. Treasury Department. All this can be looked up any time on Firstgov. 31 U.S.C. Chapter 3 does not list the IRS as an agency or part of the Treasury Department. 31 U.S.C. Subtitle VI
section 9101 does not show the IRS as a Government Owned Corporation under "Government Corporations ". 31 U.S.C. Subtitle I Chapter 9 section 901 does not list the
IRS as an authorized agency." CFTGI Research Paper

120. Fractional Reserve Banking: What It Is and How It Works. S. Nevil. 2024. Investopedia.com.

121. Banks Have Begun Freezing Accounts Linked to Trucker Protest. K. Fung. 2022. Newsweek.

122. A future with no individual ownership is not a happy one: Property theory shows why. R. Stewart, M.B. Charles, J. Page. 2023. Article.

123. Music Tuned to 440 Hz Versus 432 Hz and the Health Effects: A Double-blind Cross-over Pilot Study. D. Calamassi, G.P. Pomponi. 2019. Science Direct.

124. Six Corporations Control 90% of the Media Outlets in America. N. Louise. 2020. Article.

125. Desmet, M. *The Psychology of Totalitarianism*. 2022. Chelsea Green Publishing.

126. Stanley Milgram. Harvard Psychology Department.

127. About Solomon Asch. Swarthmore Psychology.

128. About the Stanford Prison Experiment. Stanford.Edu.

129. Electromagnetic Fields Fact Sheet. National Cancer Institute.

130. For an overview and comprehensive list of studies, see Effects of Exposure to Electromagnetic Fields: Thirty Years of Research. J.M. Moskowitz, PhD. 2024. Article.

131. Number of Patents for Weather Control and Geoengineering. ResearchGate.net.

132. The Origins of Ecocide: Revisiting the Ho Chi Minh Train in the Vietnam War. P. McElwee. 2020. Environment and Society.

133. Ex-Researcher says US Seeded Clouds over Cuba. Geoengineering Monitor.

134. Playing God with the Atmosphere. M. Koren. 2024. The Atlantic.

135. You can find regular updates through an app. Schumann-resonance.org.

136. About Community Water Fluoridation. CDC.gov.

137. The Untold Story of Fluoridation: Revisiting the Changing Perspectives. M.P. Unde, R.U. Patil, P.P. Dastoor. 2018. NIH Article.

138. Federal Court Orders EPA to Regulate Fluoridation of Drinking Water under TSCA. M.N. Duvall, T. Richichi, E.H. Spanton, J.B. Zietman. 2024. The National Law Review.

139. The Hundredth Monkey Revisited. Elaine Myers. 1985. Article.

140. Autism Spectrum Disorder Reclassified: A Second Look at the 1980s Utah/ UCLA Autism Epidemiologic Study. J.S. Miller, D. Bilder, M. Farley, H. Coon, J. Pinborough-Zimmerman, W. Jenson, C.E Rice, E. Fombonne, C.B. Pingree, E. Ritvo, R-A. Ritvo, W.M. McHahon. 2013. Article.

141. Data and Statistic on Autism Spectrum Disorder. CDC.

142. The Genetics of Sex Differences in Brain and Behavior. T. C. Ngun, N. Ghahramani, F. J. Sánchez, S. Bocklandt, E. Vilain. 2012. Article.

143. The Cult of the Individual is a theory put forth by Emile Durkheim to explain the foundation of a new 'religion' based on individual democratic rights and modern science. Modern Democracy as the Cult of the Individual: Durkheim on religious coexistence and conflict. P. Carls. 2019. Article.

144. Culture and the evolution of human cooperation. R. Boyd, P. J. Richardson. 2009. Article.

145. World Population Review: Most Christian Countries 2024. Site.

146. McCannon, T. *Return of the Divine Sophie: Healing the Earth through the Lost Wisdom Teachings of Jesus, Isis, and Mary Magdalene.* (2015) Bear & Company.

147. How Many Books of the Bible did Paul Write? P. Palmer. 2023. Article.

148. The Gnostic Society Library. About the Nag Hammadi Library. Article.

149. *The Nag Hammadi Library: The Gospel of Thomas.* Translated by Thomas. O. Lambdin. Gnosis.org

150. Secret Gospel of Mary. Sophian.org.

151. *The Real Reason why Mary Magdalene is Such a Controversial Figure.* F. Carr. 2018. Time Article.

152. Vatican Decree: *Sanctae M Magdalenae Decretum (En)* Link

153. Refer again to *Return of the Divine Sophia*, above, for an in depth discussion on the witch hunts and persecution of the feminine.

154. *The Map of Consciousness Explained: A Proven Energy Scale to Actualize Your Ultimate Potential.* D. R. Hawkins, MD, PhD. (2020) Hay House LLC.

155. Artificial Intelligence Specialist Demographics and Statistics in the US. Site.

156. New Study Confirms Atrazine's Effects Across a Range of Species (Including Us). A. Wetzler. 2011. Article.

157. A review of the endocrine disrupting effects of micro and nano plastic and their associated chemicals in mammals. S. Ullah, S. Ahmad, X. Guo, S. Ullah, S. Ullah, G. Nabi, K. Wanghe. 2023. Article.

158. Why Are Men's Testosterone Levels Decreasing? Dr. Joshua Smith, Reviewed by Dr. Sam Rogers. 2024. Medichecks.

159. I regret that I did not at the time of recording note the book or author on camera and a pile of books I owned disappeared from storage, so in spite of searching I have not yet been able to identify the specific book or its author. If anyone knows, please do reach out so I can properly credit!

160. Avoidance of sun exposure as a risk factor for major causes of death: a competing risk analysis of the Melanoma in Southern Sweden cohort. P.G. Lindqvist, E. Epstein, K. Nielsen, M. Landin-Olsson, C. Ingvar, H. Olsson. 2016. Article.

161. Lambert, G. W., Reid, C., Kaye, D. M., Jennings, G. L., & Esler, M. D. (2002). Effect of sunlight and season on serotonin turnover in the brain. Lancet, 360(9348), 1840-1842.

162. Cajochen, C., Kräuchi, K., & Wirz-Justice, A. (2000). Role of melatonin in the regulation of human circadian rhythms and sleep. Journal of Neuroendocrinology, 12(4), 303-317.

163. Leproult, R., Colecchia, E. F., L'Hermite-Balériaux, M., & Van Cauter, E. (2001). Transition from dim to bright light in the morning induces an immediate elevation of cortisol levels. The Journal of Clinical Endocrinology & Metabolism, 86(1), 151-157.

164. Hannuksela, M. L., & Ellahham, S. (2001). Benefits and risks of sauna bathing. The American Journal of Medicine, 110(2), 118-126.

165. What is Seasonal Affective Disorder? NIH Article.

166. Prevalence of serum vitamin D deficiency and insufficiency in cancer: Review of the epidemiological literature. D. Gupta. P.G. Vashi, K. Trukova, C.G. Lis, C.A. Lammersfeld. 2011. Article.

167. Weller, R. B. (2013). Sunlight Has Cardiovascular Benefits Independently of Vitamin D. Blood Purification, 35(1-3), 5-11.

168. Prevalence and Relevance of Vitamin D Deficiency in Newly Diagnosed Breast Cancer Patients: A Pilot Study. C. Zemlin, L. Altmayer, C. Stuhlert, J.T. Scheicher, C. Wörmann, M. Lang, L-S. Scherer, I.C. Thul, LS. Spenner, J.A. Simon, A. Wind, E. Kaiser, R. Weber, S. Godeicke-Fritz, G. Wagenpfeil, M. Zemlin, E-F. Solomayer, J. Reichrath, C. Müller. 2023. Article.

169. Does vitamin D deficiency increase the severity of Covid-19? E.K. Weir, T. Thenappan, M. Bhargava, Y. Chen. 2020. Article.

170. Seed oil, sunscreen, and sunlight: the facts you need to know. 2023. Article.

171. Weller, R. B. (2013). Sunlight Has Cardiovascular Benefits Independently of Vitamin D. Blood Purification, 35(1-3), 5-11.

172. Risk and Benefits of Sun Gazing. J. Fletcher, Reviewed by A. Varma, MD. 2022. Article.

173. Local Brain Functional Activity Following Early Deprivation: A Study of Postinstitutionalized Romanian Orphans. H. T. Chugani, M. E. Behen, O. Muzik, C. Juhász, F. Nagy, D. C. Chugani. 2001. Article.

174. Lieberman, M. *Social: Why Our Brains Are Wired to Connect.* (2014) Crown

175. What We Know Currently about Mirror Neurons. J.M. Kilner, R.N. Lemon. 2013. Article.

176. Hebbian learning and predictive mirror neurons for actions, sensations, and emotions. C. Keysers, V. Gazzola. 2014. Article.

177. Pandemic Learning Loss and Covid-19: Education Impacts. Annie. E. Casey Foundation, 2024. Article.

178. Social isolation in adults with cancer: An evolutionary concept analysis. Y. Liang, G. Hao, M. Wu, L. Hou. 2022. Article.

179. Social isolation, loneliness, and depression in young adulthood: a behavioural genetic analysis. T. Matthews, A. Danese, J. Wertz, C. L. Odgers, A. Ambler, T.E. Moffitt, L. Arseneault. 2016. Article.

180. Hyper-Independence and Trauma: What's the Connection? A. Marschall, PsyD. 2024. Article.

181. Permanent Peace.org provides a comprehensive overview and analysis of the research findings pertaining to reduction in war and violence due to mass meditation. Evidence.

182. I have learned that this is the highest protection we can call in, and the best protection against energies and entities that would attempt to interfere or corrupt the channel.

183. I offer resources and specific tools for protection and connection inside my School

184. How the Maya Imagined the World Would End or Not. B. Taub. 2023. Article.

185. Find the full Hopi Prophecy message shared by Thomas Banyacya, Sr. (1909-1999), messenger and translator for the Hopi elders on YouTube: Hopi Prophecy by Thomas Banyacya (1995) Part 1 of 2

186. The Legend of the Rainbow Warriors. The Earth Stories Collection.

187. White Buffalo Calf Prophecy. R. Estes. 2012. Native Heritage Project.

188. The Eagle and the Condor Prophecy: A Prophecy for Our Time. J. Perkins. Guide.

189. Kali Yuga – When Did it End and What Lies Ahead? Sadhguru, 2020. Article.

190. About the Haudenosaunee Confederacy. Article.

Made in the USA
Middletown, DE
13 November 2024

64456768R00163